Advertising Management

ADVERTISING MANAGEMENT

Virender S. Poonia

genNEXT Publication

Advertising Management

Rs. 180

ISBN : 978-93-80222-28-8

Published in 2010 in India by
Gennext Publication
23 Main Ansari Road, Darya Ganj,
E-Mail : GenNextpublication@hotmail.com
Phone : 23282060

Laser Type Setting : Shubh Deep Laser Printers

Printed at : Chawla Offset Printers, Delhi

Contents

Preface

As we all know that Advertising Management is one of the most important topics in today's world. Many books have been written in this topic. This modest effort is another pearl in the sequence. This book has been designed in mind the mentality of the general reader's language which is easy to understandable. The aim of this book is to provide students and lectures with a clear concise and comprehensive introduction to the theory and practice of advertising management.

The objective of the book is to bring together a balanced selection of core concepts as well as new perspectives that collectively articulate a knowledge-based view of advertising management.

Advertising management incorporates various specialized sub-functions like media strategy, message strategy, media planning, media buying, etc. While advertising management is an inseparable part of the marketing department, usually, the marketing department of an organization is concerned more with market research and evaluation of results. All the critical processes of advertising management are generally outsourced to specialized advertising agencies. It involves designing the strategies to be adopted for influencing the public, i.e., media selection and deciding on the aspect to be advertised based on the image of the company and the present marketing objective.

This book is designed to be a comprehensive text on advertising management for students in all the world. This book covers a wide range of advertising management issues, and attempt to introduce the subject in a comprehensive way. It avoids the narrow focus and considerable complexity of many other books in this area where in depth treatment is required, students are recommended to read relevant texts by leading contributors to idea about advertising management thinking and practice.

We hope that the discussion made in this book will help the readers to understand and learnt about the different aspects of "Advertising Management" in a most comprehensive way to face the present and future challenges which are occurred in this field.

Thanks

1

Introduction

This chapter includes key concepts which are described below:-

- Introduction,
- Reasons for Advertising,
- Types of Advertising,
- Communication Mix,
- Benefits of Advertising,
- Study of Advertising,
- Mediums for Advertising,
- Tools for Advertising,
- Value of advertisement,
- Advertisement Media and
- Need for Advertising.

Advertising is defined as a measure for the growth of civilization and indication of betterment and perfection that must arise in the nature of human being.

Advertising is described as a forum is of commercial mass communication that designed to promote the sale of a product or service; or a message on behalf of an institution, organization or candidate for political office. Evidence of advertising can be found in cultures that existed thousands of years ago. Advertising became a major industry in the only 20th century. Today, industry employs hundreds of thousands of people and influences the behavior and buying habits of billions of people. Now Advertisement spending worldwide exceeds $350 billion per year. In United States alone, about 6,000 advertising agencies help to create and place advertisements in wide range of media including newspapers, television, direct mail, radio, magazines, the Internet, and outdoor signs. Advertising is so common place in United States that according to some estimates, an average person may encounter from 500 to 1,000 advertisements in a single day.

Advertising is a purposeful communication, which is designed with a view to achieve the specific objectives and goals. Major objective of advertising is to make the job of sales personnel less difficult and more efficient that are measured by sales, which are achieved per person where direct selling effort is essential and helps in use of inputs.

Advertising is most used to design that promote the sale of a particular product or service. However, some advertisements are intended to promote an idea to influence the behavior, such as encouraging people not to use illegal drugs or smoke. These ads are often called public service ads (PSAs). Some ads promote an institution such, as the Red Cross States, and are known as institutional advertising. Their purpose is to encourage people to donate money or services or simply to improve the image of the institution doing the advertising. Advertising is also used to promote political parties and candidates for political office. Political advertising has become a key component of electoral campaigns in many countries.

There difference between advertising and publicity. It is necessary to make a distinction between advertising and Publicity. Advertising acts as paid forum of non-personal presentation of idea, goods and services by an identified sponsor. These also serve the purpose of disseminating information about an organization or a company and their products and services available with these organization and company. This amounts to unpaid publicity over which, the concerned company as well as organization which would have no explicit control.

Many experts believe that advertising has important economic and social benefits. However, advertising has its critics also who say that advertising is deceptive or encourages an excessively materialistic culture or reinforces harmful stereotypes. United States and many other countries regulate advertising to prevent deceptive ads or to limit the visibility of certain kinds of ads.

Advertising has become increasingly international. More than ever before, corporations are looking beyond their own country's borders for new customers. Faster modes of shipping, growth of multinational corporations, rising personal income level worldwide, and falling trade barriers, have all encouraged commerce between countries. Because corporations are opening new markets and selling their products in many regions of the globe, they are also advertising their products in those regions.

Advertising is also concerned with much more than the promotion of tangible goods. Although, the use of advertising has been made largely for promoting goods and services, it is increasingly used to further public interest as well goods and services with limited profit motive.

REASONS FOR ADVERTISING

In today's fast-paced world, consumers are everyday faced with thousands of ads. Can you remember an ad that actually stopped you, got your attention and was committed to your long term memory so you could take action? If you're like most consumers, not much sticks. Why do some ads penetrate the mental filters and why do most not? Looking at top 7 reasons campaign fail can lead us to some solid answers about making them more effective :

1. ***Confusing content.*** Successful ads don't try to tell everything in one ad the advertiser knows. The best ads are focused around one or two main ideas:

First reason is confusing content which tends to the main ideas and involving the confused material, their concepts already define them and don't try to tell each and every thing about the ad.

2. ***Too much emphasis on price.*** Most ads are written as if the only price were variable. Consumers always want fair price but have no way of knowing if they got at the best price. Consumers don't respond to ads because of price alone.

Second reason is too much emphasis on price. This reason includes those ads which do not show the price of the product in an advertisement. Most of the consumers want the fair and good price of a product and also attractive, when the prices are displayed on the product in an advertisement.

3. ***Unrealistic expectations.*** Expecting major league results

in a time frame that's too short with a budget that's too small. Make sure expectations match up with budget and timing.

Third reason is unrealistic expectations. Some times expectations depend on budget. Generally consumer's expectation against the product is much depend on their budget (Price).

4. ***Too little frequency, repetition, consistency.*** Most advertisers stop short because they run out of patience and/or money just at the time when the campaign is about to start working. If you have a good ad, keep using it.

Fourth reason is too little frequency, repetition and consistency. When the advertisement is too short to end and this reason applies when the advertisement tends to good nature.

5. Too much about the product, not enough about the consumer. The most successful ads are about the consumer...why they should buy the product and how they benefit from using the product. Most ads waste too much time and space, talking about the product and not enough about the consumer and their needs.

Fifth reason is too much about the product and not enough about the consumer. This is the most important reason which describes that most of the successful ads contain about the consumer i.e. why they use this product and what are the benefits of their product instead of too much speech about the producer. The failure of an ad is most of the time consumes on the features of product, instead of about the consumer and their needs.

6. Not memorable. Not meaningful. Not sticky. Consumers can act only on the ads they remember. Most ads we encounter are irrelevant. The best ads break through the mental filters by talking our language, touching our emotions and creating imagery that resonates the consumer.

Reason for the advertisement fail is that, the advertiser includes the features of product, benefits of product but doesn't includes the concepts that touch the emotions and feelings of consumer by which they can't remember about the product. When a product breaks the mental concepts, languages and also the emotions of consumer, they cannot remember about the product.

7. Failure to understand and focus on the consumer. Consumers don't have a lot of patience for ads that talk only about the business or the product. No one's listening. No one cares. Speak to consumers about what they're interested in and they will respond.

This reason focuses on the consumer behavior. This describes that the ads include not only about the product or the company but also about the consumers by which they are attracted and response to it.

TYPES OF ADVERTISING

Advertising can be categorized into two broad categories:-

1. Consumer advertising.
2. Trade advertising.

Consumer advertising is directly proportional to the public i.e. consumer i.e. it is directed to the public.

Trade advertising is directed at wholesalers or distributors who resell to the public. Consumer advertising is most important in the field of advertising.

Consumer advertising can be further divided into *national advertising* and *local advertising*. National advertising is aimed at consumers throughout the entire country. National advertising usually attempts to create awareness among the public of a product or service, or it tries to build loyalty to a product or service. Local advertising is aimed at informing people in a particular area where they can purchase a product or service. Advertising to the public may also take the form of *institutional advertising*, *image advertising*, *informational advertising*, or *cooperative advertising*.

National advertising is one part of the consumer advertising. It is generally used to encourage the public about the product or service that are given by an organization or a company.

Local advertising is second part of consumer advertising. The objective of local advertising is to inform the public about the product in a particular or specified area.

Consumer advertising is directed to the public. So, there are also some advertising that are directed to the public.

Institutional advertising aims to create a favorable impression of a business or institution without trying to sell a specific product. This type of advertising is designed solely to build the prestige and public respect for their company. For nonprofit institutions, such advertising helps to support the institution's activities- example, by encouraging blood donations or cash contributions for the work of an organization like the Red Cross. For profit business, there are other reasons to improving its reputation rather than trying to sell a particular product. In some cases, a large company may sell a diversity of products. As a conclusion, there is more value and greater efficiency in building a brand image for the company itself. If consumers learn to have a high regard for the company, then they are more likely to have a favorable opinion of all diverse products of the company's.

Many advertisers prefer a strategy which are known as image advertising. These advertisers aims to give a personality to a product that is unique, appealing, and appropriate, so that the consumer would choose it over similar products that might fulfill the same need. The personality is created partly by the design and packaging of product but, more importantly, by the words and pictures the advertisements are associated with the product. This personality is often called as a brand image. Advertisers believe brand image frequently leads consumers to select one brand over another or instead of a less expensive generic product. Brand image is specially important for commodities such as detergents, jeans, hamburgers, and soft drinks, because within these product categories there are few, if any, major differences.

Informative advertising tries to promote an idea or influence behavior. These advertising are often called as public service advertising; to used to provide an information or advice to the public. It may try to discourage the young people from drugs or tobacco and also encourage to people to adopt safer and healthier life styles.

Cooperative advertising is defined as the arrangement between manufacturers and retailers in which manufacturers offer credits to their retail customers for advertising. The credits, or advertising allowances, which are based on the amount of product the retailer purchases. For example, if the retailer purchases $100,000 worth of a product from a manufacturer, the manufacturer's cooperative advertising program may allot a 1 percent credit, or $1,000, toward the cost of purchasing an ad that will feature the product. In addition, some manufacturers will match the amount that the retailer spends, sharing the cost of the ad. In United States antitrust laws enforced by the Federal Trade Commission (FTC) ensure that these ad allowances are offered on equal and proportionate terms so that large retailers are not unduly favored over small retailers. Cooperative advertising is a form of local advertising because it directs consumers to local retail outlets. Cooperative advertising is used to establish the arrangement between manufacturers and retailers in an industry.

COMMUNICATION MIX

In these days of large scale production, complexity of selling, cut-throat competition, availability of a substitute product, widely scattered consumers, frequent changes in the habits and tastes of the consumers, the problem of selling has become more sophisticated and difficult. All these factors and a host of other problems has necessitated the need for speedy and accurate flow of communication from the seller to the buyer. Transmission of information about the prospects is necessary at different stages of sales promotion activities.

Communication mix solves the problem of complexity of selling, availability of product, changes in habits and tastes of consumer. These problems are overcome with the speedy and accurate flow of communication from seller to consumer.

For instance flow of information is about the product or service to be well communicated in advance of the introduction of the product or service, to announce the introduction of a new product, information about the modification of the product, information about the price change, a new pack to make a special offer and to remind the consumer, etc. To achieve this end, several promotional mix factors are to be designed. All efforts towards sales promotion may be called as promotional activities. Various activities are designed particularly to help easy sale of goods.

These above underlined factors, are factors which are included in promotional mix. The increasing sales quantity is called as promotional activities or promotional mix. Promotional activities includes advertising, sales promotion and personal selling, which are generally involved in communication media. Media may publish the matter of publicity free of charge to inform the public about a particular topic.

Communication media consider the news value or worthiness or public importance for publicity. All publicity materials may not go into publicity. According to Kenneth A. Longman, the distinction between publicity and advertising is: If a message is sent to someone because it is newsworthy, and if it is intended to be published or broadcast without charge to the sender, it is publicity. If the sender specifies the exact content of the message and pays for the time or space required for publishing or broadcasting this message, it is advertising.

According to Robert V. Zacher: "Publicity consists of impersonally communicated messages which are designed to leave certain impressions upon the minds of persons exposed to them. Unlike advertising, however, publicity is not openly paid for. It may be carried as part of the views or other editorial content of a newspaper or magazine, or as part of the news or entertainment broadcast on radio or television."

Advertising

The major components of communication mix are advertising. Advertising is also published by the media but on given instruction by a particular individual, organization, small groups or company on the specific charge to pay for ad. Advertisement has many sources to make famous or popular, their product or services like radio, news, newspaper, television, outdoor as well press, mail and house mail and many other sources.

In a communications mix, advertising is a major component towards persuasive communication. It is a paid form of non-personal persuasive communication of ideas, goods and services. The essential element of advertising is that, the cost of advertisement is to be borne by the sponsor. The specific operations that are undertaken by the advertisement are press, outdoor, television, radio, film, direct mail, house journal, etc. It promotes presentation or the seller. It is one of the sales promotion activities like personal selling and sales promotion. It is a tool to transmit product information to the prospective customers. Though it is an impersonal and paid form of presentation, it is a powerful and effective medium of communication. Information of the product or service must be spread among the population. It brings the fact to the public notice or announces publicly.

The objectives of an advertisement are to inform the public about the introduction of a new product or service which are published into the market, or well communicating in advance of the introduction of a product or service into the market. Also modification in the product or service, price, price change, exposure of the market to the new buyers, announcement of a new pack, inviting enquiries, and in general educating and informing the public with the ultimate aim of increasing the sales volume. Advertising may be of several kinds such as primary demand advertising, institutional advertising, cooperative advertising, commercial advertising, industrial goods advertising, dealers' advertising, consumer goods advertising, etc. which are also described in this chapter.

Advertising and sales promotion are indirect and non-personal methods of communication while personal selling is direct and face-to-face conversation of sales effort. It is a personal method of sales promotion. Advertising takes place both in print media, visual, audio and audio-visual media. The object of every commercial organization is to promote sales to help the easy sale of goods. No single activity will help the purpose of achieving this end. So, effective coordination and integrated efforts of all the three promotional activitie alone can help to achieve this purpose.

These activities are also referred to as 'communication mix' because these activities involve various communication media. The promotional mix consisting of marketing activities are particularly concerned with the task of persuasive communication and to collectively form the promotional mix. The following are four major components of communications mix or promotional mix:

Promotion

Promotion is the term that is used as a word 'selling'. Selling means the transfer of goods from seller to buyer.

The term selling denotes transfer of title to goods. It involves activities concerning transfer of ownership in the property. But the term promotion is generally used synonymously for selling. The word selling is to be used in a narrow sense to mean ownership transferability. Whereas promotion is used comprehensively including several activities or efforts employed for increasing sales volume.

Promotion is divided into two activities i.e. advertising and sales promotion. Personal selling and advertising are the two forms of promotion. These activities are designed to increase sales that are known as promotional activities. Point of purchase display is yet another form of promotional programme. On the other hand, direct mail is a supplementary form of promotion. Promotion includes both direct and indirect selling methods. Promotion is broader in outlook that includes all marketing efforts which are directed to make the product informative to reach the ultimate consumers or users. According to Masson and Ruth, "Promotion consists of those activities that are designed to bringing goods or service of a company to the favourable attention of customers."

Sales Promotion

Sales promotion is a medium of communication which provides an opportunity of direct contact and face-to-face conversation with seller and user, individually or small group and mass communication with a large audience. Sales promotional activities is one of the major components of promotional mix. The expression of sales promotion activities includes all other activities, other than personal selling, advertisement and publicity. It involves marketing activities specifically designed to create stimulus of demand for a product or service. Displays, shows, exhibitions, demonstrations, demonstration-cum-sales, etc are examples of sales promotion activities. In other words, sales promotion includes the forms of mass communication, which directs towards informing the channels of distribution like distributors, retailers, wholesalers, etc. It also includes all other activities that are meant to increase and expand the market and the activities, which are additional to 'above the line', media advertising. Sales promotional activities are greatly help and strengthen the hands and provide support to sales representative, distributors or salesmen. According to Frank Jefkins, "It includes merchandising or tactical advertising and consists of 'below the line' efforts to stimulate both selling and selling out at the point of sale."

Sales promotion acts as the interface of communication that gives an opportunity of face to face as well as direct conversation which includes the communication with large number of audience. Sales promotion includes the activities that are related to marketing which are particularly designed to make demand for the product or services which are given by a company or organization. It is a long-term operation and means of selling. Sales promotion is a component of promotional mix. A form of mass communication directed towards influencing the channel of distribution, whereas advertising includes all forms of mass media communication directed towards influencing the ultimate consumer. The American Marketing Association defines the term sales promotion in the words," Sales Promotion, in a specific sense, refers to those sales activities that supplement both personal selling and advertising and coordinate them and help to make them very effectively, which helps to display shows and expositions and demonstration.

Personal Selling

Personal selling is also the component of promotional mix. This is also the part of communication but it represents the oral presentation that are used in conversation between the seller and user individually or in small groups.

Personal selling is yet another promotional tool, which is mainly concerned with the communication. It involves oral presentation in conversation with an individual small group of buyers for the purpose of making sales. It is directed to bring the right products into direct contact with the right consumers. In personal selling, there is direct personal contact, effective information flow, feedback and quick action. It is one of the vehicles of promotional mix and communication mix, which are best suited to each prospect. Product introduction is an interface, which is quite effective in this method. It ensures that the personal presentation of the product message is used for the purpose of selling. Sales personnel involves face to-face conversation with one or more prospective buyers, existing buyers or potential buyers. The American Marketing Association defines the term "the personal or impersonal process of assisting and/or persuading a prospective customer to buy a commodity or service and to act favourably upon an idea that has commercial significance to the seller."

Personal selling has some qualities like active relationships, depth of understanding the concepts, promotion of relationship, and peculiar obligation, which influence the buyer to buy the product etc. Salesmanship indicates the skills in personal selling. There are two types of salesmanship, i.e. creative salesmanship and competitive salesmanship. It discharges the functions like introduction of the product to sell the goods, to explore new customers, to create demand and to maintain demand, and to gather information about the market for the product. Selling is a career, salesmanship is a profession. A salesman may be classified as creative salesman, service salesman, detailed salesman, manufacturer's salesman, wholesaler's salesman, retailer's salesman, indoor and outdoor salesman, etc.

Here personal selling introduce in terms of salesmanship i.e. skills in personal selling. To the career of salesmanship, selling is their profession. Personal selling is defined as the direct contact, which is made by the representatives of business firms who attempt to induce the purchase of product or services.

Publicity

Publicity is a persuasive communication. The word publicity

means to make known the product message publicly or to allow to make known the message publicly. It is a non-personal influencing factor, which creates demand for a product or service. Publicity may be undertaken through print media, broadcast media, and audio-visual media. Publicity differs much from advertising. It is non-personal factor, which influence to create the demand for product or service. Publicity aims to make famous or popular a specific product or service around the public.

The term publicity is to be distinguished from advertisement. The difference between publicity and advertisement is that, advertising is paid for by its sponsor, whereas publicity is not paid. The publicity materials are of newsworthy contents and a matter of public interest and importance; the media may publish them or broadcast them free of charge. They may publish free of charge to inform the public at large. The opinion or news or message of a president or prime minister when published is publicity. In publicity, the media themselves publish information free of charge. But an advertisement form of paid is non-personal presentation. In an advertisement the message sent to the media will be printed as it is without change in case of print media or broadcasting. The media has necessarily to alter the message content in case of publicity material. Publicity is the matter of public interest, which is published by the media.

Purpose of Advertising

The advertising process consists of copy of advertising, media selection and budget of advertising. Advertising has attention value, reminding value and influencing value.

The purpose of advertising communication is to change the behaviour of the audience or their attitudes through some medium of communication. All advertising or paid announcement take the form of the following media:

- *Print Media:* Newspapers, daily, weekly, special, evening, Sunday and Sunday supplements. Magazines:
  - — Consumer magazines: general interest and special interest;
  - — Business publications: industrial publications, trade publications, institutional publications, etc; and
  - — Direct mail advertising.
- *Broadcast Media:* Radio network and spot, television network

and spot.

- *Outdoor Media:* Vehicular advertising, electronic displays, rural advertising, neon sign, sky writing, sandwichmen.
- *Audio Visual Media:* Film advertising, documentary films, straight advertising films and sponsored advertising films.
- *Point of Purchase Advertising:* Window display, counter display, showroom, etc.
- *Direct Mail Media:* Leaflets, folders, booklets, catalogues, and brochures, etc.

Thus Advertising is the coordination and integration of all communication efforts discussed above. A proper mix or blend of sales promotion, advertising, personal selling and publicity is important factor concerning the marketing or advertising manager.

BENEFITS OF ADVERTISING

- Advertising helps the manufacturers in creating demand for the products and thus increasing their sales.
- Effective advertising keeps steady demand for products round the year. The seasonal fluctuations are greatly smoothed out by good advertisement.
- Advertising stimulates demand for products. The manufacturers keep smaller inventories due to rapid turn over.
- Retailers benefit from advertising as the consumers get better information about the quality of products. Increased demand for goods from retailers enlarges the sales of the products.
- Advertising increases sales and thereby facilitates mass production. The cost per unit of production is therefore reduced.
- Consumers are better informed of the goods available in the market through advertising. Task of the salesman thus becomes easier in canvassing for the product. Advertising thus supplements salesmanship and helps in promoting the sales of the product.
- Advertising directly encourages innovation and technological advancements. Improvement and development of new products lead to higher sales and an increase in profits of the manufacturer.
- Production of higher quality of goods and the information of

their availability in the market through advertisements gives a sense of pride to the manufacturer and the other employees involved in production.

- Benefits of Advertising include the information, which is most important for the consumer before buying the product and this information about the product he gets from the advertisement.
- Advertising is used to build a brand image. Images are mental pictures of brands that may appeal to different segments of the target audience in varying degrees.
- New product launching is another benefit of advertising. The term new product includes modifications of existing products, imitations of competitive products and product line acquisitions. Advertising can be used to promote new products and to call attention to changes in old or previous products.

STUDY OF ADVERTISING

Advertising is a forum or type of communication that attempts to persuade potential customers to purchase or to consume more of a particular brand of product or service.

The question of the utility of advertising in different types of societies and at various stages of development is one, which could continue to give rise to debate and discussion.

The first concept is that, it will be necessary to create an understanding of purpose, aims and functions of advertising and then proceed to study about the process of advertising. These consideration lead to decisions on the budget, media and target audience for whom the message is intended. This will be followed by an analytical approach to the evaluation of advertising and its related campaigns.

There is usually a tendency to view the advertising in isolation from the objective set of it. Questions of selection of the advertising agency relationships that are considerably important because of the direct bearing they have on the quality of advertising.

Advertising is an integral part of marketing mix. However, it is frequently attracts the attention of the exchequer and singled out for unfavourable treatment instead of being treated on the same basis as expenditure on research and development.

MEDIUMS FOR ADVERTISING

Some media of communication are to be applied for announcements. A detailed discussion on media of communication has been covered under a separate paragraph. Here it is felt desirable to identify the media of mass communication briefly to give some coverage under mass communication process. The media of mass communication may be broadly divided into two categories — advertising media and sales promotion media. All the media of mass communication are given below:

(1) Print Media : Printed materials by which the consumer is informed about the particular topic are called print media. This category includes:

(a) Newspapers: Newspapers constitutes the leading and major medium of advertisement. This includes all the daily as well as general information which are carried. It may include:

- Daily,
- Morning,
- Evening,
- Sunday special and
- Rural newspapers.

(b) Magazines: The second category of print media includes magazines used mainly for wider circulation. It is Major types of magazine are general, industrial and trade, technical journal, farm magazines and professional journals.

(2) Broadcast Media: Broadcast media are used specifically to provide the wide coverage with a brief commercial exposer of a product. Airwaves are the channels by which media are directed to reach a wide section of the audience. This is known as broadcast media which includes mainly radio i.e. frequency modulation and television. Television has the elements of action, sights, songs and words also. Television has is also classified as network, national spot and local. These classifications are also applicable in radio.

Direct Mail Media: These media are mostly used when products are sold by mail. Under this condition, printed materials are sent through the mail directly to the selected people included in the mailing list. Opposed to print media, where printed materials have editorial content, whereas in direct mail, media, printed matter occurs without editorial content.

Point of Purchase Media: Point of purchase media also forms part and parcel of an advertising campaign. There is no doubt it is a sales promotion effort but part of a campaign. It is a type of advertisement or media designed, to draw the attention of the customer while shopping or at the time of buying. These media includes display material in stores and other incentives to the buyer.

Visual Outdoor Media : Outdoor and transit media are used to draw the attention of persons, who are passing through some spots where posters and other outdoor advertisements are installed. There are a wide variety of outdoor advertising media. The most common outdoor medium is bill board; the car cards also come under this category.

Promotional Literature: Handout cards, brochures etc., are instances included in the category of promotional literature. Promotional literature includes those materials which are carried by persons easily and which also exist in visual outdoor media.

Advertising Copy: Advertising copy means to a medium or media of communication. The word copy has several meanings because it has several elements. As we have seen, in print as well as audio-visual media, an advertisement has several elements. It refers to materials written for advertising and publicity purpose. It may cover print, audio, audio-visual and other communication symbols, which are specifically designed to reach consumers to draw their attention to make them purchase with the ultimate object of increasing sales turnover. Copy writing is an important feature in advertisement management. It includes all features of the advertising message either through print or broadcast media. Advertising copy also refer to the tool of communication. It acts as materials which are written or published for advertising or publicity i.e, make famous or popular in the surrounding. It may be print media or visual media or audio also.

Copy Elements: Copy refers to an advertising message, which are communicated by any advertising medium or media that not necessarily an advertising message in printed words. It includes the word messages of headlines, subheads, sketches.

The success or failure of an advertisement depends on copy writing. It includes the creation of an idea for advertising is, to appeal to customers, and the arrangement of various elements such as the headline, sub-head, trade name etc. It is important to recognize the role of the copy writer who is greatly concerned with visualization and layout of a copy. All elements that are included in the finished advertising message are included in the copy. Visual symbols, illustrations, text, pictures, captions, photographs, slogans, actions in graphic presentation, brand name, trade mark, price, borders, reading materials, logotype. A copy of a television commercial includes elements like motion, sight and sound. Broadly, it refers to the words which are to be spoken by the characters in the scripts, plus music and sound effects as well as illustrative materials, actions and even camera cues. The print media advertisements in newspapers, magazines, etc., rely on words and pictures to transmit their message for information. They include headings, sub-heads, picture, caption, slogan, body copy, trade mark and mascot, border and other illustrations and a visual symbol. Radio commercials employ sound effects and music and the words in the advertisement message.

Logotype: A logotype is the advertiser's name or signature of advertiser that are printed at a prominent place and in distinctive letters logotype (logas) or signature cuts. This means special design of the name of the advertiser. It may have such designs which are the same as the trade mark in the product.

Copy writer: Copy writer is a person who writes advertising copy who has to collect a lot of information to write copy.

Visualization and Layout : Visualization with reference to copy means creation of an idea for advertising to appeal to consumers to target audience. Writers, artists and production personnel are engaged in visualization, i.e., creation of an idea for advertisements. There is another term called layout which also refers to print media particularly. Layout in copy refers to the arrangement of various elements in the advertisement such as headline, illustration, trade mark, main text or body copy, film name, background, border, caption, slogan, space, price, decoration, coupon, sub-heading, product, name plate, etc.

Visualization in copy means the creation of an idea for advertisement which are used to appeal to consumers to target audience whereas layout in copy means to the arrangement of variate elements in the advertisement. Now after the discussion on visualization and layout presents in copy, the next topic, which are in process to discuss, is types of advertising copy and their description.

Types of Advertising Copy: Advertising copy contains a number of elements. All advertisement copies may not contain all the elements. Different advertisement copies may have different elements and some may include all the elements. The ultimate goal is to increase sales turnover to maximize the profit. So, different advertisements are designed to incorporate the required elements to meet different problems in reaching the maximum profit. There are various types of copy. One advertisement may contain more than one of these kinds of copy. Burton and Kreer list five kinds of copy. These are:

- *Celebrity Endorsement Copy:* These includes pictures of some persons who already enjoy the publicity which are used to convey the message. For instance, a message is supported by a sportsman, cinema star, political leader.
- *Descriptive Copy:* A type of copy which describes briefly as well as clearly and usually used for consumer products.
- *Dialogue and Monologue Copy:* In this kind the characters in the advertisement do the selling in their own words.
- *Gimmick Copy:* In this copy, effects are not classified. Humour, exaggeration and other trick devices are employed to capture attention.
- *Straight Line Copy:* In this copy, the body text starts to develop the headline.
- *Narrative Copy:* In this type of copy, a story is established or a specific situation which ultimately leads to discussion.
- *Picture and Caption Copy:* In this copy, the story or specific situation is described by a number of illustrations and captions. In other words, copy block alone is not used.
- *Questioning Copy:* Why a particular product has to be purchased. This attracts the consumers. Instances of this are Colgate paste, face powder.
- *Reason why Copy:* A kind of copy that are designed to meet a different problem. It gives a solution to the problem to encourage the people to purchase a product. For instance, a

scooter advertisement.

- *Scientific Copy:* This copy is meant to meet a target audience because it contains jargon, technical and scientific. For instance, advertising copy relating to fertilizers, pesticides, drugs, and pharmaceuticals.

As we earlier discussed about the advertising copy which may refers to the materials, which are published or written by media for advertisement or publicity to inform the public. We described above about the types of advertising copy.

TOOLS FOR ADVERTISING

There are seven tools for advertising which are shown below:-

- **Branding** - How to create and characterize a brand.
- **Direct** - How to get your clicks with direct response e-mail, DRTV, and Internet ads.
- **Positioning** - How to position a company, product or service.
- **Strategy** - How to create a communications strategy.
- **Planning** - How to write an advertising plan.
- **Theory** - How ads can make people think, feel, or act.
- **Involvement theory** - Inside the buyer's brain.

VALUE OF ADVERTISEMENT

Advertisement is the main source of a large part of newspaper revenue. Advertisement and circulation act and interact on each other. The larger the circulation, the greater the advertisement revenue. And revenue so earned is used to sustain circulation drives.

Two well-known journals only in India, which have tried to be independent of advertisements are the *Indian Social Reformer* and the *Harijan*.

As the size of newspapers has been reduced during and after the war advertisement has overflowed to the small papers, but this advantage may disappear when the size increases, as it does now.

Social value of the advertisement is undoubted. It puts the buyer of goods and services in touch with the seller of goods and services. Both help social, commercial and financial life of the country. Some kinds of advertisement have a certain news value and are of public interest.

Instances have come to the notice of members of the Federation in which the editorial staff is asked by the advertising department to keep out or soft-pedal news stories that may hurt the feeling of advertisers and so damage the paper's business. Sub-editors have got into trouble for allowing matter to appear which has meant loss of business. Neither are instances uncommon of advertisements being cancelled because of the policy of a paper.

The working of the audit bureau of circulation and its usefulness may be enquired into. Government and social agencies can keep a check on advertisements of doubtful value. There is definite need for a code of advertisement ethics.

Influence of Advertisements: Our Federation is interested primarily in the influence of advertisements on the editorial work of a newspaper, and we are stating below some important aspects of the question.

For the sake of revenue, most newspapers accept advertisements irrespective of quality and utility of the goods advertised. Few would care to reject an advertisement unless it is too bad or unless. there are limitations of space.

Advertisements may be classified into three sections: display, classified and financial. The agencies providing advertisements are Government and their allied organizations, municipalities and local authorities, tourist bureaux, company promoters, banks and insurance companies, shipping companies, transport companies, advertisers of manufactured goods of many varieties, film-makers and cinema theatres, astrological and matrimonial agencies, those who want to accept or offer services, etc.

There is a relationship between advertisement and circulation where advertisement and circulation act and interact on each other. When the circulation is greater, the advertisement revenue is also the larger.

ADVERTISEMENT MEDIA

Advertisement media is the process of selecting most of the media, which is cost- effective, by which the necessary coverage and number of exposures are achieved among the target audience. Advertising media is the process of choosing the most cost-effective media to achieve the necessary coverage, and number of exposures, among the target audience.

Media Buyers

Media Buyers defines the person who delivers the goods and special deals with media owners and purchasing the slots of best parcels to achieve the best cost, which is normally measured in terms of the cost per thousand viewers.

In the end, it is the media buyers who deliver the goods; by negotiating special deals with the media owners, and buying the best parcels of 'slots' to achieve the best cost which is normally measured in terms of the cost per thousand viewers, or per thousand household 'impressions', or per thousand impressions on the target audience. The "best cost" can also be measured by the cost per lead, in the case of direct response marketing. The growth of very large international and agencies has been partly justified or satisfied by their increased buying power over the media owners.

Styles of Media and their Characteristics

In terms of overall advertising expenditures, media advertising is still dominated by Press and television, which are of comparable size (by value of 'sales'). Posters and radio follow some way behind, with cinema representing a very specialist medium.

Cinema

Although the numbers in the national audience are now small, this may be the most effective medium for extending coverage to the younger age groups, since the core audience is aged 15-24. Cinema featured by national audience mostly includes the younger age groups i.e. age lies between 15 and 24.

Internet/web Advertising

This is a rapidly growing force in the marketing. It is varied in form, but much of it still follows the example of Press advertising. The most effective usage which are now adopted by the 'search engines' is interactive. Indeed, in its own field, it demonstrates how effective such an approach can become. As per the current market trends Ad agencies are using a new mixed method called media ripples to gain a higher brand recall among the target audience.

Mobile Advertising

It is one of the most popular types of Advertisement Media.

Although the personal mobile phone is becoming very attractive as an important advertising media to the network operators, it is relatively unproven and therefore still remains in the media buyers' sidelines.

In the United Kingdom, spending is dominated by the national and regional newspapers, the latter taking almost all the classified advertising revenue. The magazines and trade or technical journal markets are about the same size as each other, but are less than half that of the newspaper sectors.

National newspapers are supposed to carry more weight with their readers by which, an advertisement place in one, is taken more seriously than a comparable one in a Regional Newspaper whereas Regional Newspaper is performing like daily newspapers or weeklies. These are usually more advertising competing for the attention of the reader.

- **National newspapers** —From the media buyer's viewpoint, these are still traditionally categorized on the basis of class; even though this is declining the importance to many advertisers. For example,'Quality' newspapers tend to have a readership profile in excess of 80 per cent of ABC1 readers, though it is more typical to segment readerships by age categories. These are obviously best matched to national advertisers who are happy with black and white advertisements, although color is now available. High-quality color is available in some supplements of Newspaper. National newspapers and the quality Press in particular, are supposed to carry more 'weight' with their readers, since they are deliberately read, not treated just as 'background'). Therefore, an advertisement placed in one is taken more seriously than a comparable one in a regional newspaper, although it may be more transitory since it is not kept for some reference as some local weeklies may be.

- **Regional newspapers** —These may be dailies, which look and perform much like the nationals, or weeklies, which are rather more specialized, although they dominate the market for classified advertising. Indeed, there is usually much more advertising competing for the reader's attention, and the weekly newspaper are now largely the province of the 'free-sheet' - which is typically delivered free to all homes in a given area - obtaining all their revenue from the very high proportion of advertising, which they carry, and accordingly having the least 'weight' of all.

Magazines

Magazines are designed to keep public interest in the mind. Advertisers have the ability to include all the material which contain in the magazine covers the whole matter about the public interest. Magazines can also include the color printing with five stuff of paper. These magazines offer a more selective audience which is more 'involved' with the editorial content at least. Magazines are traditionally categorized into general interest, special interest and trade or technical. The advertiser will, therefore, be able to select those which match the specific profile demanded by the advertising strategy. The weight, or 'authority', of magazines is correspondingly high, and they may be kept for a considerable time for use as reference and passed to other readers (so that 'readership' figures may be much higher than 'circulation' figures). They can offer excellent color printing; but again, the clutter of many competing advertisements may reduce the impact of the advertiser's message.

Trade or Technical Journals

Trade or Technical Journals are like the free press in which they are delivered the free informations to the recipients at least in theory. In the trade and professional fields, there are now a significant number of 'controlled circulation' magazines. These are like the 'free Press', in that they are delivered free to the recipients; but, at least in theory, those recipients should have been carefully screened to ensure that they are of value to the advertisers — Their circulation can, if properly controlled, represent a wide cross-section of the buyers, and influencers, in the advertiser's target audience. The rates for positioning are usually more varied than for newspapers, with premiums being paid for facing editorial matter and, of course, for color.

Posters

These are famous advertising Media by which people can attracts and responds on it. This is something of a specialist medium, which is commonly used in support of campaigns using other media. On the other hand, some advertisers, particularly those in brewing and tobacco, have successfully made significant use of the medium;

although, to achieve this, they have developed the requisite expertise to make efficient use of its peculiarities.

The main roadside posters are described in terms of how the poster is physically posted on, to them pasted on one sheet at a time, by a bill-poster; as 16 sheet the main, 10' x 68" size in vertical format and 48 sheet 10' x 20', in horizontal/landscape format. Those smaller ones, seen in pedestrian areas, are typically four sheet (5' x 34"). The best sites are typically reserved for the long-term clients, mainly the brewers and tobacco companies (hence one reason for their success in use of the medium), so that new users may find this a relatively unattractive medium.

This industry is also known as Out of Home Media. However, this category is not limited to posters and billboards. It may involve the use of media space in airports, malls, convenience stores, etc, and it could even tie into guerilla marketing, a nontraditional approach to advertising that may involve grassroots tactics (e.g. posting branded stickers or static clings to buildings, restrooms, and other surfaces in metropolitan areas).

In Malaysia, there are numerous sizes from 10x40', 20x60', 20x80' to 40x60'. In both formats. Landscape and portrait. Current Outdoor Media Owners include Seni Jaya and Big Tree.

Radio

In today's time, the radio is most efficient source of advertising because most of the people have interest in listening radio or FM. So this is the best media of advertising.

The use of radio has increased rapidly in recent years, with the granting of many more licences. It typically generates specific audiences at different times of the day, for instance, adults at breakfast, housewives thereafter, and motorists during rush hours. It can be a very cost-effective way of reaching these audiences especially as production costs can also be much cheaper, although the types of message conveyed will be limited dut to lack of any visual elements, and may have a 'lightweight' image.

Television

This is generally the most expensive medium, which is generally open only to the major advertisers, although some regional contractors offer more affordable packages to their local advertisers. It offers by far the widest coverage, particularly at peak hours (roughly 7.00—10.30 p.m.) and especially of family audiences. Offering sight, sound, movement and color, it has the greatest impact, which are especially for those products or services where a 'demonstration' is essential, since it combines the virtues of both the 'story-teller' and the 'demonstrator'. However, to be effective, these messages must be kept simple — and have the impact to overcome the surrounding distractions of family life; especially the attraction of the remote control — which has caused more problems for advertisers than any other development.

The price structures can be complicated, with the 'rate card'or the price list which are offering different prices for different times throughout the day. This is further complicated by a wide range of special promotional packages, and individual negotiations. It is truly the province of the specialist media buyer.

Advertising- free Media

Advertising free media is defined as the media out puts by which they are not funded or subsidized by sale of advertising.

Advertising-free media refers to media outlets whose output is not funded or subsidised by the sale of advertising space. It includes in its scope of mass media entities such as websites, television and radio networks, and magazines.

The public broadcasters of a number of countries, air without commercials. Perhaps the best known example of this is the United Kingdom's public broadcaster, the BBC, whose domestic networks do not carry commercials. Instead, the BBC, in common with most other public broadcasters in Europe, is funded by a television license fee levied on the owners of all television sets.

NEED FOR ADVERTISING

When we think about the need for advertising, then a question arises why does a developing country like India need advertising?

All businesses need advertising for their business at some point or another. Whether it's word of mouth or a Television ad, more than you will likely find any number of businesses advertising.

When a business considers need to advertising, or most advertising is when sales are slow.

The new way of advertising for companies is through digital promotions. There is a company that specializes in this, particularly.

Promotional Currency. They have grown into the leading aggregator of digital content for promotional marketing purposes. They bring a powerful combination of music downloads, ringtones, wallpaper, mobile games, PC games, instant win games and artist licensing — offering their brand partners, the first one-stop source for all online and wireless digital promotions.

There are some answers of the above question:

Advertising is the most economical means by which a manfacturer of an institutional body can communicate to an audience, whether to sell a product or promote a cause of social welfare.

Advertising is necessary, essential and integral part of marketing system. It is sometimes maintained that the marketing system is nothing but the consequences of social and economic growth of country. The fact is that marketing and advertising are key tools that are used to cure the growth of country.

Advertising being a necessary means of communication which is an inseparable part of free speech.

Advertising is the way of communicating to the consumer, information which enables him or her to compare and select the products and services from them.

Advertising can help in improving the economy of developed and developing country. It can help to stabilize the prices and thus lead to wider distribution and greater availability of goods and services.

Case Study

Note : knowing more about "An Introduction" reader can study documentation process of Microsoft company by visiting their site : www.members.microsoft.com

http://www.kristofcreative.com/experience/case studies/examples.shtml

http://www.icmrindia.org/casestudies/Case Studies Concept Wise.asp?cat=Advertising

http://www.terrakon.com/ppc-case-study/

http://harvardbusiness.org/search/Advertising%20management/0/

http://www.dbs-uk.co.uk/print/case-studies.html

2

Evaluation of Advertising

This chapter includes the key concepts that are described below:-

- Introduction
- Objectives and Functions of Advertising
- Pre-testing
- Campaign Pre-testing
- Post-testing
- Media Buying
- Methods of Advertising
- Advertising Campaign
- Advertising Research Foundation
- Advertising Engagement
- Public Service Advertising
- Contextual Advertising
- Editorial Related Advertising
- Advertising Network
- Ad Serving

INTRODUCTION

Any evaluation of an Advertising campaign will depend on the objectives of the campaign. In order to use any measure of Advertising campaign, it is also necessary to take the degree and direction of change that takes place in the market due to variations in the patterns of demand and supply and in buyer behavior as well as result of promotional efforts of advertising.

Advertising is a management function. While advertising is the event, advertising management is the whole process - a function of marketing starting from market research, continuing through advertising; leading to actual sales or achievement of objective. It goes further in regard to evaluation of the whole cost-benefits that were involved in the whole exercise.

This means that if there is a public service Ad with an objective to increase domestic saving, the evaluation would take place in terms of the actual increase in domestic savings as can be found from banks and other financial institutions. If it's about launch of a new product, then the evaluation would be in terms of benefits derived from the cost sunk in the advertising campaign. Advertising management incorporates the different specialized sub functions like media strategy, message strategy, media planning, media buying etc.

While advertising management is an inseparable part of the marketing department, usually, the marketing department of an organization is concerned more with market research and evaluation of results. All the critical processes of advertising management are generally outsourced to specialised advertising agencies. For example the media buying is done in bulk by these Ad agencies on which they receive discount/commission, that goes into their earning. It involves designing the strategies to be adopted for influencing the public i.e, media selection and deciding on the aspect to be advertised based on the image of the company and the present marketing objective.

Advertising agencies employ research for both *strategic* and *evaluative* purposes. Strategic research enables the agency to better understand how consumers use a product or service and how they regard the product or service. Strategic research also determines the types of people most likely to buy the product. That group of people is called the target market. Advertisers have limited budgets, so knowing who is most likely to buy a particular product helps them spend their advertising budget more efficiently. Evaluative research is used after the advertising has run and seeks to determine how well consumers remember the advertising message and how persuasive it was. Evaluative research is expensive, and as a result, many advertisers do not employ it. Instead, they try to measure the advertising's effectiveness by analyzing sales results.

Here, advertising is the integral part of marketing system and it is sometimes managed that the marketing system is nothing but the consequence of social and economic growth of country. It is the fact that both marketing and advertising are most of the famous tools that are used in growth of country.

Marketing is concerned with market research and Advertising companies or departments employes the strategic and evaluation researches because with the help of strategic research, advertising agency have the ability to know how consumers use a product and how they regard that product, whereas Evaluation research is applied when adverting has run and helps to know about how consumers easily remember the message of advertisement and how it is persuasive.

Agencies use both qualitative and quantitative research methods. Agencies employ *qualitative research* to gain an initial understanding of the marketing situation. This research method uses open-ended questions that allow consumers to explain their values, beliefs, and behaviors at length. One of the most common qualitative research techniques is the *focus group* in which a moderator leads a small group of consumers in a candid discussion of a particular product category, service, or marketing situation.

Agencies use quantitative research to determine a final course of action. One of the most common quantitative research techniques is the survey in which researchers use a questionnaire to gain information from a large group of people, called a sample. Statistical studies show that if the sample is large enough, about 1,000 people, and is representative of a particular group (for example, working mothers who buy disposable diapers), then the findings from the sample are considered true, or statistically valid, and can be extended to the entire group of consumers in that category. The findings provided by quantitative research are therefore conclusive in a way that qualitative research cannot be.

Therefore, after the discussion of Research, it is determined that advertisement employs four types of research i.e strategic, evaluation, qualitative and quantitative research.

OBJECTIVES AND FUNCTIONS OF ADVERTISING

Objectives of Advertising should be followed by defining and prioritizing the expectations of the advertiser from an advertising programme. Sometimes lack of clarity of defining the objectives may arise due some factors. These factors are included:-

- Inability in identifying the target audience.
- Problem of stating objectives in quantifiable terms.
- Inadequate information about media, its qualitative focus and reach.
- Apparent failure in realizing that results of advertising cannot be measured in order of sales.

Advertising objectives are the communication tasks to be accomplished with specific customers that a company is trying to reach during a particular time frame. A company that advertises usually strives to achieve one of the four advertising objectives: trial, continuity, brand switching, and switchback. Which of the four advertising objectives is selected, usually depends on where the product is in its life cycle.

Trial

The purpose of the trial objective is to encourage customers to make an initial purchase of a new product. Companies will typically employ creative advertising strategies in order to cut through other competing advertisements. The reason is simple: Without the first trial of a product by customers, there will not be any repeat purchases.

Trial objective is the initial step of purchasing of a new product. It is much benefited to the customer because if the trial is successful to use, then customer also make repurchase of product and if trial gets failed, then there will not be repurchase of the product.

Continuity

Continuity advertising is a strategy to keep current customers using a particular product. Existing customers are targeted and are usually provided new and different information about a product that is designed to build consumer loyalty. This type of advertising is used to make permanent customer of the existing product, it is necessary to inform them and build consumer loyalty.

Brand Switching

Companies adopt brand switching as an objective when they want customers to switch from competitors' brands to their brands. A common strategy is for a company to compare product price or quality in order to convince customers to switch to its product brand.

Switch Back

Companies subscribe to this advertising objective when they want to get back to former users of their product brand. A company might highlight new product features, price reductions, or other important product information in order to get former customers of its product to switchback. The term switch back means to inform their customers about the modification or updation that occurs in their product and provides new featured the product to their of consumers of product.

Informative

Informative advertising, seeks to tell the market about the product, explain how the product works, provide information on pricing, and build awareness of both the product and the company. Such objectives are normally pursued at the launch of a new product, re-launch is up-date of an existing product.

Informative advertising are used to inform and for to the consumers of their product and tell them about the working of product, pricing information and also about the company of that product. This type of advertising is used at the launching of new product, re-launch or updating of the existing product.

Example: The Dyson Contrarotator

This is type of informative advertising, which shows the features of Dyson contrarotator washing machine.

Persuade Advertising

This type of advertising is used to encourage the audience for the product's purchasing. Objectives of persuade are to encourage the target audience to switch the brands, make the purchase, and create a preference in the market for the product as opposed to its competition. Advertising of this nature is required in highly competitive markets, where a range of products compete directly with each other. In such circumstances businesses often seek to variate their product through Comparison Advertising either directly or indirectly comparing its product to that of its competitors.

Persuade Advertising supports the comparison Advertising. This is the type of objectives where the product of a company is compared with the product of their rival company's product and makes the preference of their product in the market. This is example of comparison advertising showing Halifax Banks for saving.

Campaign has been an extremely successful example of Comparative Advertising, used to Persuade savers to switch Banks. In a highly competitive market, the aim of the work is to show the extra value the bank delivers to customers across a range of financial services, and was produced by the Delaney Lund Knox Warren & Partners agency.

PRE-TESTING

A pre-test may be carried out employing relatively small samples. However, it is important to stimulate the actual environment as the one in which the audience would read, hear and also see the advertisement.

Pre-testing is also known as copy testing, is a form of customized research that predicts in-market performance of an ad, before it airs, by analyzing audience levels of attention, brand linkage, motivation, entertainment, and communication, as well as breaking down the ad's Flow of Attention and Flow of Emotion. Pre-testing is also used on ads still in rough form – e.g., animatics or ripomatics. Pre-testing is also used to identify weak spots within an ad to improve performance, to more effectively edit 60's to 30's or 30's to 15's, to select images from the spot to use in an integrated campaign's print ad, to pull out the key moments for use in ad tracking, and to identify branding moments.

Copy testing is a specialized field of marketing research, it is the study of television commercials prior to airing them. It is defined as research to determine an ad's effectiveness based on consumers' responses to the ad and covers all media including print, TV, radio, Internet etc. Although also known as copy testing, pre-testing is considered the more accurate for the prediction of how effectively an ad will perform, based on the analysis of feedback gathered from the target audience. Each test will either qualify the ad as strong enough to meet company action standards for airing or identify opportunities to improve the performance of the ad through editing.

The basic purpose of pre-testing various possible advertisements is to establish whether the message content and presentation are likely to perform their allocated task efficiently.

Pretests are held in following situations:

- When there are uncertainties or contradiction are expressed about the content of an advertisement.
- To introduce a product or a band
- To substitute an ongoing campaign with a new campaign.

Pre-testing is also used to identify weak spots within an ad campaign, to more effectively edit 60-second ads to 30-second ads or 30's to 15's, to select images from the spot to use in an integrated campaign's print ad, to pull out the key moments for use in ad tracking, and to identify branding moments.

Features of Pretesting

- It provides measurements which are relevant to the objectives of the advertising
- It requires agreements about how the results will be used in advance of each specific test.
- It provides multiple measurements – because single measurements are generally inadequate to assess the performance of an advertisement
- Pretesting is based on a model of human response to communications – the reception of a stimulus, the

comprehension of the stimulus and the response to the stimulus.

- It allows for consideration of whether the advertising stimulus should be exposed more than once.
- It recognizes that the more finished a piece of copy is, the more soundly it can be evaluated and requires, as a minimum, that alternative executions be tested in the same degree of finish.
- It provides controls to avoid the biasing effects of the exposure context.
- Pretesting takes into account basic considerations of sample definition.
- It demonstrates reliability and validity.

These are features of Pretesting in which pretesting are done.

CAMPAIGN PRE-TESTING

This is the type of pretesting which incorporates one of the leading media planning tools that are developed by media modeling.

A new area of pre-testing driven by the realization that what works on TV does not necessarily translate in other media. Greater budgets allocated to digital media in particular have driven the need for campaing pre-testing. The first to market with a product to test integrated campaigns was OTX in association with Sequent Partners with the introduction of MediaCEP™. The latest generation of this product incorporates one of the leading media planning tools developed by a media modeling and software company Pointlogic. The addition of a media planning tool to this testing approach allows advertisers to test the whole campaign, creative and media, and measures the synergies expected with an integrated campaign.

POST-TESTING

Post testing is also known as Ad- Tracking. Post- testing aims at ascertaining the extent to which advertising achieves its specified objectives following its release.

Post-testing/Ad tracking provide either periodic or continuous in-market research monitoring a brand's performance, including brand awareness, brand preference, product usage and attitudes. Some post-testing approaches simply track changes over time, while others use various methods to quantify the specific changes produced by advertising—either the campaign as a whole or by the different media utilized.

Overall, advertisers use post-testing to plan future advertising campaigns, so the approaches that provide the most detailed information on the accomplishments of the campaign are most valued. The two types of campaign post-testing that have achieved the greatest use among major advertisers include continuous tracking, in which changes in advertising spending are correlated with changes in brand awareness, and longitudinal studies, in which the same group of respondents are tracked over time. With the longitudinal approach, it is possible to go beyond brand awareness, and to isolate the campaign's impact on specific behavioral and perceptual dimensions, and to isolate campaign impact by medium.

Ad tracking is also refers to Ad effectiveness tracking is in market research that monitors a performance including brand and advertising awareness, product trial and usage, also the attitudes about the brand and their product's rival.

Purpose of Ad- Tracking

The purpose of post testing i.e. Ad-tracking is commonly provides a measure of the combined effect of the media weight or spending level, effectiveness of media buy or targeting and the quality of advertising execution.

Advertisers use the results of ad tracking to estimate the return on investment (ROI) of advertising, and to refine advertising plans. Sometimes, tracking data are used to provide inputs to Marketing Mix Models which marketing science statisticians build to estimate the role of advertising, as compared to pricing, distribution and other marketplace variables on sales of the brand.

Today, most ad tracking studies are conducted via the Internet. Some ad tracking studies are conducted continuously and others are conducted at specific points in time (typically before the advertising appears in market, and then again after the advertising has been running for some period of time). The two approaches use different types of analyses, although both start by measuring advertising awareness. Typically, the respondent is either shown a brief portion of a commercial, or a few memorable still images from the TV ad.

Continuous tracking design analyzes the advertising awareness over the time, in relation to ad spending this design is able to track the brand awareness and then develops the indices of effectiveness which are based on the strength of the correlation between ad spending and brand awareness of the product.

The most popular alternate approach to the continuous tracking design is the Communicus System longitudinal design, in which the same people are interviewed at two points in time. Changes in brand measures (for example, brand purchasing and future purchase intentions) exhibited among those who have seen the advertising are compared to the changes in brand measures that occurred among those unaware of advertising. By means of this method, the researchers can isolate those marketplace changes that were produced by advertising versus those that would have occurred without advertising.

MEDIA BUYING

Each and every agency has their own media department by which an agency can capable to advertise their product and identified that product towards the audience. These media department of an agency have the capability to find the most effective way to identified the product in the market.

Once the target audience has been identified, an agency's media department determines the most effective way of delivering the message to that target. The *media planner* is the person who decides which media will be used. The media planner must consider three factors:

- the number of people to be exposed to the message, known as the reach,
- the number of times each person needs to be exposed to the message in order to remember it, known as the frequency, and
- the costs.

According to these factors, media planner can be capable various functions by it.

The media planner wants to reach the largest possible percentage of the target audience. To accomplish that goal, the media planner must employ the media that have audiences closely resembling the target audience. If the target is very broad, such as the national market for medium-priced automobiles, the media planner will probably select network television, which has a broad reach. If the target is more narrow and specialized, then the media that reach a more specialized audience, such as magazines, would be selected. Moreover, since not all members of the narrow target audience read the same magazines, the media planner might employ a range of magazines to reach a larger percentage of the intended consumer. Media planner must also determine that how the advertising should run in each medium very frequently. Frequency is most important because repetition helps the consumer remember both the product and advertising message.

Finally, because no advertiser has an unlimited amount of money to spend, cost is also a factor. The media planner must choose those media that will enable the advertiser to reach the largest percentage of the target with enough frequency for the message to be remembered without exceeding the advertiser's budget. Once this media plan has been put together, the agency's *media buyer* contacts the media on behalf of the client in order to purchase advertising space or time at the best possible rate.

Creative Work

Once the types of media have been determined, the agency's creative department develops the presentation of the ads. The principal figures in the creative department are the *copywriter* and the *art director*. The copywriter is the person who writes the advertising message. The art director is the person who oversees the design of the ad. The copywriter and the art director work together to find creative ways to deliver the message that research found would have the greatest appeal to the target audience.

Each agency have their creative department which consists of two main concepts i.e. copywriter and second one is art director from the aspects of creative department, copy writer is one of the person are capable to write the message in advertising and art director is the person which are capable to oversee the design of advertisement. Both figures are most important for the advertising agency. Print ads and television communicate use a variety of techniques to deliver their messages.

Production

In the Creative department, production is main feature of advertisement. The Creative department of agency has the cut director and copywriters, both are capable and helpful to make the concepts of ad instead of advertisement.

Art directors and copywriters create the concepts behind the ads, but they do not literally make the advertising. Making the ads is the job of the production department. In print advertising, the art director works with the print production manager to hire a photographer or illustrator and then supervises the work. Once the photograph has been taken or the illustration completed, the image is scanned into a computer and placed in the proper position. The art director also selects typefaces for the headline and body copy and then, using the computer, correctly positions the headline and body copy. Once all the elements are in place, the computer file is sent to the newspaper or magazine in which the ad will run. The publication then prints the ad directly from the computer file.

After a client approves a television storyboard, the creative team works with the broadcast producer to hire a director for the commercial. In consultation with the agency and the client, the director selects the actors who will appear in the commercial. The director also hires the crew, including the camera and sound people who will film and record the commercial. After the commercial has been filmed, the creative team works with an editor to put the commercial's various scenes together. When that task is completed, the copywriter and art director supervise the addition of music and sound effects. Once the ad is completed, numerous videotape copies called dubs are made. A dub is then sent to each television station that will air the commercial.

To make the advertisement, there is need of production department in an agency. In print advertising, print production manager helps to create an ad. The production of ad is done by whole team of production. There is also the role of creative department i.e. copywriter and Art director who provides the music and sound effects on the ad.

METHODS OF ADVERTISING

Television

In United States—To reach the consumer, advertisers employ a wide variety of media. In the United States, the most popular media, as measured by the amount of ad spending, are television, newspapers, direct mail, radio, Yellow Pages, magazines, the Internet, outdoor advertising, and a variety of other media, including transit ads, novelties, and point-of-purchase displays. (These rankings are measured each year by *Advertising Age*, an advertising trade magazine, and seldom vary, although Internet advertising continues to grow significantly. In the first half of 2005, ad spending on the Internet increased 26 percent, far greater than the 4.5 percent growth for the entire advertising market.) There are various numbers of sources available for advertising but also an expensive source to advertise.

Newspaper

In Canada—In Canada, newspapers are the most popular advertising medium, followed by television, magazines, radio, and outdoor advertising. Canada is the ninth largest advertising market in the world. Newspapers are most famous and major source in Canada instead of television, magazines, radio and other advertising.

To run commercials on television, advertisers buy units of time known as spots. The standard units of time are 15, 30, or 60 seconds in length. These spots are purchased either locally or from a national network. Because of the high cost of national network spots, ranging from hundreds of thousands of dollars to millions of dollars, only large national advertisers can afford to run network television spots. Advertisers wishing to reach a local audience can buy time from an individual station. But even these spots cost so much to produce and run that small and even many mid-sized companies cannot afford them.

In United States—Newspapers are the second source of advertising after the television. It receives 22% dollars whereas television receives 23% dollars of advertising.

Because television commercials combine sight, sound, and motion, they are more dramatic than any other form of advertising and lend excitement and appeal to ordinary products. Advertisers consider television an excellent medium to build a product's brand image or to create excitement around a particular event such as a year-end auto sale. But TV spots are too brief to provide much product information. As a result, television works best for products such as automobiles, fashion, food, beverages, and credit cards that viewers are familiar with and easily understand.

In the United States, newspapers are the second most popular advertising medium after television, receiving about 22 percent of all advertising dollars. Newspapers enable advertisers to reach readers of all age groups, ethnic backgrounds, and income levels. Two types of advertising appear in newspapers: classified advertising, such as the want ads, and display advertising. Display ads range in size from as large as a full page to as small as one column in width and less than one centimeter (less than one inch) in length. Display ads often contain illustrations or photographs and usually provide information about where the product or service being advertised can be purchased. Typically, advertising makes up about 65 percent of a newspaper's content and generates about 65 percent of a newspaper's revenue. About 88 percent of this revenue comes from local businesses.

Newspaper provides the display ads and these ads are generally very attractive to see and they provides the power and ideal content about the product or service. Most advertisers believe that newspaper ads fail to convey the kind of emotional images that build brand image. As a result, most newspaper advertising is done by retailers who use newspaper ads to provide timely information that can lead to immediate sales. Newspapers are particularly well suited to this role because most are published daily. Readers can clip coupons from the newspaper and cash them in quickly at local stores. People also turn to newspapers for immediately useful information about product discounts, bank interest rates, restaurant specials, and entertainment.

Direct Mail

Direct mail is the third medium of advertising which receives the 20% dollars instead of 23% or 22% of Television and Newspaper. Direct mail is sent by mailing system directly to the people through Postal system.

Direct mail is the third largest advertising medium, attracting about 20 percent of all U.S. advertising dollars. Direct mail advertising, as the name implies, is advertising that is sent directly to people by mail, usually through the postal system. Increasingly, however, electronic mail (e-mail) is being used as a direct mail device. Direct mail can be as simple as a single letter or as involved as a catalog or an elaborate e-mail known as HTML mail that offers graphics and links to more information.

From the advertiser's point of view, the key to a successful direct mail program is the mailing list. The mailing list contains the names and addresses of people who share certain common characteristics that suggest they will be likely to buy a particular product or service. Because advertisers are speaking directly to those who are most likely to buy their product or service, many advertisers consider direct mail the most effective of all advertising media for generating immediate results. Direct mail through the U.S. postal system, however, is the most expensive form of advertising, costing about 14 times as much per exposure as most magazine and newspaper ads. But because of the results it produces, many advertisers believe the expense is justified.

Radio

Radio attracts about 8 percent of all U.S. advertising dollars, making it the fourth largest advertising medium. Although national advertisers can buy national network radio time, 90 percent of all radio advertising is local. Unlike television which reaches a broad audience, the specialized programming of radio stations enables advertisers to reach a narrow, highly specific audience such as people who like sports or urban teenagers who listen to the latest styles of popular music. Because many people listen to radio while in their cars, radio also enables advertisers to reach prospects just before they go shopping. But because people listen to the radio while doing something else such as driving or working, radio commercials can be easily misunderstood. As a result, radio ads work best when the messages are relatively simple ones for familiar, easily understood products.

Radio is the fourth source of advertising that receives the 8% of dollars of advertising. Most of the people have the interest to listen the radio so this is the best way to advertise their product or services.

Yellow Pages

Yellow Pages, the thick directories of telephone listings and display advertisements, represent the fifth most popular advertising medium, attracting about 6 percent of total advertising spending. Almost all advertising in the Yellow Pages is local advertising. Here yellow pages are the fifth source of advertising which refers to the directories of telephone. It receives the 6% of dollars which is less than radio. Yellow pages acts as local advertising.

Magazines

Magazines have the sixth place or source of advertising which receives the 5% dollars of US. Magazines rank sixth in total U.S. ad spending, representing about 5 percent. Although newspapers reach all different kinds of readers, a magazine's specialized editorial content generally reaches readers who have similar interests. The relatively specialized, narrow audience of a magazine enables an advertiser to speak to those most likely to buy a particular product. For example, a manufacturer of mascara who advertises to teenage girls could use a magazine with editorial content aimed especially at teenage girls to reach that audience exclusively.

A magazine advertising is the very effective way to represents their product in front of public. A magazine's editorial environment can also lend a product credibility and prestige, and the magazine's ability to reproduce beautiful color photographs can enhance a product's appearance. As a result, magazine advertising is an effective way to build a product's brand image. Because such advertising is expensive and because most magazines are distributed regionally or nationally, they generally feature national advertising rather than local advertising. Magazines generate 63 percent of their revenue from advertising.

Internet Advertising

In 2004 the Internet accounted for $9.6 billion in advertising spending in the United States, or 3.7 percent of total ad spending, an increase from 3 percent in 2003, according to data gathered by the accounting firm of PricewaterhouseCoopers LLP for the Interactive Advertising Bureau. About 96 percent of ad spending on the Internet goes to 50 Web companies, mostly to four sites maintained by Yahoo, Google, America Online, and the Microsoft Network. It is the seventh source of advertising.

Advertisements on the Internet often take the form of banners, buttons, pop-ups, and sponsorships. But the most important aspect of Internet marketing is that the World Wide Web allows advertisers to personalize their messages for individual customers. For example, when a customer visits a commercial Web site that person is often welcomed by name and is offered information about new products based on the type of products the person has purchased in the past. Moreover, the customer can then order the product immediately without venturing out to a store. By allowing advertisers to customize their advertising, the Internet enables them to build customer loyalty and generate stronger sales results. Google pioneered the technique of providing customized ads when someone enters a search term. Advertisers take part in an auction to have their ads placed next to relevant search results and pay only when someone clicks on the ad.

In this type of advertising, each person gets the information of the product who visits on that commercial site. By this advertising, it is easy to sell their product online which is called e-shopping.

Outdoor Advertising

It is eighth source of advertising which receives less than 10% dollars of advertising.

Outdoor advertising amounts to less than 1 percent of total ad spending in the United States. Outdoor advertising is an effective way to reach a highly mobile audience that spends a lot of time on the road—for example, in commuting to and from work or as part of their job. It offers the lowest cost per exposure of any major advertising medium, and it produces a major impact, because it is big, colorful, and hard to ignore. The messages on outdoor boards have to be very brief. So outdoor advertising primarily serves as a reminder medium and one that can trigger an impulse buy.

Outdoors advertising refers to the advertising through the marketing team or salesman who introduces their product infront of public by communicating with them face-to-face and provides the whole information about their product & convinces them to purchase it.

Other Advertising

A wide variety of other advertising media make up the remainder of total ad spending. Transit advertising is mainly an urban advertising form that uses buses and taxi tops as well as posters placed in bus shelters, airports, and subway stations. Like outdoor boards, transit is a form of reminder advertising that helps advertisers place their name before a local audience. Finally, point-of-purchase advertising places attention-getting displays, streamers, banners, and price cards in the store near where the product is sold to explain product benefits and promote impulse buys.

ADVERTISING CAMPAIGN

An advertising campaign is a series of advertisement messages that share a single idea and theme which make up an integrated marketing communication (IMC). Advertising campaigns appear in different media across a specific time frame.

The critical part of making an advertising campaign is determining a *champion theme*, as it sets the tone for the individual advertisements and other forms of marketing communications that will be used. The campaign theme is the central message that will be communicated in the promotional activities. The campaign themes are usually developed with the intention of being used for a substantial period but many of them are short lived due to factors such as being ineffective or market conditions and/or competition in the marketplace and marketing mix. Advertising campaign is used to build the IMC i.e. integrated marketing communication means the series of advertising messages which shares into a single idea or theme (IMC).

ADVERTISING RESEARCH FOUNDATION

It is the association for creating and developing, also managing the fields of advertising. These are abbreviated by ARF. It conducts the various numbers of advertisers, advertising agency & departments, institutions also.

The Advertising Research Foundation (ARF) is a nonprofit industry association for creating, aggregating, synthesizing and sharing the knowledge in the fields of advertising and media. It was founded in 1936 by the Association of National Advertisers and the American Association of Advertising Agencies. Its stated mission is to improve the practice of advertising, marketing and media research in pursuit of more effective marketing and advertising communications. Its membership consists of over 400 advertisers, advertising agencies, research firms, media companies, educational institutions, and international organizations.

The ARF conducts several research initiatives. It also sponsors a variety of advertising related marketing research endeavours.

During the 1990s the ARF spearheaded notable primary research in studies such as the Copy Research Validity Project, which redefined the area of copy testing, and the ARF/Ad Council Study to determine the impact of public service advertising. More recently the ARF has pioneered efforts to define advertising engagement and to measure consumers' emotional response to advertising. ARF includes two important Advertiser naming association of national advertisers and American association of advertising agencies i.e. (ANA & AAAA)

ADVERTISING ENGAGEMENT

Advertising Engagement measures the extent to which a consumer has a meaningful brand experience when exposed to commercial advertising, sponsorship, television contact, or other experience.

In March 2006 the Advertising Research Foundation defined Engagement as "turning on a prospect to a brand idea enhanced by the surrounding context". The ARF has also defined the function whereby engagement impacts a brand:

Advertising engagement refers to those method which is used to measures the extent to which a consumer has brand experience.

Engagement + **Trust** x **Targeted Contacts** = **Brand Impact**

idea message media

This chart shows that the engagement refers to three figures i.e. idea, message, message media when these figures combines with trust and it includes the targeted contacts then they all concludes the impact of brand of the product.

Engagement is complex because a variety of exposure and relationship factors affect engagement, making simplified rankings misleading. Typically, engagement with a medium often differs from engagement with advertising, according to an analysis conducted by the Magazine Publishers of America.

PUBLIC SERVICE ADVERTISING

It is the techniques of commercial advertising which are used for non-commercial purposes. These advertisements are used to encourage the people to safe themselves and to provide the ideal services or offers that they deserve.

Public Service Advertising is the use of commercial advertising techniques for non-commercial purposes. Typical topics for public service advertising include public health/public safety issues, emergency preparedness instructions, natural resources conservation information, and other topics of broad interest.

Public service advertising campaigns are widespread around the world. Such advertising is generally produced and distributed on a cooperative basis by governmental agencies or nonprofit organizations acting in concert with private advertising and mass media companies. In most cases, the nonprofit provides the programming that is to be advertised, while the participating advertising agency and media companies provide creative services, media planning, and dissemination services on a *pro bono* basis.

One of the best-known forms of public service advertising is that which is broadcast on television. These televised "spot" announcements, known in the USA as public service announcements (PSAs) and in the UK as public information film (PIFs), are often striking in their presentation and occasionally become well-known aspects of popular culture among their audiences.

CONTEXTUAL ADVERTISING

It is also the type of targeted advertisement for those advertisements which are appeared on websites.

Contextual Advertising is a form of targeted advertising for advertisements appearing on websites or other media, such as content displayed in mobile browsers. The advertisements themselves are selected and served by automated systems based on the content displayed to the user.

Contextual advertising has made a major impact on earnings of many websites. Because the advertisements are more targeted, they are more likely to be clicked, thus generating revenue for the owner of the website (and the server of the advertisement). A large part of Google's earnings is from its share of the contextual advertisements served on the millions of webpages running the AdSense program. Contextual advertising has major impacts of selling the products only through many sites.

A contextual advertising system scans the text of a website for keywords and returns advertisements to the webpage based on what the user is viewing. The advertisements may be displayed on the webpage or as pop-up ads. For example, if the user is viewing a website pertaining to sports and that website uses contextual advertising, the user may see advertisements for sports-related companies, such as memorabilia dealers or ticket sellers. Contextual advertising is also used by search engines to display advertisements on their search results pages based on the keywords in the user's query.

EDITORIAL RELATED ADVERTISING

This type of advertising are associated with contextual advertising.

Editorial Related Advertising is associated with the concept of Contextual Advertising but differs in its ability to match advertising to content in a much more specific manner. Where Contextual Advertising is keyword based, Editorial Related Advertising is able to also take in the content of the whole article and match on a conceptual level, rather than simply looking for the existence of pre-selected words. For example, there is no chance that an Auto Mechanic could advertise next to an article about the Detroit Pistons.

This specificity also ensures that:

- Advertisers do not advertise next to defamatory articles (or they can create content that will offer a right of reply)

- Advertisers do not advertise next to inappropriate content such as obituaries or negative news articles
- Advertisers can appear next to articles in the general subject area of interest, for example for keywords that are not actually included in the on page text

Advertisers can supply a number of specifically targeted pages, each with their own message to attract users to their 'microsite'. This 'microsite' is housed within a publication on a searchable vertical directory. Advertisers who are not completely related to the publication will not be considered for the program. This creates a directory resource of related suppliers within the publication's website that is also optimized for search engine traffic.

ADVERTISING NETWORK

Advertising network is a type of company that makes the interaction between the websites. for this networking, a company have to pay to the software developers to establish the connections between websites.

An advertising network or ad network is a company that connects web sites that want to host advertisements with advertisers who want to run advertisements. Increasingly Ad networks are companies that pay software developers as well as web sites money for allowing their ads to be shown when people use their software or visit their sites. This type of network has to establish because of its, people gets the information about the product when they use that software or visit their sites.

Online advertising inventory comes in many different forms. This inventory can be found on websites, in RSS feeds, on blogs, in instant messaging applications, in adware, in e-mails, and on other sources. Some examples of advertising inventory include: banner ads, rich media, text links, and e-mails.

An advertiser can buy a run of network package, or a run of category package within the network. The advertising network serves advertisements from its ad server, which responds to a site once a page is called. A snippet of code is called from the ad server, that represents the advertising banner.

Advertising networks are used to serves the advertisements to a site when ever page called.

Large publishers often sell only their remnant inventory through ad networks. Typical numbers range from 10% to 60% of total inventory being remnant and sold through advertising networks.

Smaller publishers often sell all of their inventory through ad networks. One type of *ad network*, known as a *blind network*, is such that advertisers place ads, but do not know the exact places where their ads are being placed.

In most cases, ad networks deliver their content through the use of a central ad server. Large ad networks include a mixture of search engines, media companies, and technology vendors.

There are much more difference between large and small industries in inventory of them. Large industries frequently sell only then remnant inventory via ad networks whereas small groups are frequently sell all of the inventories through ad networks.

Types of ad networks:-

- Representative or Rep Networks
- Blind Networks
- Targeted Networks

Representative (or Rep) Networks

They represent the publications in their portfolio, with full transparency for the advertiser about where their ads will run. They typically promote high quality traffic at market prices and are heavily used by brand marketers. The economic model is generally revenue share.

Blind Networks

These companies offer low pricing to direct marketers in exchange for those marketers relinquishing control over where their ads will run. Blind networks achieve their low pricing through large bulk buys of typically remnant inventory combined with campaign optimization and ad targeting technology. The financial model is arbitrage.

Targeted Networks

Sometimes called "next generation" or "2.0" ad networks,

these focus on specific targeting technologies such as behavioral or contextual. Targeted networks specialize in using consumer click stream data to enhance the value of the inventory they purchase. Targeted networks are also known as next generation ad networks.

There are two types of advertising networks: first-tier and second-tier networks. First-tier advertising networks have a large number of their own advertisers and publishers, they have high quality traffic, and they serve ads and traffic to second-tier networks. Examples of first-tier networks include the major search engines. Second-tier advertising networks may have some of their own advertisers and publishers, but their main source of revenue comes from syndicating ads from other advertising networks.

First – tier networks have then own publishers and advertiser, it is independent network and also traffic is also in high quality and serve ads to second- tier network but second- tier network is depend on syndicating ads.

AD SERVING

Ad serving describes the technology and service that places advertisements on web sites. Ad serving technology companies provide software to web sites and advertisers to serve ads, count them, choose the ads that will make the website or advertiser most money, and monitor progress of different advertising campaigns.

Ad serving is the concept that describes the technology and service that establish the advertisements on sites. Ad serving is provided by advertising companies, they provides the software to websites which count the number of visitors on sits, and choose ads that will make the websites.

Ad Server

It is a server that acts like web server and stores the all advertisements that are publish on site and also delivers them to visitors.

An ad server is a computer server, specifically a web server, that stores advertisements used in online marketing and delivers them to website visitors.

The content of the webserver is constantly updated so that the website or webpage on which the ads are displayed contains new advertisements — e.g., banners (static images/animations) or text — when the site or page is visited or refreshed by a user.

In addition, the ad server also performs various other tasks like counting the number of impressions/clicks for an ad campaign and report generation, which helps in determining the ROI for an advertiser on a particular website.

Ad servers come in two flavors: local ad servers and third-party or remote ad servers. Local ad servers are typically run by a single publisher and serve ads to that publisher's domains, allowing fine-grained creative, formatting, and content control by that publisher. Remote ad servers can serve ads across domains owned by multiple publishers. They deliver the ads from one central source so that advertisers and publishers can track the distribution of their online advertisements, and have one location for controlling the rotation and distribution of their advertisements across the web.

Functions of Ad Server—There are number of functions that are performed by ad server are following below:-

- Tuning and optimization based on results.
- Reporting impressions, clicks, post-click & post-impression activities, and interaction metrics.
- Uploading advertisements and rich media.
- Frequency capping so users only see messages a limited amount of time.
- Trafficking ads according to differing business rules.
- Targeting ads to different users, or content.
- Sequencing ads so users see messages in a specific order often called as surround sessions).
- Displaying ads so an advertiser can own 100% of the inventory on a page (sometimes known as roadblocks).
- Targeting ads to users based on their previous behavior (behavioral marketing or behavioral targeting).
- Excluding competition so users do not see competitors' ads directly next to one another.

Case Study

Note : knowing more about "Evaluation of Advertising" reader can study documentation process of Microsoft company by visiting their site : www.members.microsoft.com

3

Implications of Advertising

This chapter includes the key concepts that are described below—

- Introduction
- Economic Effects of Advertising
- Impacts of Advertising
- Criticisms of Advertising
- Role of Advertising
- Socio-issues of Advertising
- Opposition and Campaigns
- Taxation as Revenue and Control

INTRODUCTION

Advertising may be useful for consumers, considering that dissemination of information is necessary when buyers have to make a choice from the various products and services. It may be useful to look separately into the economic and social effects of advertising.

Advertising has an important effect on a country's economy, society, culture, and political system. This is especially true in the United States where the advertising industry plays such a prominent role.

The cumulative effect of Advertising is particularly relevant to the discussion of both economic and social implications. The role of Advertising in society has often been a subject of services debate. As systematic as well as susceptibility to change are essential ingredients of aimful advertising.

ECONOMIC EFFECTS OF ADVERTISING

Advertising is closely linked with economic development in the long term which are considering that it can be a vital marketing input for new product introductions.

Most economists believe that advertising has a positive impact on the economy because it stimulates demand for products and services, strengthening the economy by promoting the sale of goods and services. Manufacturers know that advertising can help sell a new product quickly, enabling them to recoup the costs of developing new products. By stimulating the development of new products, advertising helps increase competition. Many economists believe that increased competition leads to lower prices, thereby benefiting consumers and the economy as a whole. These economists also argue that by interesting consumers in purchasing goods, advertising enables manufacturers and others to sell their products in larger quantities. The increased volume of sales enables companies to produce individual units at lower costs and therefore, sell them at a lower price. Advertising thus benefits consumers by helping lower prices.

Economic growth is the outcome of expansion in demand on the one hand and augmenting of resources on the other. Economic systems are basically constituted of a series of transactions between individual, organizations and sectors.

Other economists, however, believe that advertising is wasteful. They argue that the cost of advertising adds to the cost of goods and that most advertising simply encourages consumers to buy one brand rather than another. According to this view, advertising simply moves sales from one company to another, rather than increasing sales overall and thereby benefiting the economy as a whole.

Business Environment and Advertising

Utility of advertising in periods of economic recession. Recession refers to the period of economic and industrial activity when the rate of growth of the market served is substantially lower than the long term. The Deviations of short-term trend from the long-term market trend indicates the periods of expansion and recession.

The Deviation chart between short-term and long term trends are shown below:—

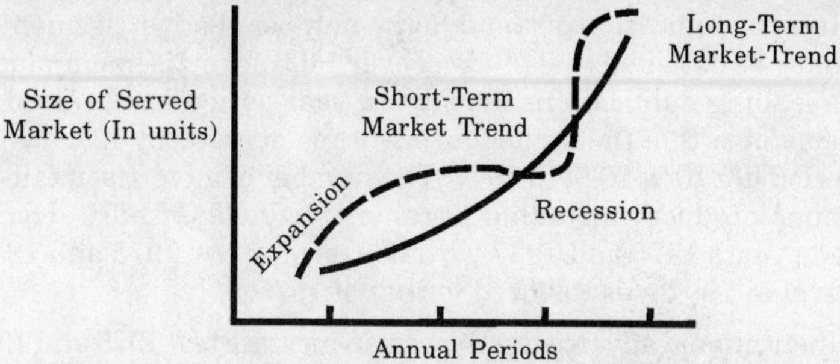

Business can help improve the value of their market shares by increasing the expenditures on media advertising. The below chart shows the business which have difficulty in meeting growing demand, thus allowing competitors an easier entry into the market.

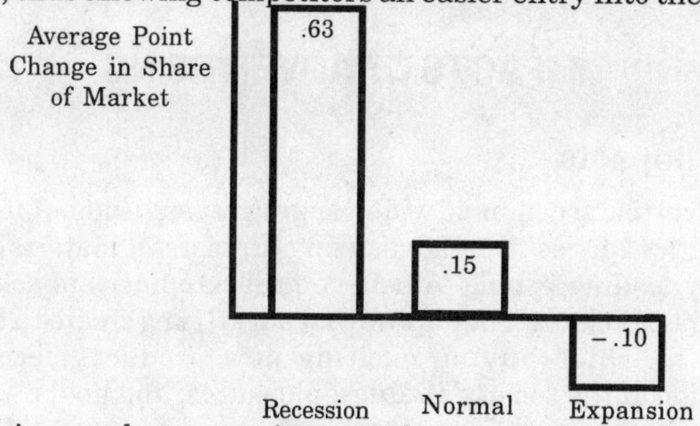

During market expansion periods, over 50% of the businesses increased advertising expenditure and no spectacular gains in market shares were achieved. The chart which are shown below describes those business which reduced the media advertising expenditures during the expansion phase on the other hand suffered from losses in market shares:—

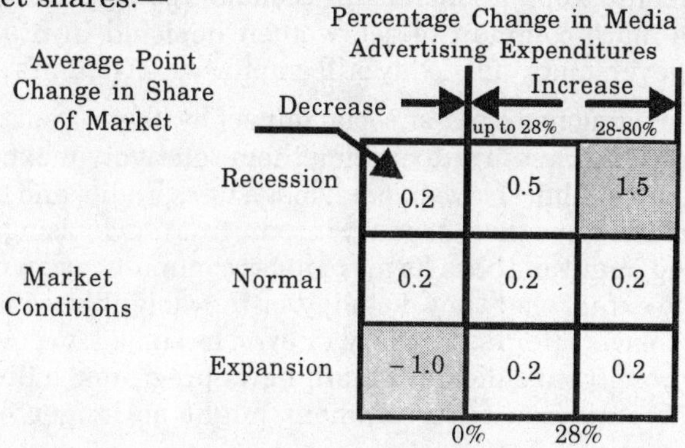

It is the indication of trend in the number of advertisement in India may be obtained that study of over 1400 advertisement placed in two leading publications during ten year period i.e. 1971-80. It was remember that the number of advertisement fell by 42% during the period lies b / w 1974 to 1977. The number of advertisements of consumer products including durables recorded a sharp decline between years 1975 and 1977 with less decline b/w 1975 and 1976. The level in 1977 was restored to that of 1975.

Institutional advertising showed an increase b/w 1975 and 1976 and then sharp declined in 1977 largest number of advertisement appeared in 1974 which are following by Indian economy in 1973 and lowest during decade was reached in 1977. A distinct upward trend in 1980.

IMPACTS OF ADVERTISING

Social Impacts

Advertising can have wide-ranging repercussions on a society. Some critics suggest that advertising promotes a materialistic way of life by leading people to believe that happiness is achieved by purchasing products. They argue that advertising creates a consumer culture in which buying exciting new products becomes the foundation of the society's values, pleasures, and goals.

Other critics express concern over the way advertising has affected women and racial minority groups. Ads in the 1950s depicted women primarily as decoration or sex objects. Although millions of women worked outside the home in the 1960s, ads continued to focus on their role as homemakers. Whether owing to the feminist movement or to women's increasing economic power, after the 1960s it became more common to see women depicted in professional roles. However, many ads today still emphasize a woman's sexuality.

Advertising has a major social impact by helping sustain mass communications media and making them relatively inexpensive, if not free, to the public. Newspapers, magazines, radio, and broadcast television all receive their primary income from advertising. Without advertising, many of these forms of mass communication might not exist to the extent that they do today, or they might be considerably more expensive, offer less variety, or even be subject to government control through subsidies. In-depth news programs, a diversity of magazines, and free entertainment might no longer be widely available.

Advertising has various impacts in society i.e. social impacts. It affects the social aspects of Advertising.

Advertisers may affect media programming in other ways, too, critics charge. For example, companies that sponsor TV programs prefer relatively wholesome, noncontroversial programming to avoid offending a mass audience. This preference causes TV networks to emphasize this type of programming. The result is that society may be denied the benefits of being able to view challenging or highly original entertainment programs or news programs on controversial issues. Because advertisers are especially interested in attracting the 18 to 34 year olds who account for most consumer spending, television shows are often developed with this audience in mind. If the ratings show that a program is not attracting large audiences, particularly among 18 to 34 year olds, advertisers often withdraw support, which causes a program to be canceled. As a result, shows that are more likely to interest and to be of value to older audiences are not produced.

The impact of television on young children has received much attention. Research suggests that children see television advertising as just another form of programming and react uncritically to its messages, which makes them especially vulnerable to advertising. There is also concern about the way in which adolescent girls respond to advertising that features beautiful, thin models. Research indicates that many adolescent girls are unduly influenced by this standard of beauty, become dissatisfied with their own bodies, and may develop eating disorders in pursuit of a thin figure. New research suggests that adolescent boys are also being influenced by advertising images of bulked-up, buffed bodies. As a result, many become dissatisfied with their own body image, devote large amounts of time to weightlifting, and may even take drugs that have harmful side effects in order to develop more muscle. Those over the age of 60 are thought to be less influenced by advertising, but some elderly people no longer process messages as easily as younger people, making them more susceptible to questionable advertising claims.

Economic Impact

At the same time, however, some critics warn that because advertising plays such a major economic role, it may exercise undue influence on the news media and thereby curtail the free flow of information in a free society. Reporters and editors, for example, may be hesitant to develop a news story that criticizes a major advertiser. As a result, society might not be alerted to harmful or potentially harmful conduct by the advertiser. Most members of the news media deny that pressure from an advertiser prevents them from pursuing news stories involving that advertiser, but some members of the media acknowledge that they might not be inclined to investigate an issue aggressively if it threatened to offend a major advertiser. Advertising has then economic impacts. These impacts are also described in previous topic of this chapter.

Political Impact

Advertising is now a major component of political campaigns and therefore has a big influence on the democratic process itself. In 1998 more than $467 million was spent on election campaigns in the United States. That amount of spending placed political advertising in the ranks of the country's 30 leading advertisers that year. Political advertising is a relatively new development in U.S. history. Advertising professionals did not become involved in electoral campaigns until the 1950s. But since then, political advertising has grown in sophistication and complexity.

Political Impact has occurred in very difficult time. It occurs in the condition of sophistication and also in complexity. This impact has a big influence on the democratic process of political campaigns

Political advertising enables candidates to convey their positions on important issues and to acquaint voters with their accomplishments and personalities. Television advertising is especially effective for candidates running for national or statewide office because it can reach so many people at once. Candidates can also use advertising to respond effectively to the charges of their opponents.

Critics of political advertising also charge that the 30-second television spot has become more important to a political campaign than a thorough discussion of the issues. As a result, voters are bombarded with image advertising rather than being acquainted with the candidate's positions. They contend that this practice is harmful to good government. Issues are simplified, and candidates are "packaged and sold" much like a consumer product, thereby distorting the political process.

Because of the high cost of television ads, the costs of political campaigns have sky rocketed, making it necessary for candidates to raise money continually even after they have been elected to office.

Cultural Impact

Advertising can affect cultural values. Some advertising messages, for example, encourage aggressive individualism, which may clash with the traditional cultural values of a country where the collective or group is emphasized over the individual or humility or modesty is preferred to aggressiveness. With the globalization of the world economy, multinational corporations often use the same advertising to sell to consumers around the world. Some critics argue that advertising messages are thus helping to break down distinct cultural differences and traditional values, causing the world to become increasingly homogeneous.

Advertising has also its cultural impacts. Some criticisms find that advertising messages tend to breakdown the various cultural differences and traditional values and cause the world with shortage of cultural aspects of different countries.

Many advertising campaigns, however, have universal appeal, overriding cultural differences, or they contribute to culture in a positive way. Humor in advertising has made many ad campaigns widely popular, in some cases achieving the status of folklore or taking on new life in another arena. For example, a popular ad campaign for a fast-food chain with the slogan "Where's the beef?" became part of the 1980 Democratic presidential primary campaign between Gary Hart and Walter Mondale. The ad ridiculed a competitor by depicting a small hamburger patty dwarfed by a huge bun. During a primary debate one of the candidates used the ad slogan to suggest that his opponent's campaign lacked substance.

CRITICISMS OF ADVERTISING

Advertising invites a lot of criticism from various quarters. There are various criticisms of advertising:—

- Influencing and conditioning
- Price of attention and hidden costs
- Hyper- commercialism and commercial tidal wave.
- Product proliferation
- Barriers to entry
- Prosperity to consume
- Advertising and constitutional rights.

Influencing and Conditioning

The first criticism of advertising is influencing and conditioning.

The most important element of advertising is not information but suggestion more or less making use of associations, emotions (appeal to emotion) and drives dormant in the sub-conscience of people, such as sex drive, herd instinct, of desires, such as happiness, health, fitness, appearance, self-esteem, reputation, belonging, social status, identity, adventure, distraction, reward, of fears (appeal to fear), such as illness, weaknesses, loneliness, need, uncertainty, security or of prejudices, learned opinions and comforts. "All human needs, relationships, and fears – the deepest recesses of the human psyche – become mere means for the expansion of the commodity universe under the force of modern marketing. With the rise to prominence of modern marketing, commercialism – the translation of human relations into commodity relations – although a phenomenon intrinsic to capitalism, has expanded exponentially." Cause-related marketing' in which advertisers link their product to some worthy social cause has boomed over the past decade.

For advertising critics another serious problem is that "the long standing notion of separation between advertising and editorial/ creative sides of media is rapidly crumbling" and advertising is increasingly hard to tell apart from news, information or entertainment. The boundaries between advertising and programming are becoming blurred. According to the media firms all this commercial involvement has no influence over actual media content.

Price of attention and hidden costs

Advertising has developed into a billion-dollar business on which many depend. In 2006 391 billion US dollars were spent worldwide for advertising. In Germany, for example, the advertising industry contributes 1.5% of the gross national income; the figures for other developed countries are similar. Thus, advertising and growth are directly and causally linked. As far as a growth based economy can be blamed for the harmful human lifestyle (affluent society) advertising has to be considered in this aspect concerning its negative impact, because its main purpose is to raise consumption. "The industry is accused of being one of the engines powering a convoluted economic mass production system which promotes consumption."

There are many billion dollars spending for advertising on the business depend. Each business spends on advertising for the success of their company because growth of business and advertising are directly linked.

Hyper commercialism and commercial tidal waves

Criticism of advertising is closely linked with criticism of media and often interchangeable. They can refer to its audio-visual aspects (e. g. cluttering of public spaces and airwaves), environmental aspects (e. g. pollution, oversize packaging, increasing consumption), political aspects (e. g. media dependency, free speech, censorship), financial aspects (costs), ethical/moral/social aspects (e. g. sub-conscious influencing, invasion of privacy, increasing consumption and waste, target groups, certain products, honesty) and, of course, a mix thereof. Some aspects can be subdivided further and some can cover more than one category.

Criticisms of advertising include the concepts of hyper commercialism. This criticism is directly involved with criticism of media and generally refers to interchangeable.

Attention and attentiveness have become a new commodity for which a market developed. "The amount of attention that is absorbed by the media and redistributed in the competition for quotas and reach is not identical with the amount of attention, that is available in society. The total amount circulating in society is made up of the attention exchanged among the people themselves and the attention given to media information. Only the latter is homogenised by quantitative measuring and only the latter takes on the character of an anonymous currency." According to Franck, any surface of presentation that can guarantee a certain degree of attentiveness works as magnet for attention, e. g. media which are actually meant for information and entertainment, culture and the arts, public space etc. It is this attraction which is sold to the advertising business. The German Advertising Association stated that in 2007 30.78 billion Euros were spent on advertising in Germany, 26% in newspapers, 21% on television, 15% by mail and 15% in magazines. In 2002 there were 360.000 people employed in the advertising business. The internet revenues for advertising doubled to almost 1 billion Euros from 2006 to 2007, giving it the highest growth rates.

Here, Hyper commercialism is the concept which refers that many peoples are employed to increased their career from advertising i.e. the term hyper commercialism is defined that many people employed in advertising business because it has much more scope in future and each business start their career or scope through advertising and launch their product infront of public through the help of advertising.

In 2008, Spiegel-Online reported that in the USA in 2008 for the first time more money was spent for advertising on internet (105.3 billion US dollars) than on television (98.5 billion US dollars). The largest amount in 2008 was still spent in the print media (147 billion US dollars). For that same year, Welt-Online reported that the US pharmaceutical industry spent almost double the amount on advertising (57.7 billion dollars) than it did on research (31.5 billion dollars). But Marc-André Gagnon and Joel Lexchin of York University, Toronto, estimate that the actual expenses for advertising are higher yet, because not all entries are recorded by the research institutions. Not included are indirect advertising campaigns such as sales, rebates and price reductions. Few consumers are aware of the fact that they are the ones paying for every cent spent for public relations, advertisements, rebates, packaging etc. since they ordinarily get included in the price calculation.

Product Proliferation

A critic of advertising point out that advertising encourages unnecessary product proliferation. It leads to the multiplication of products that are almost identical, resulting in wastage of resources which could otherwise have been used to produce other product.

Barriers to Entry

There is a general concept that advertisements promote industrial concentration to a greater or lesser degree. The extent of these concentrations may vary with the character of the individual trade, the advertising of the product and the technical conditions of its production.

Prosperity to Consume

Advertising generally raises the prosperity to consume. There are following reasons by which advertising favors the higher prosperity:-

- Advertising for mass consumption goods can help in gradually reducing disparities and breaking down barriers as those between the urban elite and others, by making more products which are available in rural areas.

- Consumptions refer to the productivity because people are inspired to work hard and earn more in order to satisfy their needs. This effort on their part also increases productivity and helps to develop the country.

It is generally argued that if the propensity to consume get higher then the savings will be lesser i.e. propensity to consume is inversely proportional to the savings

Propensity to consume – 1 / saving

This problem tends to the problem of capital formulation.

Advertising and Constitutional Rights

Advertising is equated with constitutionally guaranteed freedom of opinion and speech. Therefore criticizing advertising or any attempt to restrict or ban advertising is almost always considered to be an attack on fundamental rights (First Amendment in the USA) and meets the combined and concentrated resistance of the business and especially the advertising community. "Currently or in the near future, any number of cases are and will be working their way through the court system that would seek to prohibit any government regulation of ... commercial speech (e. g. advertising or food labelling) on the grounds that such regulation would violate citizens' and corporations' First Amendment rights to free speech or free press." An example for this debate is advertising for tobacco or alcohol but also advertising by mail or fliers (clogged mail boxes), advertising on the phone, in the internet and advertising for children. Various legal restrictions concerning spanning, advertising on mobile phones, addressing children, tobacco, alcohol have been introduced by the US, the EU and various other countries. Not only the business community resists restrictions of advertising. Advertising as a means of free expression has firmly established itself in western society. Surveys e. g. reveal that advertising is generally seen as a welcome information and seldom as a nuisance. At worst it is seen as a necessary evil to be endured and most often its entertaining value is pointed out. Hardly any by-law restricting advertising fails to appease possible critics by pointing out the positive effects and the necessity of advertising in its foreword. McChesney argues, that the government deserves constant vigilance when it comes to such regulations, but that it is certainly not "the only antidemocratic force in our society. ...corporations and the wealthy enjoy a power every bit as immense as that enjoyed by the lords and royalty of feudal times" and "markets are not value-free or neutral; they not only tend to work to the advantage of those with the most money, but they also by their very nature emphasize profit over all else...Hence, today the debate is over whether advertising or food labelling, or campaign contributions are speech, if the rights to be protected by the First Amendment can only be effectively employed by a fraction of the citizenry, and their exercise of these rights gives them undue political power and undermines the ability of the balance of the citizenry to exercise the same rights and/or constitutional rights, then it is not necessarily legitimately protected by the First Amendment." In addition, "those with the capacity to engage in free press are in a position to determine who can speak to the great mass of citizens and who cannot". Critics in turn argue, that advertising invades privacy which is a constitutional right. For, on the one hand, advertising physically invades privacy, on the other, it increasingly uses relevant, information-based communication with private data assembled without the knowledge or consent of consumers or target groups.

For Georg Franck at Vienna University of Technology advertising is part of what he calls "mental capitalism", taking up a term (mental) which has been used by groups concerned with the mental environment, such as Adbusters. Franck blends the "Economy of Attention" with Christopher Lasch's culture of narcissm into the mental capitalism.

Advertising is very powerful system which affects the culture, Politics and social aspects of the country. It will also be the responsible for destroying the world.

ROLE OF ADVERTISING

Role of advertising in society has been a subject of much debate or issue.

Advertising is one of the key elements in building a brand personality, which is equally important to the marketer & consumers. Brand personality is distinct, non pre-emptible enduring and associates the brand with certain values. Brand personality acts a potent brand differentiator and offers sustainable competitive advantage.

Brand personality give the famous product and make the image of the company. This could be possible with Advertising. Brand personality is necessary for both the company and also the consumer.

Advertising by creating or reinforcing brand's personality enhances brand value or equity , which in turn can be leveraged through brand extension. Brand personality also helps brands to gain market share, command price premium and insulates from discounting Brands.

Consumers as part of self-defining process, use possessions to describe themselves and also to which group they belong, especially in socially conspicuous product categories such as clothing, automobiles etc. (what is me is related to what I have) Brands make personality statements, users associate a brand with a strong personality.

Role of advertising in creating Brand Personality

Like human personality that is essentially a summation of traits. Brand personality is described as sum of tangible and intangible aspects of the brand. Brand personality also emphasizes on emotion, human and tangible aspects of brand.

Even for industrial product like steel, SAIL uses emotional connect with 'punch line' there is bit of SAIL in everybody's life. Brand personality, is process of transforming the brand into a person or humanizing the brand. Thus brands can also have characteristics (Ex: Sex, Gender, skills & abilities etc.). Marketers deliver the personality using advertising, features, packaging etc.

Users and non users differ in perceptions with respect to Brand personality users attach a distinct personality to the brand. Established brands have unique personality which is generally consistent and may be implicit. Brand personality enables to establish relationship between brand & consumer with emotional content. The degree of proximity between brand and consumer personality, will influence the purchase intension and brand loyalty. Brands need to update personality to stay contemporary and relevant, as target audience personality may change over a period of time, due to changes in cultural, economic, media exposure etc. Brand personality should not be confused with target audience characteristics. Personality may be existing or aspirational. Projective techniques can be used to describe brands. Consumers can be asked to associate the brand, with adjectives (word association, sentence completion etc.) and also can be asked about user imagery.

For example—

Brands	:	Personality
Moods	:	Sensitivity
Thumbs up	:	bravery / daring
Amul	:	humour
MTV	:	wacky
Indiakings	:	Sophistication (upper class)
Woodlands	:	Ruggedness & outdoorsy
Mahindra Scorpio	:	Ruggedness
Marlboro	:	Ruggedness
Ruff & Tuff	:	Bravery
Sona chandi Chavanprash	:	Bravery
Britania little hearts	:	Love & Affection
Brand	**:**	**Adjective**
Liril	:	freshness & Lime
Lux	:	Beauty, softness
Dove	:	Softness
Bisleri	:	Safety
Bajaj Pulsar	:	Power
Yamaha	:	Power
Titan	:	Style, elegance
Cintho	:	Freshness
Mysore Sandal	:	Traditional
Medimix	:	Traditional

These above examples show the popular brands with their adjectives and personality.

In all the above brands, advertisement elements such as selection of endorsers and execution etc. are delivered the Brand Personality.

Using of Film stars for the Lux beauty soap is logical and the attractiveness of celebrity is high. This is critical and leads to credibility. Endorser personality gets transferred to the brand . Thumb up soft drink has distinct personality owing to chivalry based ads, which also communicates about user imagery. The name 'Marlboro' evokes Wild West imagery, thanks to ads and consistency of the marketers in maintaining the same brand personality. Ads for multi utility vehicles like Mahendra scorpio , shows the ruggedness personality. For Example, 'Nokia' one the world's most valuable brand has distinct personality. The slogans.' We call this human technology', 'only Nokia human technology enables you to get more out of life' and 'connecting people' emphasize human side of technology, thereby resulting in brand personality of trusted friend. It also stands for reliability and quality. The ads also played prominent role in contributing to the distinct personality.

Elements of Brand Personality

Key advertising elements such as endorser, user imagery, symbols and execution which are contribute to Brand Personality.

Endorser—Endorser is one of the important elements of Brand-Personality. Its selection is much typical.

The selection of an endorser is critical, as the personality of the endorser can get transferred to the brand. Hathway shirts has acquired strong image owing to presence of sophisticated and mysterious endorser. Marlboro cowboy gave macho image to the brand. Endorser may be real or fictional. Using celebrities as brand endorser has advantages & disadvantages celebrity enjoys instant recognition & goodwill that can be transferred to the brand. Local celebrities can be used in local / Regional markets Ex. Pavan Kalyan for Pepsi in A.P. Celebrities can also be experts in some situations such as Michael Jordan expert in basketball shoes. The using of Film stars for Lux beauty soap and highly successful sports persons for Nike is logical and shows brand fit.

Sachin, Shahrukh Khan and Big 'B' endorse number of brands. Choosing the right celebrity & levering their qualities is important, otherwise celebrity endorsement may end up as futile exercise also involving wastage of money.

Sachin stands for style, power play, technique and excellence or performance. Sharukh Khan represents energy & entertainment and style. They cut across all demographic groups and have mass appeal.

For 'Boost' Health beverage brand fit with Sachin is excellent. Similarly, King Khan is also played role in the success of 'Santro small car' Rahul Dravid was brand endorser for Max New York life insurance, as he stands for trust, reliability, Which can be transferred to the brand. The same is the case with Steve Waugh endorsing ANP SANMAR Life insurance.

Exide has signed the new batting sensation MS Dhoni for his power play and talent. John Abraham endorse the brands of Yamaha and Samsung because of his look, good physique and youthfulness.

The term endorser stands for certain favourable values of the brand such as performance, style and reliability etc. these endorsers will be provide much needed assurance to the consumers and also protect brand images and their values.

Personality of the brand and celebrity should complement each other. Reliable celebrity ensures instant awareness, acceptability and positive attitude towards the brand, which is precursor to buying.

The element of creativity is critical while using celebrity endorsements. Otherwise celebrity may overpower, and overshadow the brand (vampiring effect). Boost advertisement featuring Sachin etc. is a classic example of effective celebrity endorsement.

User Imagery—User-Imagery defines about the who or what type of person, might use the product or brand.

It describes who or what type of person, might use that product / brand. Somebody may identify himself as Mercedes owner or Volvo driver. The recent TVC of Raymonds,(playing with puppies) focuses on soft side of man (i.e. caring and loving) and also on subtle aspects of life styles of executives. Here the focus is on emotional aspects rather than on functional attributes).

User imagery also communicates about the life style of the user. User imagery results in user-driven image which is transferred to the Brand. Brand personality needs to be updated with change in user imagery and information so that the brand remains contemporary and relevant.

It describes the image of the user i.e. endorser who endorse the advertisement and shows the lifestyle of that endorser by which consumer inspired by them.

The Thumbsup, Marlboro, are classic examples for 'user imagery' contributing to brand personality & success. In fact, some of the brands have become cult brands in which brand personally played prominent role.

Kingfisher attained distinct personality as fun, frolic and lively supported by their ads and event sponsorships. Smirnoff attained youthful and innovative personality and all their innovative promotions are in tune with the brand personality. MTV has become coolest brand among the youth as channel, with sensible promotions (MTV youth icon award) and believed in talking to the audience/ youth and localization of the content.

Execution Elements—These elements generally described to show the visual appearance. It usually focuses on the color, layout and visual appearance as well as music which are apply in the ad.

The elements like layout, color etc. (in print ads) and visual appeal, music etc. in broad cast advertising also contribute to the Brand personality. Intelligent and creative ads deliver brand personality. IBM. Intel are excellent techno brands, in which advertising also played prominent role in their success. Mozart symphony played in Titan Ad. Complements the brand personality of Titan as sophistiscation, elegance etc. success of absolute Vodka in U.S.A. is also attributed to clever execution of the advt in which bottle image figures always in intelligent way.

Tangible aspects of the Brand

A tangible aspect of brand includes package, pricing etc. Brand's tangible aspects like package and other elements like price are also key elements. Nirma's price & transparent package, Yellow color of the detergent powder, symbolize 'Down to Earth' personality of Nirma.

Smell package of Medimix and Mysore Sandal (including soap shape) gives distinct personality to them. Absolute Vodka, transparent liquid and shape of the bottle played key role in brand personality.

Symbols and logos

Each company has their own logo of the product. Each product is donated by their own symbol or mascots. Symbols can also be used effectively to communicate brand values and characteristics. Mascots may also be part of the logo of a brand. Eicher uses head of the horse in the past , representing power and sturdiness of the Tractor. Eicher now uses galloping horse after diversifying its operations. Goodlands Nerolac uses Guddy tiger, signifying bright lasting colours.

LIC is the insurance company that use the hands of logo where represents the safety whereas UTI has logo of Kalash which are considered as signals of good things. Royal stag uses horse for naturality and purity.

There are some features that defines the logo should be:-

- Unique but easy to understandable.
- Simple looking and has perfect meaning.
- Worth remembering and represents ideas.

Following are the brand personality with their attributes:-

Peter England	-	Honest Shirt (sincerity)
LIC	-	Try – Thy name is LIC (Trust)
L & T switch gear	-	Safe & Sure (Trust)
Bajaj	-	Inspiring confidence (Competence)
Videocon	-	The Indian Multinational (Competence)
Vantlensen	-	Power Evolved (Sophistication- upper class)
Bank of Rajasthan	-	Dare to Dream (Excitement)
The New India Assurance Co. Ltd.	-	Assurance of the leader (Competence)
Mahindra Scropio	-	Nothing else will do – (Ruggedness)
Bank of India	-	Bank that cares (empathy)
Nike	-	Just do it (Motivation, excitement)

Slogans enhance brand recall and have strong linkage with brand's essence / key values. Logos support brand names, provide ease in processing visual information lead to brand recall. Logo can be textual, abstract design and may be real.

They convey a clear meaning or suggest something about product category / brand / values / features / benefits of the brand.

Conclusion of Brand Personality

To conclude, Brand Personality being potent tool that needs to be leveraged to achieve key objectives for existing and new brands.

Consistency is also important, failing which dilution of brand personality or absence of it may occur. Other mix elements like distribution, pricing, promotion and packaging (apart from advertising) should support and strengthen brand personality.

Controversial Effects of Advertising

In the terms of ill-effects of advertising, there still remains he issue of whether advertising creates such negative effects or whether it merely reflects the values and attitudes which are caused by more significant sociological effects.

Dependency of the Media and Corporate Censorship

Almost all mass media are advertising media and many of them are exclusively advertising media and, with the exception of public service broadcasting are privately owned. Their income is predominantly generated through advertising; in the case of newspapers and magazines from 50 to 80%. Public service broadcasting in some countries can also heavily depend on advertising as a source of income (up to 40%). In the view of critics no media that spreads advertisements can be independent and the higher the proportion of advertising, the higher the dependency. This dependency has "distinct implications for the nature of media content... In the business press, the media are often referred to in exactly the way they present themselves in their candid moments: as a branch of the advertising industry."

Advertising is directly proportional to dependency that has different implications for the nature of the media contact.

"Journalists have long faced pressure to shape stories to suit advertisers and owners ... the vast majority of TV station executives found their news departments 'cooperative' in shaping the news to assist in 'non-traditional revenue development." Negative and undesired reporting can be prevented or influenced when advertisers threaten to cancel orders or simply when there is a danger of such a cancellation. Media dependency and such a threat becomes very real when there is only one dominant or very few large advertisers. The influence of advertisers is not only in regard to news or information on their own products or services but expands to articles or shows not directly linked to them. In order to secure their advertising revenues the media has to create the best possible 'advertising environment'. Another problem considered censorship by critics is the refusal of media to accept advertisements that are not in their interest. A striking example of this is the refusal of TV stations to broadcast ads by Adbusters. Groups try to place advertisements and are refused by networks.

It is principally the viewing rates which decide upon the programme in the private radio and television business. "Their business is to absorb as much attention as possible. The viewing rate measures the attention the media trades for the information offered. The service of this attraction is sold to the advertising business" and the viewing rates determine the price that can be demanded for advertising.

There are two problems with advertising i.e. dependency of the media and second is censorship. First problem includes that advertising depends on the media i.e. advertising dependency of media. Second problem is censorship which arises when the refusal of media is done to accept the advertisements that are not interested in them.

Advertising and information are increasingly hard to distinguish from each other. "The borders between advertising and media become more and more blurred. What August Fischer, chairman of the board of Axel Springer publishing company considers to be a 'proven partnership between the media and advertising business' critics regard as nothing but the infiltration of journalistic duties and freedoms". According to RTL-executive Helmut Thoma "private stations shall not and cannot serve any mission but only the goal of the company which is the 'acceptance by the advertising business and the viewer'. The setting of priorities in this order actually says everything about the 'design of the programmes' by private television." Patrick Le Lay, former managing director of TF1, a private French television channel with a market share of 25 to 35%, said: There are many ways to talk about television. But from the business point of view, let's be realistic: basically, the job of TF1 is, e. g. to help Coca Cola sell its product. For an advertising message to be perceived the brain of the viewer must be at our disposal. The job of our programmes is to make it available, that is to say, to distract it, to relax it and get it ready between two messages. It is disposable human brain time that we sell to Coca Cola."

Because of these dependencies a widespread and fundamental public debate about advertising and its influence on information and freedom of speech is difficult to obtain, at least through the usual media channels; otherwise these would saw off the branch they are sitting on. "The notion that the commercial basis of media, journalism, and communication could have troubling implications for democracy is excluded from the range of legitimate debate" just as "capitalism is off-limits as a topic of legitimate debate in U.S. political culture".

Commercialization of Culture and Sports

Advertising itself is extensively considered to be a contribution to culture. Advertising is integrated into fashion. On many pieces of clothing the company logo is the only design or is an important part of it. There is only little room left outside the consumption economy, in which culture and art can develop independently and where alternative values can be expressed. A last important sphere, the universities, is under strong pressure to open up for business and its interests.

Performances, exhibitions, shows, concerts, conventions and most other events can hardly take place without sponsoring. The increasing lack arts and culture they buy the service of attraction. Artists are graded and paid according to their art's value for commercial purposes. Corporations promote renown artists, therefore getting exclusive rights in global advertising campaigns. Broadway shows, like 'La Bohème' featured commercial props in its set.

Competitive sports have become unthinkable without sponsoring and there is a mutual dependency. High income with advertising is only possible with a comparable number of spectators or viewers. On the other hand, the poor performance of a team or a sportsman results in less advertising revenues. 'Sports/Media Complex which is a complicated mix of media, agencies, managers, sports promoters, advertising etc. with partially common and partially diverging interests but in any case with common commercial interests. The media presumably is at centre stage because it can supply the other parties involved with a rare commodity, namely (potential) public attention. In sports "the media are able to generate enormous sales in both circulation and advertising." **There is no scope of competitive sports without sponsoring with mutual dependency.**

"Sports sponsorship is acknowledged by the tobacco industry to be valuable advertising. A Tobacco Industry journal in 1994 described the Formula One car as 'The most powerful advertising space in the world'. In a cohort study carried out in 22 secondary schools in England in 1994 and 1995 boys whose favourite television sport was motor racing had a 12.8% risk of becoming regular smokers compared to 7.0% of boys who did not follow motor racing." **It is in the very much interest of the media and sports to counter this danger because media sports can only work as long as sport exists.**

Occupation and Commercialization of Public Space

Every visually perceptible place has potential for advertising. Especially urban areas with their structures but also landscapes in sight of through fares are more and more turning into media for advertisements. Signs, posters, billboards, flags have become decisive factors in the urban appearance and their numbers are still on the increase. "Outdoor advertising has become unavoidable. Traditional billboards and transit shelters have cleared the way for more pervasive methods such as wrapped vehicles, sides of buildings, electronic signs, kiosks, taxis, posters, sides of buses, and more. Digital technologies are used on buildings to sport 'urban wall displays'. In urban areas commercial content is placed in our sight and into our consciousness every moment we are in public space. The German Newspaper 'Zeit' called it a new kind of 'dictatorship that one cannot escape'. Over time, this domination of the surroundings has become the "natural" state. Through long-term commercial saturation, it has become implicitly understood by the public that advertising has the right to own, occupy and control every inch of available space. The steady normalization of invasive advertising dulls the public's perception of their surroundings, re-enforcing a general attitude of powerlessness toward creativity and change, thus a cycle develops enabling advertisers to slowly and consistently increase the saturation of advertising with little or no public outcry."

The massive optical orientation toward advertising changes the function of public spaces which are utilised by brands. Urban landmarks are turned into trademarks. The highest pressure is exerted on renown and highly frequented public spaces which are also important for the identity of a city (e. g. Piccadilly Circus, Times Square, Alexanderplatz). Urban spaces are public commodities and in this capacity they are subject to "aesthetical environment protection", mainly through building regulations, heritage protection and landscape protection. "It is in this capacity that these spaces are now being privatised. They are peppered with billboards and signs, they are remodelled into media for advertising." This is the controversial effects of advertising which includes the public space of urban areas and about its structures including landscapes.

SOCIO-ISSUES OF ADVERTISING

"Advertising has an "agenda setting function" which is the ability, with huge sums of money, to put consumption as the only item on the agenda. In the battle for a share of the public conscience this amounts to non-treatment (ignorance) of whatever is not commercial and whatever is not advertised for. Advertsing should be reflection of society norms and give clear picture of target market. Spheres without commerce and advertising serving the muses and relaxation remain without respect. With increasing force advertising makes itself comfortable in the private sphere so that the voice of commerce becomes the dominant way of expression in society." Advertising critics see advertising as the leading light in our culture. Advertising aims to do something.

As public funds are drained from the non-commercial cultural sector, art galleries, museums and symphonies bid for corporate sponsorship." In the same way effected is the education system and advertising is increasingly penetrating schools and universities. Cities, such as New York, accept sponsors for public playgrounds. "Even the pope has been commercialized. The pope's 4-day visit to Mexico in 1999 was sponsored by Frito-Lay and PepsiCo. The industry is accused of being one of the engines powering a convoluted economic mass production system which promotes consumption. As far as social effects are concerned it does not matter whether advertising fuels consumption but which values, patterns of behaviour and assignments of meaning it propagates. Advertising is accused of hijacking the language and means of pop culture, of protest movements and even of subversive criticism and does not shy away from scandalizing and breaking taboos (e. g. Benneton).

A great part of advertising is the promotion of products dealing with the appearance of people which are mainly for women. Media put the sphere of girls and women under high pressure to compare themselves to propagate the ideal beauty. Politics is increasingly concerned about the negative aspects of advertising.

Social issues in advertising cover the means of advertising as well as its effects. Matters of taste in advertising are possible pre-occupation with exploiting all other appeals.

There are three social issues in advertising i.e. deception, manipulation and taste also.

Deception

It occurs when an advertisement is described into the perpetual process of audience and the outcomes or conclusion of this perpetual process is differed from the reality of the situation or circumstances.

Manipulation

It is also the critics of advertising that feel the freedom of selection of consumer are very much restricted by the power of advertising wherever it can update or manipulate buyers into the decision against this interest. There is also a view that advertisers have the power to manipulate their audience also. Almost the large companies have the ability to get large number of exposures for their advertisement of their product or services.

Taste

It is the third critics in social issues of advertising that have the adverse effect that may not always be in perfect taste there is moral concern about the advertising related to the product itself e.g.- "Cigarettes", alcohol etc. there is also an objections to appeal employed and also to the techniques of advertising strategy like repetition of the claim.

OPPOSITION AND CAMPAIGNS

According to critics, the total commercialization of all fields of society, the privatization of public space, the acceleration of consumption and waste of resources including the negative influence on lifestyles and on the environment has not been noticed to the necessary extent. The "hyper-commercialization of the culture is recognized and roundly detested by the citizenry, although the topic scarcely receives a whiff of attention in the media or political culture". "The greatest damage done by advertising is precisely that it incessantly demonstrates the prostitution of men and women who lend their intellects, their voices, their artistic skills to purposes in which they themselves do not believe, and ... that it helps to shatter and ultimately destroy our most precious non-material possessions: the confidence in the existence of meaningful purposes of human activity and respect for the integrity of man." "The struggle against advertising is therefore essential if we are to overcome the pervasive alienation from all genuine human needs that currently plays such a corrosive role in our society. But in resisting this type of hyper-commercialism we should not be under any illusions. Advertising may seem at times to be an almost trivial of omnipresent aspect of our economic system. Yet, as economist A. C. Pigou pointed out, it could only be 'removed altogether' if 'conditions of monopolistic competition' inherent to corporate capitalism were removed. To resist it is to resist the inner logic of capitalism itself, of which it is the pure expression."

"Visual pollution, much of it in the form of advertising, is an issue in all the world's large cities. But what is pollution to some is a vibrant part of a city's fabric to others. Other cities like Moscow have reached their limit and have begun to crack down on over the top outdoor advertising. Many communities have chosen to regulate the billboards to protect and enhance their scenic character.

America estimates the nationwide total of cities and communities prohibiting the construction of new billboards to be at least 1500. A number of States in the USA prohibit all billboards:

- Vermont - Removed all billboards in 1970s
- Hawaii - Removed all billboards in 1920s
- Maine - Removed all billboards in 1970s and early 80s
- Alaska - State referendum passed in 1998 prohibits billboards

- Almost two years ago the city of São Paulo, Brazil, ordered the downsizing or removal of all billboards and most other forms of commercial advertising in the city."

Technical appliances, such as Spam filters, TV-Zappers, Ad-Blockers for TV's and stickers on mail boxes: "No Advertising" and an increasing number of court cases indicate a growing interest of people to restrict or rid themselves of unwelcome advertising.

TAXATION AS REVENUE AND CONTROL

This topic includes the concepts that include the taxation on advertising to control on them. Each advertiser has to pay to advertise and this is paid to members of the public who are intruded upon it. This type of tax is known as Pigovian tax

Public interest groups suggest that "access to the mental space targeted by advertisers should be taxed, in that at the present moment that space is being freely taken advantage of by advertisers with no compensation paid to the members of the public who are thus being intruded upon. This kind of tax would be a Pigovian tax in that it would act to reduce what is now increasingly seen as a public nuisance. Efforts to that end are gathering more momentum, with Arkansas and Maine considering bills to implement such a taxation. Florida enacted such a tax in 1987 but was forced to repeal it after six months, as a result of a concerted effort by national commercial interests, which withdrew planned conventions, causing major losses to the tourism industry, and cancelled advertising, causing a loss of 12 million dollars to the broadcast industry alone".

In the U. S., for example, advertising is tax deductible and suggestions for possible limits to the advertising tax deduction are met with fierce opposition from the business sector, not to mention suggestions for a special taxation. In other countries, advertising at least is taxed in the same manner services are taxed and in some advertising is subject to special taxation although on a very low level. In many cases the taxation refers especially to media with advertising (e. g. Austria, Italy, Greece, Netherlands, Turkey, Estonia). Tax on advertising in European countries:

- Belgium: Advertising or billboard tax (taxe d'affichage or aanplakkingstaks) on public posters depending on size and kind of paper as well as on neon signs

- France: Tax on television commercials (taxe sur la publicité télévisée) based on the cost of the advertising unit
- Italy: Municipal tax on acoustic and visual kinds of advertisements within the municipality (imposta communale sulla publicità) and municipal tax on signs, posters and other kinds of advertisements (diritti sulle pubbliche offisioni), the tariffs of which are under the jurisdiction of the municipalities
- Netherlands: Advertising tax (reclamebelastingen) with varying tariffs on certain advertising measures (excluding ads in newspapers and magazines) which can be levied by municipalities depending on the kind of advertising (billboards, neon signs etc.)
- Austria: Municipal announcement levies on advertising through writing, pictures or lights in public areas or publicly accessible areas with varying tariffs depending on the fee, the surface or the duration of the advertising measure as well as advertising tariffs on paid ads in printed media of usually 10% of the fee.
- Sweden: Advertising tax (reklamskatt) on ads and other kinds of advertising (billboards, film, television, advertising at fairs and exhibitions, flyers) in the range of 4% for ads in newspapers and 11% in all other cases. In the case of flyers the tariffs are based on the production costs, else on the fee
- Spain: Municipalities can tax advertising measures in their territory with a rather unimportant taxes and fees of various kinds.

Above are the major taxes that are applied on advertising in European countries.

Case Study

Note : knowing more about "Implications of Advertising" reader can study documentation process of Microsoft company by visiting their site : www.members.microsoft.com

http://www.marketingscoop.com/advertising-casestudies.htm

http://www.icmrindia.org/casestudies/Case_Studies_Concept_Wise.asp?cat=Advertising

http://www.kristofcreative.com/experience/case_studies/examples.shtml

http://www.quasar.co.in/pdfs/samsungcasestudy.pdf
http://www.magazine.org/advertising/case_studies/index.aspx
http://advertising.microsoft.com/adcenter-case-studies
http://www.meed.com/advertising/meed-advertising-case-studies/300040

4

Advertising Agency

This chapter includes the key concepts that are described below:-

- Introduction
- Functions of Advertising Agency
- Types of Advertising Agency
- Full Service Agencies
- Interactive Agencies
- Search Engine Agencies
- Social Media Agencies
- Online Reputation Management
- Other Agencies
- Departments in Advertising Agency
- Functions of Advertising Departments
- Role of Consultant

INTRODUCTION

Advertising Agency refers to the business or a company who are whole responsible for making the advertisement which have some functionalities, role and also their department which includes all the members of each department who are involve in creating, planning, designing and also handling all the process of advertisement. It is also known as Ad agency.

An advertising agency or ad agency is a service business dedicated to creating, planning and handling advertising (and sometimes other forms of promotion) for its clients. An ad agency is independent from the client and provides an outside point of view to the effort of selling the client's products or services. An agency can also handle overall marketing and branding strategies and sales promotions for its clients.

Typical ad agency clients include businesses and corporations, non-profit organizations and government agencies. Agencies may be hired to produce an advertising campaign.

Advertising campaign is also discussed in chapter 2. An ad agency has the ability to maintain whole of the programme of an advertisement without any dependence.

FUNCTIONS OF ADVERTISING AGENCY

There are so many reasons for having an advertising agency which has concluded in the growth of the advertising professionals and business.

Professionals in advertising agency will be in a position to take an objective view of advertiser's plans and proposals. These professionals offer a number of functions that includes a account management, creative team, researchers and also the media planners.

- **Account Management** – Within an advertising agency the account manager or account executive is tasked with handling all major decisions related to a specific client. These responsibilities include locating and negotiating to acquire clients. Once the client has agreed to work with the agency, the account manager works closely with the client to develop an advertising strategy. For very large clients, such as large consumer products companies, an advertising agency may assign an account manager to work full-time with only one client and, possibly, with only one of the client's product lines. For smaller accounts an account manager may simultaneously manage several different, though non-competing, accounts.

- **Creative Team** –The principle role of account managers is to manage the overall advertising campaign for a client, which often includes delegating selective tasks to specialists. For large accounts one task account managers routinely delegate involves generating ideas, designing concepts and creating the final advertisement, which generally becomes the responsibility of the agency's creative team. An agency's creative team consists of specialists in graphic design, film and audio production, copywriting, computer programming, and much more.

- **Researchers** – Full-service advertising agencies employ market researchers who assess a client's market situation, including understanding customers and competitors, and also are used to test creative ideas. For instance, in the early stages of an advertising campaign researchers may run focus group sessions with selected members of the client's target market in order to get their reaction to several advertising concepts. Researchers are also used following the completion of an advertising campaign to measure whether the campaign reached its objectives.

- **Media Planners** – Once an advertisement is created, it must be placed through an appropriate advertising media. Each advertising media, of which there are thousands, has its own unique methods for accepting advertisements, such as different advertising cost structures (i.e., what it costs marketers to place an ad), different requirements for accepting ad designs (e.g., size of ad), different ways placements can be purchased (e.g., direct contact with media or through third-party seller), and different time schedules (i.e., when ad will be run). Understanding the nuances of different media is the role of a media planner, who looks for the best media match for a client and also negotiates the best deals.

Above these are the professionals who have their own and different functionalities in an advertising agency. An advertising agency has another function that it can perform especially to those advertisers who may not have the essential or necessary expertise in the use of advertising.

TYPES OF ADVERTISING AGENCY

There are various types of advertising agency who have the ability to maintain the creation of an advertisement.

Ad agencies come in all sizes and include everything from one or two-person shops (which rely mostly on freelance talent to perform most functions), small to medium sized agencies, large independents such as SMART and TAXI, and multi-national, multi-agency conglomerates such as Omnicom Group, WPP Group, Publicis, Interpublic Group of Companies and Havas.

FULL SERVICE AGENCIES

This is type of advertising agencies which are worked with fee base and commission based processes. Full Service Agencies are also known as Media-Neutral Agencies as well as traditional advertising agencies.

Full-service agencies are also known as traditional advertising agencies for the client, wherein the client satisfies almost all their advertising or promotional needs with the same organization. This type of agency provides advertising services such as strategic planning, creative development, production, media planning, media buying, and other related services such as sales promotionals, direct selling, design, and branding, etc.

These are the agencies where the client satisfies with the work of them that the agencies have the ability to fulfill the requirements of the client.

Most *full-service agencies* work on a combination of fee-based and commission based compensation. The fee is paid by the entity for which the marketing is being done. The commission is a payment from the media to the agency and is usually equal to 15% of the cost of the advertisement. The broadcast media, radio and television, traditionally pay a commission.

Full-service, or media-neutral advertising agencies produce work for many types of media, creating integrated marketing communications, or through-the-line (TTL) advertising. The "line", in this case, is the traditional marker between the media that pay a commission to the agency and the media that do not.

INTERACTIVE AGENCIES

When the traditional advertising agencies means full service agencies are embraced with the internet at that time Interactive agencies worked. These types of agencies grew very rapidly. These are the agencies which provide the specialized advertising with marketing services for the digital space.

Interactive agencies may differentiate themselves by offering a mix of web design/development, search engine marketing, internet advertising/marketing, or e-business/e-commerce consulting. Interactive agencies rose to prominence before the traditional advertising agencies fully embraced the Internet. Offering a wide range of services, some of the interactive agencies grew very rapidly, although some have downsized just as rapidly due to changing market conditions. Today, the most successful interactive agencies are defined as companies that provide specialized advertising and marketing services for the digital space. The digital space is defined as any multimedia-enabled electronic channel that an advertiser's message can be seen or heard from. The 'digital space' translates to the Internet, kiosks, CD-ROMs, DVDs, and lifestyle devices (iPod, PSP, and mobile). Interactive agencies function similarly to advertising agencies, although they focus solely on interactive advertising services. They deliver services such as strategy, creative, design, video, development, programming (Flash and otherwise), deployment, management, and fulfillment reporting. Often, interactive agencies provide: digital lead generation, digital brand development, interactive marketing and communications strategy, rich media campaigns, interactive video brand experiences, Web 2.0 website design and development, e-learning Tools, e-mail marketing, SEO/SEM services, PPC campaign management, content management services, web application development, and overall data mining & ROI assessment.

The recent boost in the interactive agencies can also be attributed to the rising popularity of web-based social networking and community sites. The creation of sites such as MySpace, Facebook and YouTube have sparked market interest, as some interactive agencies have started offering personal and corporate community site development as one of their service offerings. It still may be too early to tell how agencies will use this type of marketing to monetize client ROI, but all signs point to online networking as the future of brand marketing.

Due to the social networking explosion, new types of companies are doing reputation management. This type of agency is especially important if a company needs online damage control. If a customer becomes disgruntled, it is very easy to damage a companies reputation over social networking sites. Because of how rapidly the information spreads, it becomes absolutely necessary to address any rumors, gossip or other negative online press immediately. The interactive agencies are much important when a company needs the active control of damage.

Examples of interactive agencies include, Razorfish, R/GA, AKQA, Freedom + Partners, Rokkan, Night Agency, B-Reel, Fantasy Interactive, Your Majesty, Big Fuel, Core Industries, Domani, Big Spaceship, Agencynet, Firstborn Interactive, Odopod, eROI, ZOO. Digital and EVB, among others.

SEARCH ENGINE AGENCIES

Lately, search engine marketing (SEM) and search engine optimization (SEO) firms have been classified by some as 'agencies' because they create media and implement media purchases of text based (or image based, in some instances of search marketing) ads. This relatively young industry has been slow to adopt the term 'agency', however with the creation of ads (either text or image) and media purchases, they do technically qualify as 'advertising agencies'. Recent studies suggest that both SEO and SEM are set to outpace more traditional channels of media spending over the next 3-5 years.

Search engine agencies include both search engine marketing and search engine optimization. These are the firms which classified by source agencies because they both create media as well as implementation of that media of text as well as image based.

SOCIAL MEDIA AGENCIES

Social media is defined as the online content which is created by people who are using highly accessible and sealable publishing technologies. Social media agencies are specialized in promotion of brands in social media platform.

Social media

Information outputs and Human interaction in social media

Social media depends on interaction between people as the discussion and interaction to build shared meaning.

User Generated Media

User generated content (UGC) is also known user created content (UCC) which refers to the different kinds of media content and publicly available that are produced by end-users. In UGC, consumers have been willing to receive free content through internet, commercial radio & television broadcast in exchange for advertising.

The term

In this type of sites, cach and every user the rights to make the on this topic and advise the concepts of that particular topic or subject.

ONLINE REPUTATION MANAGEMENT

Online Reputation Management (ORM) is the practice of consistent research and analysis of one of the personal or professional, business or industry reputation which are represented by the control across all types of online media. It is also known as online Reputation monitoring. ORM party formed from a held to mange the consumer generated media i.e. CGM which described earlier in this chapter.

As CGM grew with the rise of social media and other similar user-based online content aggregators, it began to effect search results more and more, bringing with it increased attention to the matter of managing these results.

ORM is a relatively new industry but has been brought to the forefront of professionals' consciousness due to the overwhelming and many times unpredictable nature of both professional journalistic content *and* amateur user-generated content (or UGC), the latter of which there is far more, and not the least because of the wide number websites that offer such an opportunity to visitors, typically with very low barriers to entry—often just by creating a screen name, registering one's birthday and a geographical location, and providing a valid e-mail address to complete the account-creation process. Thus, the type of online content monitored in ORM spans professional, journalism sponsored by traditional news and media giants as well as user-created and user-generated blogs, ratings, reviews, and comments, and all manner of specialized websites about any particular subject, be it a person, group, company, business, product, event, concept, or trend.

The market in UK for ORM will grow by around 30% in 2008 to an estimated value of L 60 million.

EBay was one of the first web companies to harness the power of CGM feedback. By using user generated feedback ratings buyers and sellers were given reputations that helped other users make purchasing and selling decisions. ReputationDefender was one of the first companies that offered to proactively manage online reputations. ClaimID is another company that early on presented services designed to promote personal ORM. Other ORM tools include: Trackur, BrandsEye and Google Alerts.

Online Media Monitored with ORM

The online media that is monitored in ORM is :-

- Traditional/mainstream websites
- Social networks (e.g. Facebook, MySpace, Bebo)
- Consumer Review sites such as epinions.com, MouthShut.com yelp
- User-generated content (UGC)/Consumer Generated Media (CGM)
- Blogs
- Blogging communities (e.g. Open Diary, LiveJournal, Xanga)
- Microblogs (e.g. Twitter, Jaiku, Plurk)
- Sites like DontDateHimGirl and PersonRatings.com which allow reviews of individuals.
- Social news/bookmarking sites
- Collaborative Research sites such as Yahoo Answers, Rediff Q&A
- Independent discussion forums

Effects of ORM

There are various numbers of effects of ORM.

- Provide early warning systems for reactive and defensive PR.

  Reduce marketing spend by learning how to reach out to customers more cheaply.
- Reduce internal costs by employing services which save time and effort, as well as money.
- Improve customer satisfaction by gaining insights from consumers about what is good and bad about their product or services.
- Increase perceptions of brand by creating opportunities to listen to and engage consumers.
- Gain insights about competitors and their customers' perceptions about their products and services.
- Help identify gaps for products and services which can be developed for profitable niche markets.
- Gain insight into online networks and keywords and key phrases found in user-generated content, which can help to

bolster *natural* search results about the person, product, or business.

- Maintain shareholder value by mitigating risk by having ears close to the ground where opinions about a business are being formed and propagated.
- Engage in more effective public relations by understanding who the real influencers are.
- Gain understanding of the relationship between user generated content and traditional forms of online media, e.g. news, print, etc.

OTHER AGENCIES

While not advertising agencies, *enterprise technology agencies* often work in tandem with advertising agencies to provide a specialized subset of services offered by some interactive agencies: Web 2.0 website design and development, Content Management Services, web application development, and other intuitive technology solutions for the web, mobile devices and emerging digital platforms. The descriptions of interactive agencies are early discussed in this chapter.

DEPARTMENTS IN ADVERTISING AGENCY

There are various types of departments in advertising agencies that supports to provide a creative advertisement.

Creative Department

This department includes the creation of ad and provides the initial or core structure of an ad. This department includes two most important figures i.e. copywriters and art directors. They both are helpful in providing the concepts to an advertisement.

The people who create the actual ads form the core of an advertising agency. Modern advertising agencies usually form their copywriters and art directors into creative teams. Creative teams may be permanent partnerships or formed on a project-by-project basis. The art director and copywriter report to a creative director, usually a creative employee with several years of experience. Although copywriters have the word "write" in their job title, and art directors have the word "art", one does not necessarily write the words and the other draw the pictures; they both generate creative ideas to represent the proposition (the advertisement or campaign's key message). Creative departments frequently work with outside design or production studios to develop and implement their ideas. Creative departments may employ production artists as entry-level positions, as well as for operations and maintenance.

Account Services

The other major department in ad agencies is *account services* or *account management*. Account Services or account management is somewhat the sales arm of the advertising agency. An account executive (one who works within the account services department) meets with the client to determine sales goals and creative strategy. They are then responsible for coordinating the creative, media, and production staff behind the campaign. Throughout the creative process, they keep in touch with the client to update them on the ad's progress and gain feedback. Upon completion of the creative work, it is their job to ensure the ad's production and placement.

Account services includes the person have the job profile of account executive who works with in this department. It has the responsibility to coordinate the creative and production staff behind the campaign.

Media Services

The *media services* department may not be so well known, but its employees are the people who have contacts with the suppliers of various creative media. For example, they will be able to advise upon and negotiate with printers if an agency is producing flyers for a client. However, when dealing with the major media (broadcast media, outdoor, and the press), this work is usually outsourced to a media agency which can advise on *media planning* and is normally large enough to negotiate prices down further than a single agency or client can.

It is the department where employees are those persons who have the contacts with the supplier of media. These teams have the right to make the media planning with their own ideas. Modern Agencies might have a media planning department that are integrated which all the planning & placements in the company.

Other Department and Personnel

In small agencies, employees may do both creative and account service work. Larger agencies attract people who specialize in one or the other, and indeed include a number of people in specialized positions: production work, Internet advertising, planning, or research, for example.

The traffic department regulates the flow of work in the agency. It is typically headed by a traffic manager (or system administrator). Traffic increases an agency's efficiency and profitability through the reduction of false job starts, inappropriate job initiation, incomplete information sharing, over- and under-cost estimation, and the need for media extensions. In small agencies without a dedicated traffic manager, one employee may be responsible for managing workflow, gathering cost estimates and answering the phone, for example. Large agencies may have a traffic department of five or more employees.

Advertising Interns—Advertising interns are typically university juniors and seniors who are genuinely interested in and have an aptitude for advertising. Internships at advertising agencies most commonly fall into one of six areas of expertise: account services, creative, interactive, media, public relations and traffic.

Interns often take part in the internal creative process, where they may be charged with creating and managing a website as well as developing an advertising campaign. Hands on projects such as these help interns learn how strategy and well-developed marketing are essential to a sound advertising and communications plan.

During their internship, the intern will experience the development of an ad, brochure and broadcast or communications project from beginning to end. During the internship, the intern should be exposed to as much as possible within the agency and advertising process.

An internship program in account services usually involves fundamental work within account management as well as offering exposure to other facets of the agency. The primary responsibility of this position is to assist account managers. Functions of the account management intern may include:

- Research and analysis: Gathering information regarding industry, competition, customer product or service; as well as presenting findings in verbal/written form with recommendations

- Involvement in internal meetings and, when appropriate, client meetings
- Assisting account services in the management of creative projects

Role of Advertising Agency or Department

Advertising agencies create most advertisements and are the core of the advertising industry. Some companies, however, have their own advertising departments which function much like an agency. The development, production, and placement of a single ad can be a time-consuming process involving a large number of people with a variety of business and creative skills. Advertising agencies not only create the advertisements but also pay for the cost of placing the ad in a newspaper or magazine or on television or radio. A large advertising agency or department may employ hundreds or thousands of people, including advertising and marketing specialists, designers, writers known as copywriters, artists, economists, psychologists, researchers, media analysts, product testers, librarians, accountants and bookkeepers, and mathematicians.

In the beginning of the 21st century Advertising Agencies are playing a very important role in the business of advertising. A lot of water has flown past the Ganges during the last 5 decade since the foundation of the first professional agency in India in 1950's by JW Thompson & DJ Keeymer.

Gone are those days when advertising agencies were only playing a vital role in **Planning the campaign** for their clients, **preparing the campaign** and **placing it** in suitable media on behalf of their clients. In today's competitive situation it is evident that reputed ad agencies are not restricting themselves to the above services but are also willing to offer something extra to their clients in the areas of marketing research, Sales promotion & Merchandising activities and Public Relation oriented services.

Advertising Agencies being the prime facilitator in the business of advertising have rightly understood the need of the hour. It plays a key role in business of advertising.

National and reputed Advertising Agencies are increasingly going for 360 degree approach in their communications and are prepared to walk the extra yard to understand their client's business in a better manner in order to communicate with the target audience effectively and efficiently.

A typical advertising agency is divided into a number of departments, such as account service, research, media planning and buying, the creative department, and production. A multinational advertising agency with clients that spend hundreds of millions of dollars on advertising may employ as many as 8,000 people worldwide and up to 900 people in a major office. A local agency with clients that spend about $15 million a year on advertising may employ only about 25 people.

Once a company selects an agency, the agency assigns an *account executive* to act as liaison between it and the client. The account executive manages all of the services conducted on behalf of the client and coordinates the team assigned to the client's business. The account executive directs the preparation of the advertising strategy, which includes deciding how and to whom the product or service will be presented. The account executive also assigns priorities, oversees the budget, reviews and approves all recommendations before they are taken to the client, and makes sure that the agency meets all deadlines.

FUNCTIONS OF ADVERTISING DEPARTMENTS

Each advertising agency as department has a particular function. Once the function has completed, then it pass to the next level of department. There is organization chart by which the processing is transfer from one level to next level.

Each advertising department has a specific function or assignment. Once one department has completed its work, it hands off the completed assignment to the next department in the advertising process until the ad campaign is completed. The first department that becomes involved in an advertising campaign is the research department.

Research

The first function is Research which includes both strategic as well as evaluation research. Strategic research helps to understand the concepts that how consumers use a product and Evaluation research helps to understand the concepts that what are methods by which consumers attracts to buy them and how they remember about the product.

Advertising agencies employ research for both *strategic* and *evaluative* purposes. Strategic research enables the agency to better understand how consumers use a product or service and how they regard the product or service. Strategic research also determines the types of people most likely to buy the product. That group of people is called the target market. Advertisers have limited budgets so knowing who is most likely to buy a particular product helps them spend their advertising budget more efficiently. Evaluative research is used after the advertising has run and seeks to determine how well consumers remember the advertising message and how persuasive it was. Evaluative research is expensive, and as a result, many advertisers do not employ it. Instead, they try to measure the advertising's effectiveness by analyzing sales results.

Agencies use both qualitative and quantitative research methods. Agencies employ *qualitative research* to gain an initial understanding of the marketing situation (*see* Marketing). This research method uses open-ended questions that allow consumers to explain their values, beliefs, and behaviors at length. One of the most common qualitative research techniques is the *focus group* in which a moderator leads a small group of consumers in a candid discussion of a particular product category, service, or marketing situation.

Agencies use *quantitative research* to determine a final course of action. This type of research uses close-ended questions in which answers are selected from a set list. This enables the researcher to determine the exact percentage of people who answered yes or no to a question or the exact percentage choosing answer a, b, or c. One of the most common quantitative research techniques is the survey in which researchers use a questionnaire to gain information from a large group of people, called a sample. Statistical studies show that if the sample is large enough, about 1,000 people, and is representative of a particular group (for example, working mothers who buy disposable diapers), then the findings from the sample are considered true, or statistically valid, and can be extended to the entire group of consumers in that category. The findings provided by quantitative research are therefore conclusive in a way that qualitative research cannot be.

Media buying

It is second function of Department.Once the target audience has been identified, an agency's media department determines the most effective way of delivering the message to that target. The *media planner* is the person who decides which media wil.)e used.

The media planner must consider three factors: (1) the number of people to be exposed to the message, known as the reach, (2) the number of times each person needs to be exposed to the message in order to remember it, known as the frequency, and (3) the costs.

The media planner wants to reach the largest possible percentage of the target audience. To accomplish that goal, the media planner must employ the media that have audiences closely resembling the target audience. If the target is very broad, such as the national market for medium-priced automobiles, the media planner will probably select network television, which has a broad reach. If the target is more narrow and specialized, then the media that reach a more specialized audience, such as magazines, would be selected. Moreover, since not all members of the narrow target audience read the same magazines, the media planner might employ a range of magazines to reach a larger percentage of the intended consumer.

Media planner must also determiners how frequently the advertising should run in each medium. Frequency is important because repetition helps the consumer that remember both the product and the advertising message.

Often an advertising campaign will employ many types of media. For example, to help advertise a medium-priced automobile, the ad campaign may consist initially of national television advertising to raise brand awareness, followed by local newspaper and radio advertising to reinforce the message and to direct consumers to a special sale at a local dealer.

Finally, because no advertiser has an unlimited amount of money to spend, cost is also a factor. The media planner must choose those media that will enable the advertiser to reach the largest percentage of the target with enough frequency for the message to be remembered without exceeding the advertiser's budget. Once this media plan has been put together, the agency's *media buyer* contacts the media on behalf of the client in order to purchase advertising space or time at the best possible rate.

Creative work

It is the third function of advertising department. Once the types of media have been determined, the agency's creative department develops the presentation of the ads. The principal figures in the creative department are the *copywriter* and the *art director*. The copywriter is the person who writes the advertising message. The art director is the person who oversees the design of the ad. The copywriter and the art director work together to find creative ways to deliver the message that research found would have the greatest appeal to the target audience.

The creative team begins by familiarizing itself with the product and the research. Often the creative team will 'kick around ideas' or "brainstorm," a process in which one idea is allowed to stimulate another without reaching a decision about whether any of the ideas are valid.

In the creative work, department includes copywriter and art director. Copywriter is the person who writer the advertising message whereas the art director is the person who make the design of the advertisement. These both are the person who has the ability to give the concepts to the advertisement.

Most advertising appeals to people's emotions, particularly the emotional needs for love and belonging, prestige and self-esteem. Manufacturers of luxury and fashion products, for example, frequently appeal to the desire for esteem and prestige. Advertising for a line of clothing, such as Ralph Lauren's Polo clothes, may associate the product with the lifestyle of wealthy landowners. Those who buy the clothing purchase it, in part, because they want to be identified with that prestigious lifestyle. Makers of personal care products, on the other hand, often suggest that buying their products will enable consumers to experience love and acceptance. Advertising for perfume or cologne conveys the message that the product makes users more sexually attractive. Personal care products such as breath mints and dandruff shampoos, on the other hand, usually play upon consumers' fears and dramatize the rejection that results from failing to use the product. The implication is that product usage brings love and acceptance.

Print ads and television commercials use a variety of techniques to deliver their messages. Testimonials and endorsements can lend both prestige and credibility to a product. Seeing an athletic superstar, for example, endorse a particular brand of athletic shoe makes the brand seem more prestigious and suggests that it must be good because a professional uses it. Superiority is also often demonstrated through product comparisons–for example, by showing that one brand of paper towels absorbs more spilled liquid than another or that in consumer taste tests one beverage is preferred over another. But because more and more competing products are virtually identical to one another, advertisers frequently use image advertising to distinguish their products. Image advertising surrounds the product with a 'halo of positive associations' by using the same character or theme year after year.

Production

Art directors and copywriters create the concepts behind the ads, but they do not literally make the advertising. Making the ads is the job of the production department. In print advertising, the art director works with the print production manager to hire a photographer or illustrator and then supervises the work. Once the photograph has been taken or the illustration completed, the image is scanned into a computer and placed in the proper position. The art director also selects typefaces for the headline and body copy and then, using the computer, correctly positions the headline and body copy.

In creative department, copywriters and art directors have the ability to give the concept to an advertisement not make the advertising. To make an ad, it should be necessary to take the help of production department. Production department includes production manager is the person who have all the responsibility to make an advertisement. He / she has the responsibility to tire a photographer or illustrator and supervises the work. Once all the elements are in place, the computer file is sent to the newspaper or magazine in which the ad will run. The publication then prints the ad directly from the computer file.

ROLE OF CONSULTANT

An advertising agency acts as a consultant to its client, the advertiser in formulating the advertising plans and translating them into advertising campaigns. The other role of agency namely placing the advertisements arises from its traditional association with the media. Advertising is primarily oriented towards the goals and objectives of the advertiser and the corresponding future operations. There is an inherent element of confidentially in advertising and its implementation.

Case Study

Note : knowing more about "Advertising Agency" reader can

study documentation process of Microsoft company by visiting their site : www.members.microsoft.com

http://www.websitebiz.com/google-case-study.asp

http://www.blogcasestudies.com/2009/03/i-was-down-at-an-rebus-event-in-st-louis-attending-at-the-ngage-headquarters-and-was-happily-surprised-with-some-excellent.html

http://www.findmillions.net/documents/Success_Story_Financial_Services_AARM.pdf

http://www.academon.com/Essay-Aquarius-Advertising-Agency-Case-Study/37036

http://adwordsagency.blogspot.com/2009/07/new-case-study-connect-with-youtube-for.html

http://www.firstlightnet.com/ba_case_studies

http://www.azavar.com/Web-Design-Work/Case-Studies/noble.aspx

http://www.transforming.com/case_studies/advertising_agency.html

5

Creative Strategy and Execution

This chapter includes the key concepts that are described below—

- Introduction
- Purchase Proposition
- Creative Execution
- Core Concept
- Reinforcement of Message
- Evaluation of Advertising Messages
- Creative Process
- Copy Writing
- Copy Research

INTRODUCTION

The end product of advertising planning and creative strategy and its execution is the from in which an advertising appears. The basic principle of developing a message, considering the budget provides boundary parameters so that the formulation of a message or package of messages may be trimmed down.

In advertising, different creative strategies are used in order to obtain consumer attention and provoke shoppers to purchase or use a specific product. Advertisers use different ways of thinking to create catchy slogans that capture consumer attention. Creative strategies promote publicity, public relations, personal selling and sales promotion.

These ways of thinking are divided into three basic descriptions: Weak strategies, mid-strength strategies and strong strategies. The strategies labeled "strong, mid-strength, and weak are generic phrases used in the text books referenced below to help students understand the intensity of each different type of advertising strategy. Advertisements, weak, mid-strength, and strong can be found in television, radio, and magazines/print.

Since the beginning of advertising, strategies have been created which are starting with the simplest or weak strategies in 1940s.

There are three types of creative strategies including simplest or weak strategies, middle- strength strategies and also strong strategies.

Weak Strategies

Generic and Pre-emptive strategies describe the two weakest forms of advertising that were most popular through the 1940s.

Generic Strategy:-

A generic strategy gives a product attribution. An example of this would be how the beef industry chose to advertise their product. With their slogan, "Beef, it's what's for dinner," consumers aren't learning anything new about the product. The Beef slogan simply states beef as a dinner item. It enhances the product in no other way.

Weak strategies are also known as simplest. It is first strategy in advertising. This types of strategy are divided into two weakest forms i.e. generic and preemptive strategy makes the generic claims stronger.

A pre-emptive strategy is a form of advertising that makes a generic claim stronger. An example of a pre-emptive strategy can be found in Folgers Coffee. As many of us know, most all coffee is grown in the mountains. Folgers took that fact and claimed it as their own with their slogan, "Folgers: Mountain Grown Coffee."

Middle–strength Strategies

Middle strength strategies are the second strategy which are used in advertising. This type of strategies are divided into three form i.e. unique positioning strategy, brand image and Positioning.

Unique Positioning Strategy : A unique positioning strategy is proving that something about your product is truly unique. This is commonly found when producers take an average product and add a new, unique element to it. An example of Unique Positioning

Strategy would be in Crest toothpaste. Crest added the unique feature of Scope in their product to differentiate it from other brands of toothpaste.

Brand Image : Brand Image is another very common way companies choose to advertise. In brand image, an advertiser is not trying to create rational thinking. This type of advertising strives to create emotion and give a brand a personality. A common way of doing this is by using a celebrity as a spokesperson.

Brand image is early discussed in previous chapter. To make a brand personality, it is necessary to take an endorser i.e. a famous celebrity who has passion to make that product as a brand personality.

A great example of brand image is found in Proactive Acne Solutions. In each of their commercials they have celebrities sharing their Proactive experiences, giving the brand a face people want to be.

Positioning : Positioning is one of the most common forms of advertising. It was developed in the 1970s and is still widely used today. In positioning one brand will take its product and "position" it against a competing product. It is one of the part of middle strength strategy in advertising.

An example of positioning can be found in the rental car company "Avis'" store slogan. With "Hertz" car company being the leader in rental car services, Avis took their number two position and used it to their advantage by creating the slogan, "When you're number two, you try harder."

Strong Strategies

This is third and very strong i.e. strongest strategy in advertising which includes affective advertising and resonance advertising.

Making people feel really good about a product is called affective advertising. This is difficult to do, but often humor and an honest character can make affective advertising possible.

A great example of affective advertising is found in the "Geico" commercials. By creating a friendly, honest, funny gecko as a spokesperson, consumers tend to trust what the gecko is saying and find humor in his actions. This creates a good feeling about the actual service "Geico" offers.

Resonance Advertising : Lastly, resonance advertising is a way of identifying with consumers. If an advertiser can create a campaign that certain target markets identify with, then resonance advertising has been achieved.

An example of resonance advertising is in "Tide" detergent ads. Many times mothers are busy doing laundry in between sports practices and driving their children around in mini vans. Their recognition with soccer moms makes "Tide" a favorite pick among women with children who are very involved in activities.

PURCHASE PROPOSITION

The first step in creative strategy consists with purchase proposition. The use of expression purchase proposition a fact that the advertising practitioner must put the customer and try to look at the product or service that are offered for sale or acceptance from their view point. It is not merely the product which concerns the advertiser. The origin of purchase proposition for a brand thus calls not merely for knowledge of the composition of the product its properties and utilities, but also a creative and meaningful search for brand identity.

Unique selling Proposition

Unique Selling Proposition is known as Unique Selling Point i.e. USP. Rosser Reaves, who switched from journalism to advertising who starting their new cover as a copywriter and joined the well-known advertising agency named Ted Bates and company carried out extensive market research on successful advertising campaigns in early 1940s.

The Unique Selling Proposition (also Unique Selling Point) is a marketing concept that was first proposed as a theory to explain a pattern among successful advertising campaigns of the early 1940s. It states that such campaigns made unique propositions to the customer and that this convinced them to switch brands. The term was invented by Rosser Reeves of Ted Bates & Company. Today the term is used in other fields or just casually to refer to any aspect of an object that differentiates it from similar objects.

Today, a number of businesses and corporations currently use USPs as a basis for their marketing campaigns.

USP has three features:-

- Each advertisement must make a proposition to the consumer. Not just words, not just product puffery, not just show-window advertising. Each advertisement must say to each reader: "Buy this product, and you will get *this specific benefit.*"
- The proposition must be one that the competition either cannot, or does not, offer. It must be unique—either a uniqueness of the brand or a claim not otherwise made in that particular field of advertising.
- The proposition must be so strong that it can move the mass millions, i.e., pull over new customers to your product.

It may not be possible for an advertising agency to get a readymade USP. That is where innovativeness and creativity come into play.

Some unique propositions that were pioneers when they were introduced:

- Domino's Pizza: "You get fresh, hot pizza delivered to your door in 30 minutes or less — or it's free."
- FedEx: "When your package absolutely, positively has to get there overnight"
- M&M's: "The milk chocolate melts in your mouth, not in your hand"
- Wonder Bread: "Wonder Bread Helps Build Strong Bodies 12 Ways"

CREATIVE EXECUTION

The process of creative execution begins in the advertising agency. It is not intended to go into details of creative execution such as art work, size of type face in case of Print media or the type of animation as for audio-visual media.

Creative Execution entails the actual development and execution of all marketing activities which are proposed in the **Marketing Initiatives** section. Typically, this will include company logo and company identity and corporate documents, advertising, brochure design and sales collateral production, sell sheet design, corporate video production or training video production, Web site design, Web site development, web site optimization, and Web site automation, public relations, media kit production, media relations, internal communication, catalog design and production, etc.

A main issue in developing an innovative message lies in the same advertisement for an audience of great diversity, and other issue is that of arousing interest and catching the attention of the audience in the face of diversions that are arising from competitive advertising. There is not a shortcut to the formulation for developing an effective message.

Your marketing plan must include innovative and effective sales tools that an used to support your sales team, enhance your brand and communicate your key success factors and capabilities.

Beneficial Influences on Creative Execution—Simplified list of key beneficial influences the client has on the creative process and creative execution :

- Discloses much of the strategic and competitive and even tatctical information that are required to devise a sound and hard-hitting advertising of marketing campaign.
- Provides business objectives for consideration in the overall marketing communication plan.
- Provides the budgetary support system and limitations for creative production.
- Offers feedback on the creative brief – advocates proposed direction or approach.
- Offers resources for further information or support for the campaign.
- Provides the motivation and enthusiasm for the anticipate results of the marketing activity.

CORE CONCEPT

There are four stages of memory in terms of learning, retention, recall and recognition. An advertisement seeks to stimulate all these stages of memory. The Core concept or the theme of advertisement should emerge from various considerations. These considerations including the concept of defining the mass desire that makeup the market and selecting one performance in your product that satisfies that decision most deeply. This core concept provided by the psychologist Schwartz.

There are two prospects of theme or core concept of advertising i.e. thematic classification and Motivational appeal.

Thematic Classification

The major theme of an advertisement runs by the entire advertising department or advertisement. The selection of the theme is related to a specific or particular appeal which may be employed in the formulation of any message. These classifications were identified by the following themes:-

1. Utilitarian—The emphasis of main message that contained in the advertisement was on the value of that product / service.

2. Focused—The focused theme was defined as the are which was used for formulating messages which would appeal to specific market or audience segment

3. Informative— This theme consists primarily of important information about the product or service or the advertiser and doesn't project a selling stance.

4. Non-specific—The non – specific theme was identified as one which was somewhat vague and diffuse.

5. Achievement Orientation—The purpose of message was to advertise the achievement of advertiser such as increase in turnover that is winning an award or some other kind of acclaim.

6. Descriptive and Projective—This category is a combination of information and achievement orientation themes. The message contain around this theme would contain information about the advertiser and product / service and achievement of advertiser.

7. New product, service or scheme—This theme refers to the advertisement for launching new products, service or schemes.

These above thematic classifications are by no means comprehensive. However, if extends the classification approach beyond the much simpler approach of classifying advertisement merely by informative versus persuasive bias.

Motivational Appeals

An advertisement must contain an appeal for creating human interest so that it may be followed up by the audience. Hettwick has proposed two levels cf needs including primary and secondary needs.

Primary needs are known as Basic needs these are:-

- Food and Drink
- Comfort
- Freedom from fear and danger
- To be superior
- To attract the opposite sex
- Welfare of loved ones
- To live longer
- Social Approval

These Eights needs are basic needs which are suggested by Hettwick

Secondary needs includes:-

- Bargains
- Informative
- Cleanliness
- Efficiency
- Convenience
- Quality
- Style or Beauty
- Economy or Profit
- Curiosity.

These nine needs are included in secondary needs that suggested by Hettwick.

REINFORCEMENT OF MESSAGE

An advertising message must arouse the attention in the first place and be comprehensible to the target audience. This is in the domain of copy-writing, or making an audio-visual for cinema or television. It is also essential that the reception of the message must be reinforced. The background, i.e. the specific media vehicle and more specifically the setting of the advertisement on a certain page or a television commercial in certain slots; can effect the reception of the message. Furthermote, the same audience may have to be expose to a message more than once and the too in different media vehicles for reinforcing the message. Bogart Points out that a message may change character completely, depending on its environment. An advertisement from the *life* magazine may have a completely different effect when seen again in the *Time* magazine than if it were repreated in the *Life* a second time.

Advertising message occurs when the attentions are comprehensible to the audience. It is necessary to receive the message that must be reinforced. These audiences may have to expose that message more than onetime and that message too indifferent media for reinforcing that message.

There are three aspects of reinforcement of message including Repetition of message, facilitatory factors and also obstructive features.

Repetition of Message

It is necessary to repeat the message that has been emphasized by advertising the practitioners all along. The determination of ideal interval consists in estimating the likelihood that a successive exposure that doesn't come too soon, or else it will annoy and put off the prospect. Thomas Smith proposed the twenty scheduling strategy in 1885. His plan presents the basic principle that frequency of exposure to advertising messages helps in registration and including the prospect towards the stage of action.

Following are the 20-stages of scheduling stages which was proposed by Thomas smith:-

- The first time a man looks at an advertisement, he does not seet it.
- The second time he does not notice it.
- The third time he is conscious of its existence.
- The fourth time he faintly remembers having seen it before.
- The fifth time be reads it.
- The sixth time be turns up his nose at it.
- The seventh time he reads it through and says, "Oh bother!"
- The eighth time he says, "Here's that confounded thing again!"
- The ninth time he wonders if it amounts to anything.
- The tenth time he thinks he will ask his neighbour if be has tried it.

- The eleventh time he wonders how the advertiser makes it pay.
- The twelfth time he thinks perhaps it may be worth something.
- The thirteenth time he thinks it must be a good thing.
- The fourteenth time he remembers that he has wanted such a thing for a long time.
- The fifteenth time he is tantalized because he cannot afford to buy it.
- The sixteenth time he thinks he will buy it some day.
- The seventeenth time he makes a memorandum of it.
- The eighteenth time he swears at his property.
- The ninetennth time he counts his money carefully.
- The twentieth time he sees it he buys the article or instructs his wife to do so.

Facilitatory Factors—It is ambitious that effective advertising messages have some characteristics. Even has proposed that an effective advertising message have following features:-

- Capability – It must carry conviction
- Identity- The identity of the product, service or the company advertised may be clearly quickly and easily indicated.
- Impact – The advertisement must attract attention.
- Reason – Its selling message must be backed by an authentic justification.
- Relevance – It must be relevant to the needs of the target audience.
- Single mindedness – This feature is also known as specificness. It must concentrate on a single selling proposition.
- Topicality – It must be appropriate in respect of place or time.

Obstructive Feature—There are various factors which are come in the congenial reception of an advertising message.

There are following factors—

- Apathy – Laziness, indifference or inertia of audience.
- Competitive activity – More convincing proposition that are presented by competing advertising.

- Forgetfulness – Loss of memory of the propositions.
- Incomprehensibility – There is lack of understanding of the purchase proposition or its relevance.
- Hostility – This factor includes the rejection of antipathy to the proposition presented
- Product Similarity – Too many similar products with indistinguishable advertising claims in the same market.
- Unfavourable Market conditions – Change in the structure and character of the market.

EVALUATION OF ADVERTISING MESSAGES

Advertising supports the research methods like qualitative methods, these includes intrinsic qualitative characteristics and extrinsic qualitative characteristics.

Imtrinsic qualitative characteristics of advertising messages will help or hinder their ultimate effectiveness. However, an explicit qualitative characteristic doesn't necessarily ensure the success of advertising as measured by the results that are related to the marketing objectives it is expected to achieve.

CREATIVE PROCESS

The creative team has the critical responsibility of not missing out on the substances and yet making the advertising appealing and credible. There is an inherent systematic approach which must be followed in order to avoid pitfalls. There is always considerable scope for exercising executive judgment in respect of creative work. The topic of creative work is early discussed in this chapter.

In final analysis, the responsibility for making delusions has to be borne by the managers that are concerned and it is to them that success or failure is attributed. The basic principle of evolving a purchase proposition and putting it across cogently and effectively is applicable all through. These creative processes are included all through. These creative processes are included in creative work as well as creative Execution.

COPY WRITING

Copywriting is the use of words to promote a person, business, opinion or idea. Although the word *copy* may be applied to any content intended for printing (as in the body of a newspaper article or book), the term *copywriter* is generally limited to such promotional situations, regardless of media (as advertisements for print, television, radio or other media). The author of newspaper or magazine copy, for example, is generally called a reporter or writer, not a copywriter.

Copywriting is the words to convey the message having commercial, informative or persuasive value through various media and its success is indicated by the acceptance by the audience of the idea or claims made for goods or services. Conclusion comes from what are the words to convey in terms of benefits and satisfaction. This helps to establish the links between advertisers and their prospects. It may also be used to promote the acceptance of an idea, as in the case of non-commercial advertising.

Thus, the purpose of marketing copy, or promotional text, is to persuade the reader, listener or viewer to act — for example, to buy a product or subscribe to a certain viewpoint. Alternatively, copy might also be intended to dissuade a reader. Copywriting is "getting across the perfect message, with the perfect words."

On websites, copywriting may also refer to content writing for the purpose of achieving higher rankings in search engines. This practice includes the strategic placement and repetition of keywords and keyword phrases on webpages. Known as "organic" *search engine optimization* (SEO), it is best done in a way that does not distract, bore or confuse the human reader.

Copywriting can appear in direct mail pieces, taglines, jingle lyrics, web page content (although if the purpose is not ultimately promotional, its author might prefer to be called a *content writer.*), online ads, e-mail and other Internet content, television or radio commercial scripts, press releases, white papers, catalogs, billboards, brochures, postcards, sales letters, and other marketing communications media.

Copywriting Strategy and Copywriter

A copywriter performs a highly responsible role of understanding the marketing strategy and integrating it, through creative strategy in copy. The job of copywriter involves coordination with visualisers for bringing in suitable examples which will highlight they effect of the copy and make it appealing and completely comprehensible.

Most copywriters are employees within organizations such as advertising agencies, public relations firms, web developers, company advertising departments, large stores, broadcasters, online marketing firms and cable providers, newspapers and magazines. Copywriters can also be independent contractors freelancing for a variety of clients, at the clients' offices or working from home.

Copywriters are similar to technical writers and the careers may overlap. Broadly speaking, however, technical writing is dedicated to informing readers rather than persuading them. For example, a copywriter writes an ad to sell a car, while a technical writer writes the operator's manual explaining how to use it.

Therefore, a copywriter must be totally familiar with the marking goals of the advertisers and particular advertising objectives. Copywriting skills require the command over the language and an intellectual and creative mentality. For example, it is necessary to assume the role of salesman to understand the marketing perspective from the advertiser's view point as well as point of view of audience. The account executive works with copywriter and with other members of creative team for providing them necessary inputs and including in them.

A copywriter usually works as part of a creative team. Agencies and advertising departments partner copywriters with art directors. The copywriter has ultimate responsibility for the advertisement's verbal or textual content, which often includes receiving the copy information from the client. (Where this formally extends into the role of account executive, the job may be described as "copy/contact.") The art director has ultimate responsibility for visual communication and, particularly in the case of print work, may oversee production. Either person may come up with the overall idea for the advertisement or commercial (typically referred to as the concept or "big idea"), and the process of collaboration often improves the work.

Writing Strategy

Creativity is important in initiating the process of writing a copy, especially in evolving the basic approach. Following are the purpose of writing strategy:-

- Abstracting- It includes the relevant data that are obtained from the market situation, prospects and relevant media.

- Coalescence- It includes the decisions that are made for transference of ideation to physical expression i.e. writing.
- Gestation- It resolves the objections and difficulties. It may involve the discussion with others or reference to sources of information.
- Hypothesizing- It includes the ideas which are formulated into experimental patterns culminating in a working statement.
- Performance – it includes the action that are taken in the form of actual writing.
- Synthesizing – it includes the elements that are blended and combined, ideas and approaches that are accepted, revised or rejected.

Criteria of Effective Copy

An ideal copy should involve the following guideless that includes :-

- It must be precise.
- It must be concise
- It must create desire
- It must inspire confidence
- It must be addressed according to the type of the audience.
- It must aims to sell.
- It must be sincere.
- It must stimulate the interest.

COPY RESEARCH

An effective copy usually a combination of description, narration, exposition and persuasion. Copy writers have to draw upon experience, judgments, intuitive sensitivity, knowledge of research findings and methods that are used to judge whether a piece of copy would be effective.

Copy research is an aspect of advertising research and includes both the pretesting and the post-testing of advertisements or commercials in print or broadcast. Pretesting explores the product claims, technical aspects, target audience , and other areas affected by the copy, before or at the very beginning of the advertising campaign . Post-testing will explore the effectiveness of the copy in communicating the advertising message and its meaning, at the conclusion of an advertising campaign.

Copy research is concerned with development of methodology for measuring the effectiveness of copy. This may be done as pretest, before its appearance in print, in radio commercials or as a post test for analyzing the extent of its impact after its appearance. Copy research techniques may be applied before publications or after publications.

There are various pre-publication techniques that are applied before publication. Following are the pre publication techniques that are commonly used:-

- consumer Jury
- split Run
- Flesh formula
- Eye camera
- Portfolio test
- Motivation Research

Consumer Jury :- Jury consist of sample of target market segment for the product and the rating of the jury of an advertisement that helps in determining the possible reader-reaction before the publication. The Jury can also rank various versions of the copy for the same products.

Split run :- it refers to the practice of testing the advertisement by running either two copy that are alternatively designed for an advertisement or new ad against an existing ad on that press run.

Technique used to test the effectiveness of advertising copy. Two different versions of the same advertisement are printed in the same press run of an issue of a particular publication, so that some of the copies contain one version of the ad and the others contain the other version. The publication is distributed normally, but the distribution of the advertisements is split according to the request of the advertiser. Some advertisers split their run in alternate bundles; (*see* alternate bundles run) others prefer to split by geographic location or by subscription versus newsstand sales. The purpose of the split run is to compare the effectiveness of the two alternate ad copies. Advertisers will take advantage of this option when they desire to learn which of two elements used in the advertising will achieve the desired objectives. Elements that are often tested are prices, copy appeal, layout, type of illustration, coupon offered or no coupon offered, or premium or rebate offered or not. The results of split-run testing are revealed by the number of responses to each advertisement. The split-run option is offered as a convenience to advertisers. However, not all publications offer this option.

Flesh formula :- Dr. flesh who was the former Vienna lawyer was developed readability formula that are based on average sentence length, average number of syllabus and proportions of personal sentences and personal words. The commonly acceptable syllable count per sentence was 139.

Eye camera :- it measures the attention value of diffluent elements of an advertisement, through recording that are made on film of eye movements when exposed to a person.

Portfolio Test :- Various advertisements for different products are assembled and two identical portfolios including typical editorial matter are prepared. Each portfolio will contain one of the test advertisement, which is possible to get an indication of the confirmative advantage b/w two advertisements that are being studied.

Motivation Research:- it draws on psychological research or techniques which seeks to find out the underlying motives of potential consumer. It only concentrates on " why" of actual and possibly contemplated actions. It is interpretive rather than descriptive.

Case Study

Note : knowing more about "Creative Strategy and Execution" reader can study documentation process of Microsoft company by visiting their site : www.members.microsoft.com

http://craftingbree.blogspot.com/2009/01/crafting-and-executing-strategy-case.html

http://ahacreative.com/case-studies/

http://conference.imp-lore.org/statements/presentations/Remotti.pdf

http://www.inlandims.com/case-studies/campaign-execution.aspx

http://www.marketingforsports.com/work/case.php.html

http://jobfunctions.bnet.com/abstract.aspx?docid=50984

http://www.diamondconsultants.com/PublicSite/work/services/?sub=Case%20Studies&topic=Execution+

http://www.activestrategy.com/about_us/case_studies.aspx

http://www.c3itsolutions.com/en/case-study-onsite-offshore-project-execution.html

6

Advertising Process

This chapter includes the key concepts that are described below:-

- Advertising and Psychology
- Triangle of Communication
- Effectiveness of Advertising
- Advertising and Buyer Behaviour
- Audience Perception
- Perceptual Mapping
- Consumer Adoption Models

ADVERTISING AND PSYCHOLOGY

Advertising is the way or method by which an organization interact with the public or audience about their product or services.

Advertising is a specific form of communication where the aspects of cost and corresponding benefit assume to a special significance. In terms to understand the way, advertising can work it is necessary to give some attenstion to the basic processes of communication. Invariably, one is tempted to go into the domain of psychology. It will neither be possible, nor necessary to discuss details of human psychology. It may of business, or for that decision making in the area of business, or for that matter in the domain of non-commercial active, will be influenced quite considerably by patterns of behaviour of concerned persons, individually and in groups. Human beings belongs to different types and backgrounds which have an effect on their behaviour. Furthermore, regardless of education, training and and group or organizational framework constraints, rationality may be expected only up to a limit.

To understand the concept of Advertising and Psychology, it is necessary to understand the way in advertising work i.e. communication process.

TRIANGLE OF COMMUNICATION

Process of Advertising is done through communication. The objective of averters is to communicate with the audience in order to obtain the desired conclusion that are arise from the responser of the audience.

The triangle of communication includes various part :-

- Advertiser
- Audience
- Media
- Choice and Competition
- Dynamic Concept
- Advertising Agency

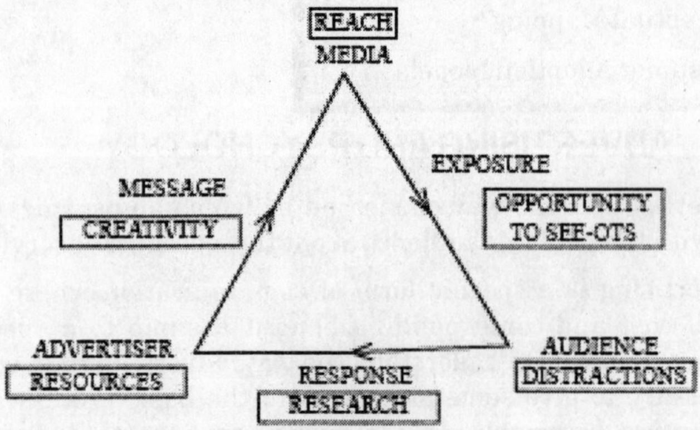

Triangle Diagram

Advertiser

Advertiser is generally interpreted as a commercial organization which has the objective of making profits out of its business activities, Profit are usually generated by marketing or business activity. However the communication logic also apply to the types of advertisers which may have social or political objectives.

Audience

Audience has to be interpreted with care. Readers of newspaper or magazines, listeners to the radio or viewers of cinema or television would not necessarily constitute the audience for an advertiser. The audience for a particular advertising has to be defined and identified by the advertiser. The need for market segmentation. Would help in defining and identifying the audience has been emphasized. There is issue of identification of audience is important for non-commercial advertising. There fore, the concept of target audience will be applicable in all situations whether an advertising campaigns for a product or service is under consideration

Choice & Competition

The creative aspect of advertising comes into play when an advertiser formulates an appropriate message to be beamed across to its target audience for a specific campaign will be necessary to formulate the message and present it in such a way that it should appeal to the audience. This is essential when there is choice and competition. The importances of appeal will obviously be less when there is limited choice, unless the advertiser has the objective of market development.

Media

Media is the third element of triangle of communication and that is where advertising tends to differ from other forms of communication. As a rule, advertisers will not the control on the media. Hence, they will have to depend on the availability of media and its appropriateness to reach their target audiences.

Dynamic Concept

Triangle of communication consists of the advertisers who are trying to convey the messages to their target audience by the help of media which are independent of advertisers. The triangle has two levels named micro level and macro level. First of all, triangle may be interpreted at both micro and macro level i.e. for an advertiser or for one campaigns and collectively for various advertisers in a community. All three elements of triangle are Advertiser, Audience and Media are subject to continuous change.

- Audiences alter their patterns of behaviors under the influence of factors such as education, occupation, mobility and so on.

- Advertisers produce and market products or services which may cater to the needs and tastes of their clientele.
- Media is influenced primarily by audience to whom they have to relate. The cost economics of media at the same time involves advertising revenues.

Advertising Agency

This topic is earlier disused in chapters. An advertising agency working with advertiser lends is professional services to the advertiser for the formulation and presentation of the messages. It is the media which provides basic sustenance to the advertising agency by allowing 15% commissions in India on billing of advertisers.

Resource Constraints

After the completion of cycle of communication, it is obvious that advertiser have their own resource constraints i.e. funds as well as time. They can afford only to spend a certain amount of money on advertising in accordance with their marketing and advertising appropriation means the preparation of advertisement s needs time. Finally the feed back from the audience is an important input for the advertisers.

EFFECTIVENESS OF ADVERTISING

The advertising industry, as a whole, has the poorest quality-assurance systems and turns out the most inconsistent product (their ads and commercials) of any industry in the world. This might seem like an overly harsh assessment, but it is based on testing thousands of ads over several decades. In our experience, only about half of all commercials actually work; that is, have any positive effects on consumers' purchasing behavior or brand choice. Moreover, a small share of ads actually appear to have negative effects on sales. How could these assertions possibly be true? Don't advertising agencies want to produce great ads? Don't clients want great advertising? Yes, yes, they do, but they face formidable barriers.

Unlike most of the business world, which is governed by numerous feedback loops, the advertising industry receives little objective, reliable feedback on its advertising. First, few ads and commercials are ever tested among consumers (less than one percent, according to some estimates). So, no one—not agency or client—knows if the advertising is any good. If no one knows when a commercial is good or bad, or why, how can the next commercial be any better? Second, once the advertising goes on air, sales response (a potential feedback loop) is a notoriously poor indicator of advertising effectiveness because there is always so much "noise" in sales data (competitive activity, out-of-stocks, weather, economic trends, promotional influences, pricing variation, etc.). Third, some of the feedback is confusing and misleading: agency and client preferences and biases, the opinions of the client's wife, feedback from dealers and franchisees, complaints from the lunatic fringe, and so on.

The test of effectiveness of advertising consists in the degree of achievement of the objectives which are set by an advertiser in consultation with the advertising agency working on the account.

Creating Better Advertising

1. The client must craft a sound strategy for its brand, based on facts, not wishful thinking and self-delusion. The client must carefully define the role of advertising in the marketing plan and set precise communication objectives for the advertising. What exactly does the client want the advertising to convey, to accomplish? Agencies are too often asked to create advertising in an informational vacuum. Agencies are not miracle workers. Once strategy and positioning alternatives are identified and tested, the strategy should be locked down..and rarely changed thereafter.

This is the first step in which drent have the sound strategy for their product & defines the role of advertising according to plan of marketing.

2. As creative executions are developed against the strategy, each execution should be pretested among members of the target audience (pretesting refers to testing advertising before it is aired, and/or before final production. When the term "testing" is used in this article, it is a shorthand term for "pretesting.") The greater the number of executions pretested, the more likely it is that great advertising will emerge. Testing the creative provides a reliable feedback loop that helps agency and client alike become smarter over time. Once a conceptual family of commercials is identified as the optimal campaign of the future, then the campaign should be locked down. Long-term continuity of advertising message is essential to maximizing effectiveness.

There is dependency in step 2nd including when the number of executions protested tends to be greater, then the advertising will also emerge to greater.

3. Use the same pretesting system consistently. There is no perfect advertising pretesting system. Some are better than others, but any system will help improve your advertising. The secret is to use one system over and over, so that everyone (client, agency, and researchers) learns how to interpret the pretesting results for the category and the specific brand.

4. If budget permits, test the advertising at an early stage in the creative process (i.e., the "storyboard" or "animatic" stage) and also test at the finished commercial stage. Early-stage testing allows rough commercials to be tweaked and fine-tuned before you spend the big dollars on final production. Early-stage testing tends to be highly predictive of finished commercial scores, but not always. Testing the finished commercials gives you extra assurance that your advertising is "on strategy" and working.

5. Build your own "action standards" over time. As you test every execution, you will begin to learn what works and what doesn't work. Think of the pretesting company's norms as very crude, rough indicators to help you get started with a testing program. But, as quickly as possible, develop your own norms for your category and your brand (yes, all of the advertising effectiveness measures vary by product category and brand). What you are searching for, long-term, are not norms, but action standards (that is, the knowledge that certain advertising testing scores will translate into actual sales increases).

6. Use a mathematical model to derive an overall score for each execution. It doesn't matter that an ad has great persuasion if it does not register the brand name. It doesn't matter that an ad registers the brand name if no one will notice the commercial itself. It doesn't matter that an ad increases short-term purchase interest if it will damage the brand's quality reputation over time. So, all of the key variables must be put together intelligently to come up with a composite or overall measure of advertising effectiveness.

7. Use the pretesting results as a guide, as an indicator, but do not become a slave to the mathematical model. Read all of the open-ended questions carefully. Make sure you really understand the underlying reasons. Base your decisions on this comprehensive assessment of the results, and leave yourself some wiggle room.

No model or system can anticipate every marketing situation, or give a 100% perfect solution every time. Informed human judgment remains important.

8. Client and agency need to accept that "continuous improvement" of the advertising is an important goal. This means that every execution is tested and tweaked based on scientific evidence from the target audience. We are not talking about changing the strategy or changing the campaign, but making sure that every execution is "on strategy" and working as hard as possible.

9. The ultimate goal of testing is an advertising success formula that works. That is, the goal of advertising creative development, and the goal of advertising testing, is to identify the elements/ideas essential to advertising effectiveness, and then to make sure that those elements/ideas are consistently communicated by all advertising executions.

Barriers to Great Advertising

Advertising testing could provide a reliable feedback loop and lead to much better advertising, but many obstacles stand in the way. The first great barrier to better advertising is self-delusion. Most of us believe, in our heart-of-hearts, that we know what good advertising is and that there is no need for any kind of independent, objective evaluation. Agencies and clients alike often think that they know how to create and judge good advertising. Besides, once agencies and clients start to fall in love with the new creative, they quickly lose interest in any objective evaluation. No need for advertising testing. Case closed.

There are eight barriers to better advertising. Each Barrier has their own functionality which helps to make or create a better advertising.

Strangely, after 40 years of testing advertising, we cannot tell you if a commercial is any good or not, just by viewing it. Sure, we have opinions, but they are almost always wrong. In our experience, advertising agencies and their clients are just as inept at judging advertising as we are. It seems that none of us is smart enough to see advertising through the eyes of the target audience, based purely on our own judgment.

A second barrier to better advertising is the belief that sales performance will tell if the advertising is working. Unless the sales response to the advertising is immediate and overwhelming, it is almost impossible to use sales data to judge the effectiveness of the advertising. So many variables are beyond our control, as noted, that it's impossible to isolate the effects of media advertising alone. Moreover, some advertising works in a few weeks, while other advertising might take many months to show positive effects, and this delayed response can confound our efforts to read the sales data. Also, advertising often has short-term effects that sales data might reflect, and long-term (years later) effects that most of us might easily overlook in subsequent sales data. Because of these limitations, sales data tends to be confusing and unreliable as an indicator of advertising effectiveness. Modeling in marketing mix is one of the way to measure these advertising effects on sales, but it often takes millions of dollars and years of effort. This modeling doesn't help us to evaluate the contribution of a single commercial but rather the cumulative affects of many different commercials over long period of time and it also dorm's tell why the advertising work or failed to work.

These barrier have their own functionality including first barrier supports judging advertising, second accept sales performance, third includes pervasive tendency. Fourth includes big creative ego, fifth includes major competitors knows what they are doing, sixth includes lack of strategy or poor strategy, seventh supports client ineptness and at last, eighth barrier includes the poor copy testing by research companies.

ADVERTISING AND BUYER BEHAVIOUR

The extent to which the process of advertising communication may conclude in affecting the buyer behavior which is subject to continuous discussion or debate. Advertising process viewed from the consumer's communication system which is aimed at reflecting there considerations by examine what people do to advertising instead of what advertising does to people. There are some elements that supports this concept which are specified Below:-

- Awareness – it is the element that includes the conditions that limiting or enabling the communication.
- Commitment – It includes the values and ideas that are taken by the consumers to unquestionably true.
- Goal Seeking – It includes the purposer for which the consumer can feels he should use advertising.

- Input System- it includes the characteristics of channels or the media that are used by the consumer for input purposes.

A third barrier to better advertising is a pervasive tendency of many (but not all) advertising agencies to delay, undermine, and thwart efforts to objectively test their creative "babies." Who wants a report card on the quality of their work? It's very threatening. The results can upset the creative folks. The results can upset clients. The agency can lose control. Agencies can be quite creative in coming up with reasons to avoid copy testing.

Third barrier is also used to make better advertising to used pervasive tendency of taking many advertising agencies to delay.

The fourth barrier to more effective advertising is the big creative ego. The belief that only the "creatives" in the agency can create advertising—and the conviction that creativity is their exclusive domain—constitute a major barrier. Great advertising tends to evolve over time, with lots of hard work, fine-tuning, and tinkering—based on objective feedback from target consumers. Big creative egos tend to resist such evolutionary improvements. We have seen great campaigns abandoned because agencies would not accept minor tweaks to the advertising. To be fair, big egos are not limited to advertising agencies. Big client egos can also be a barrier to good advertising. Research firm egos are yet another problem. Big egos create barriers because emotion is driving advertising decision making instead of logic, reason, and consumer feedback. Big egos lead to bad advertising.

A fifth barrier to better advertising is the widespread belief that one's major competitors know what they are doing. So, just copy the advertising approaches of the competition, and success will surely follow. We recently had a client who was about to copy the advertising strategy of a major competitor, but we were able to persuade the client to test all major competitive commercials as a precaution before blindly copying the competitor's advertising approach. This competitor was the industry leader in market.share and profitability. Our testing quickly revealed that this industry leader was the industry leader in spite of its bad advertising. The testing also revealed that another competitor, in contrast, had great advertising. Needless to say, the client's desire to copy the industry leader quickly vanished.

The sixth barrier to better advertising is lack of strategy, or having a poor strategy. The client is most often at fault here. The client has not done his homework, has not thought deeply about his brand and its future, and has not developed and tested strategy alternatives. The client tells the agency to go forth and create great advertising, without providing any strategy guidelines. The agency is left to guess and speculate about strategy. Great advertising is rarely created in a strategy vacuum. If the client cannot define a sound strategy, the agency cannot create great advertising. Again, the responsibility for strategy falls squarely on the client.

A seventh barrier to better advertising is client ineptness. Some clients' processes, policies, and people tend to discourage the creation of great advertising. Arrogance, ambiguity, impatience, ignorance, risk aversion, and inconsistency tend to be the hallmarks of these "agency killer" clients. Bad clients rarely stimulate or tolerate great advertising.

The eighth and last barrier to better advertising is poor copy testing by research companies. Many advertising testing systems are limited to a few markets (and cannot provide representative samples). Some systems are so expensive that the cost of testing exceeds the value of the results. Research companies have been guilty of relying on one or two simplistic measures of advertising effectiveness, while completely ignoring many other very important variables.

5. Integration – It includes those standards that are used by the consumer for purposes of maintaining the cognitive consistency.

Buyer Behaviour in Advertising Industry

In the advertising industry, the agency-client relationship recognizes the association between an advertising agency and their client. The nature of this service is a high risk and high involvement purchase which makes the information search a crucial element of the buying process. Understanding the drivers of this buying behaviour will enable the agency to become more responsive to their clients needs and tailor their services to positively influence the relationship. The foundations for a successful agency-client relationship rely on understanding:

- What are the key drivers of successful client retention?
- Are these in line with the key success factors for new client attraction?

In response to answering these questions, our report aims to investigate segmentation and buyer behavior within the advertising industry.

Selection criteria of Advertising Agency

The selection and retention criteria of advertising agencies can be described by three distinct elements:

- Relationship Management: the chemistry between the client and agency and quality of account management.
- Service Delivery: Technical and creative experience and the quality of the output.
- Cost Management: Ability to manage client budget and justify spend through added value.

An important part of marketing process is to understand the concept that why a customer or buyer makes a purchase. Without understanding this concept, business find it hard to respond to the needs of customers.

Marketing theory traditionally divides into two groups for analysis

- Consumer Buyers – Consumer Buyers are those who purchase items for their personal consumptions
- Industrial Buyers – Industrial Buyers are those who purchase items on the belay of their business or organization.

Buyer Behavior in terms of New Product

Customer buying process for new products

How do customers approach the process of buying a new product? How does this differ from the process for buying a product which the customer has bought before? What is meant by a "new product"?

A new product can be defined as:

"A good, service or idea that is "perceived" by some potential customers as new. It may have been available for some time, but many potential customers have not yet adopted the product nor decided to become a regular user of the product"

AUDIENCE PERCEPTION

There are many factors which effect the perpetual process of human beings. Following are the factors which effect perpetual process:-

1. Cultural and group factors—this factors includes the group attitude towards skin color, companies & their products spread through culture or subculture and influence the way people perceive.

2. Expectation— A tendency to expect that a stimulus situation that will exhibit certain characteristics.

3. Inner needs—It includes the internal and psychological needs of the individual affect the way he perceives the world.

4. Leveling and sharpening—In remembering things, we tends to simplify them and recall a relatively general, common and also meaningful pattern or way that is consistent without inner needs by dropping details and simplifying or sharpening others.

5. Mental set—It includes a readiness to perceive in a few way and perhaps to react in a predetermined way to the perception.

6. Mood—It includes the factors when our moods effect the way we perceive the situations, the elements on which we concentrate and the elements we ignore as well as our evaluation of the significance of this situation.

7. Past experience and primary—It includes the tendency to perceive or interpret a new experience on the basis of a previous or past experience; a tendency to organize our perception of later stimulus situations on the basis of initial impressions.

8. Perceptual constancy—It includes the tendency to perceive things in the way we are accustomed to perceiving them, even though the stimulus changes.

9. Structural factors—It includes the environmental stimuli and the physical nature of an individual. The factors may be of special importance to developing countries where the influence of groups and communities is more predominant than in advanced countries.

PERCEPTUAL MAPPING

Advertising have an effect of adding new value to the existing value of the product. It is useful to obtain the views and opinions of the target segment of uses and prospects of a product or service. A perceptual map will help the advertiser and the advertising agency in trying to look at the product or service to be advertised from the angle of the consumers. Understanding the mind of consumer in addition to the segmentation frame work can be instrumental in making the advertising process more efficient. These reasons have to be integrated into advertising communication models in terms to get a balanced perspective of how advertising works.

CONSUMER ADOPTION MODELS

Research suggests that customers go through five stages in the process of adopting a new product or services. These five stages includes Awareness, Interest, Evaluation, Trial and Adoption.

Awareness - the customer becomes aware of the new product, but lacks information about it

Interest - the customer seeks information about the new product

Evaluation - the customer considers whether trying the new product makes sense

Trial - the customer tries the new product on a limited or small scale to assess the value of the product

Adoption - the customer decides to make full and/or regular use of the new product

Role of Marketing in New Product Adoption

A marketing team looking to successfully introduce a new product or service should think about how to help customers move through the five stages.

For example, what kind of advertising or other promotional campaign can be employed to build customer awareness? If customers show a desire to trial or sample a product, how can this be arranged effectively?

Research also suggests that customers can be divided into groups according to the speed with which they adopt new products.

This graph shows 5 stages i.e. innovators, Early adopters, Early majority, Late majority and Laggards.

The **"innovators"** (those who adopt new products first) are usually relatively young, lively, intelligent, socially and geographically mobile. They are often of a high socioeconomic group ("AB's"). Conversely, the "laggards" (those who adopt last, if at all) tend to be older, less intelligent, less well-off and lower on the socioeconomic scale.

It follows from the above model that when a business launches a new product or service, the customers who buy first are likely to be significantly different from those who buy the product much later. This needs to be borne in mind when developing the marketing mix.

Innovators is 1st stage, who have the ability to adopt new product first that are relatively young, lively intelligent. Laggards is last stage figure, who adopt the new product at last, if at all, they tends to be older, less intelligent.

Case Study

Note : knowing more about "Advertising Process" reader can study documentation process of Microsoft company by visiting their site : www.members.microsoft.com

http://www.marketingscoop.com/advertising-case-study2.htm

http://www.guidonps.com/ideas-and-resources/case-studies/information-technology/Cable%20Advertising%20Case%20Study.pdf

http://www.microsoft.com/casestudies/Case_Study_Detail.aspx?CaseStudyID=4000001473

http://www.startup-review.com/blog/eharmony-case-study-offline-advertising-the-key-to-scale.php

http://www.flipkart.com/case-studies-advertising-strategies-doris/8131420167-tu23f9a3p4

http://www.aarkstore.com/reports/Case-Studies-on-Advertising-Strategies-Trends-and-Practices-13154.html

7

Advertising Strategy Planning

This chapter includes the key concepts that are described below:-

- Evolution of advertising strategy and planning
- Strategic Planning
- Vision, Mission and Values
- Goals, objectives and targets
- Approaches to Strategic Planning
- Situational Analysis
- Advertising Situation
- Strategic Planning Process
- Situational Analysis
- Advertising Strategy
- Advertising Planning
- Organizational Approach
- Factors influencing organizational features

EVOLUTION OF ADVERTISING STRATEGY AND PLANNING

Evolution of advertising strategy and planning of advertising programme that marks the meeting point of advertising theory and its practices. In previously described chapter in this book includes all the functions, objectives as well as role of advertising. The main objective of advertising in commercial level is the achievement of specific marketing objectives.

The objectives for a company of Advertising are derived from over all objectives of company. The process of setting the goal at corporate level usually extends over a period of various years and marketing goals and plans that are relate to that period.

STRATEGIC PLANNING

Planners execute and interpret research that enables the agency to keep in touch with the market and understand what the consumer wants. The Planning Department has access to social and demographic data and direct access to consumers through quantitative and qualitative research. Quantitative research deals in numbers, i.e. a large number of consumers are questioned about a client's product. This provides the agency with an objective view of the customer for the product or service on offer and gives an indication of the statistical likelihood of success or failure for a product. In qualitative research a small number of consumers discuss a product or creative concept in depth, allowing the client an insight into the consumer's attitudes.

Planning is a never-ending process of defining and redefining goals and objectives, developing strategies, and evaluating advertising results. The planning process begins before research and continues after the advertisement is run. Firstly, the Planners, usually in tandem with the account management team, meet with the client to define marketing and advertising objectives. Then the Planners meet with the agency's media planners and creative people to determine the appropriate advertising strategy. Research results are considered, and the evaluation of the agency's planning team is worked into a detailed marketing and advertising plan. With the client's approval, this plan becomes the blueprint for the agency's creative and media program.

Strategic planning is an organization's process of defining its strategy, or direction, and making decisions on allocating its resources to pursue this strategy, including its capital and people. Various business analysis techniques can be used in strategic planning, including SWOT analysis (Strengths, Weaknesses, Opportunities, and Threats) and PEST analysis (Political, Economic, Social, and Technological analysis) or STEER analysis (Socio-cultural, Technological, Economic, Ecological, and Regulatory factors) and EPISTEL (Environment, Political, Informatic, Social, Technological, Economic and Legal)

Strategic planning is the formal consideration of an organization's future course. All strategic planning deals with at least one of three key questions:

- "What do we do?"
- "For whom do we do it?"
- "How do we excel?"

In business strategic planning, the third question is better phrased "How can we beat or avoid competition?".

In many organizations, this is viewed as a process for determining where an organization is going over the next year or more -typically 3 to 5 years, although some extend their vision to 20 years

In order to determine where it is going, the organization needs to know exactly where it stands, then determine where it wants to go and how it will get there. The resulting document is called the "strategic plan".

It is also true that strategic planning may be a tool for effectively plotting the direction of a company; however, strategic planning itself cannot foretell exactly how the market will evolve and what issues will surface in the coming days in order to plan your organizational strategy. Therefore, strategic innovation and tinkering with the 'strategic plan' have to be a cornerstone strategy for an organization to survive the turbulent business climate.

VISION, MISSION AND VALUES

Vision: Defines the desired or intended future state of a specific organization or enterprise in terms of its fundamental objective and/or strategic direction.

Mission: Defines the fundamental purpose of an organization or an enterprise, basically describing why it exists.

Values: Beliefs that are shared among the stakeholders of an organization. Values drive an organization's culture and priorities.

The property of vision defines the desired future of the specific company or organization in terms of its fundamental objectives or goals.

The property of mission defines the fundamental purpose of an organization that are basically describing why it exists.

Values has the belief that are shared among the stakeholders of an organization. These value drives the culture of an organization.

Some of the most overused and misunderstood words in the planning lingo are mission, vision and values. Yet most people can relate to a personal vision, their personal values, and their mission in life even if they are not expressed in those words. Used appropriately, they can provide inspiration and momentum to a business.

Mission is the term that what you want to achieve by starting the business. This mission describes all the purpose of organization that what you do, who you do it for and how and why you do it.

Every organization is unique in its history, cu.ture, and mission. Every mission, values and vision statement should reflect that uniqueness; there is no standard model that are appropriate for every organization. Any outsider (e.g., a consultant) should be involved in a process only as a facilitator.

Developing a Mission Statement

Mission is what you want to achieve by begining the business. This must be reexamined and refreshed periodically if an organization is to remain dynamic.

Mission statements describe the overall purpose is aism of an organization : what you do, who you do it for, and how and why you do it. It sets boundaries on current activities of an organization. Reviewing the mission gets an organization back to basics. The essential activity of determining whom you serve can be a wake-up call for organizations that have started to skew their activities to meet the needs other stakeholders (such as their funders or lobby targets) and not their actual clients.

Steps for making a mission statements are following below :-

- At is most basic, the mission statement describes the overall purpose of the organization.
- If the organization elects to develop a vision statement before developing the mission statement, ask "Why does the image, the vision exist — what is it's purpose?" This purpose is often the same as the mission.
- Developing a mission statement can be quick culture-specific, i.e., participants may use methods ranging from highly

analytical and rational to highly creative and divergent, e.g., focused discussions, divergent experiences around daydreams, sharing stories, etc. Therefore, visit with the participants how they might like to arrive at description of their organizational mission.

- When wording the mission statement, consider the organization's products, services, markets, values, and concern for public image, and maybe priorities of activities for survival.
- Consider any changes that may be needed in wording of the mission statement because of any new suggested strategies during a recent strategic planning process.
- Ensure that wording of the mission is to the extent that management and employees can infer some order of priorities in how products and services are delivered.
- When refining the mission, a useful exercise is to add or delete a word from the mission to realize the change in scope of the mission statement and assess how concise is its wording.
- Does the mission statement include sufficient description that the statement clearly separates the mission of the organization from other organizations?

These are the mission statement process by which an organization decides then company's mission that what you do, who you do it for & how is it possible:

Developing a Vision Statement

Vision is what keeps us moving forward, even against discouraging odds. For example, a business may envision a community where every person has access to their product. Vision is the most powerful motivator in an organization. If it's vivid and meaningful enough, people can do astounding things to bring it to realization.

A vision statement describes an ideal future. It answers the question, "what impact do we want to have on society?" The vision of a business conveys a larger sense of organizational purpose, so that employees see themselves as "building a cathedral" rather than "laying stones."

Steps for creating a vision statement are following below:-

- The vision statement includes vivid description of the organization as it effectively carries out its operations.

- Developing a vision statement can be quick culture-specific, i.e., participants may use methods ranging from highly analytical and rational to highly creative and divergent, e.g., focused discussions, divergent experiences around daydreams, sharing stories, etc. Therefore, visit with the participants how they might like to arrive at description of their organizational vision.
- Developing the vision can be the most enjoyable part of planning, but the part where time easily gets away from you.
- Note that originally, the vision was a compelling description of the state and function of the organization once it had implemented the strategic plan, i.e., a very attractive image toward which the organization was attracted and guided by the strategic plan. Recently, the vision has become more of a motivational tool, too often including highly idealistic phrasing and activities which the organization cannot realistically aspire.

These are steps of creating a vision statement of an organization by which it decides what keeps us moving forward and describes the ideal future.

Developing a Values Statement

Following are the steps for creating value statements are shown below:

- Values represent the core priorities in the organization's culture, including what drives members' priorities and how they truly act in the organization, etc. Values are increasingly important in strategic planning. They often drive the intent and direction for "organic" planners.
- Developing a values statement can be quick culture-specific, i.e., participants may use methods ranging from highly analytical and rational to highly creative and divergent, e.g., focused discussions, divergent experiences around daydreams, sharing stories, etc. Therefore, visit with the participants how they might like to arrive at description of their organizational values.
- Establish four to six core values from which the organization would like to operate. Consider values of customers, shareholders, employees and the community.

- Notice any differences between the organization's preferred values and its true values (the values actually reflected by members' behaviors in the organization). Record each preferred value on a flash card, then have each member "rank" the values with 1, 2, or 3 in terms of the priority needed by the organization with 3 indicating the value is very important to the organization and 1 is least important. Then go through the cards again to rank how people think the values are actually being enacted in the organization with 3 indicating the values are fully enacted and 1 indicating the value is hardly reflected at all. Then address discrepancies where a value is highly preferred (ranked with a 3), but hardly enacted (ranked with a 1).
- Incorporate into the strategic plan, actions to align actual behavior with preferred behaviors.

Above are the steps which are helps in creating a values statement.

GOALS, OBJECTIVES AND TARGETS

Strategic planning is a very important business activity. It is also important in the public sector areas such as education. It is practiced widely informally and formally. Strategic planning and decision processes should end with objectives and a roadmap of ways to achieve those objectives.

The following terms have been used in strategic planning: desired end states, plans, policies, goals, objectives, strategies, tactics and actions. Definitions vary, overlap and fail to achieve clarity. The most common of these concepts are specific, time bound statements of intended future results and general and continuing statements of intended future results, which most models refer to as either goals or objectives.

One model of organizing objectives uses hierarchies. The items listed above may be organized in a hierarchy of means and ends and numbered as follows: Top Rank Objective (TRO), Second Rank Objective, Third Rank Objective, etc. From any rank, the objective in a lower rank answers to the question "How?" and the objective in a higher rank answers to the question "Why?" The exception is the Top Rank Objective (TRO): there is no answer to the "Why?" question. That is how the TRO is defined.

One approach recommends having short-term goals, medium-term goals, and long-term goals. In this model, one can expect to attain short-term goals fairly easily: they stand just slightly above one's reach. At the other extreme, long-term goals appear very difficult, almost impossible to attain.

Goal congruency

Here this term refers to the arrangement that what are the ways by which these goals are well combine with each other.

People typically have several goals at the same time. "Goal congruency" refers to how well the goals combine with each other. Does goal A appear compatible with goal B? Do they fit together to form a unified strategy? "Goal hierarchy" consists of the nesting of one or more goals within other goal(s). There are goal hierarchy in very organization and it has levels of goals.

Setting of Advertising Objectives

Each organization has their own objectives by which can reach the way of success. For achieving this factor, it is necessary to take a careful assessment of the expected contribution of various elements of marketing mix in order to get at least a crude estimate of the weightage which are attached to the advertising.

Results of Advertising are measured with the help of specific advertising objectives that are defined. Following are factors that should be considered in setting advertising objectives:-

Marketing segmentation—It is only through careful market segmentation that the target audience for advertising can be defined and identified. Market segmentation has to be a continuous exercise so that changes in consumer types, buyer behaviour and socio-economic and other environmental parameters can be kept under review. Its point to the fact that failure to recognixe the possible existence of significant differences in sensitivity levels of market segments to distinct advertising strategies that may result in an unsatisfactory return on advertising investment. Appropriate sensitivity measures have the ability to provide the advertiser with an informational basis to expand, limit or reduce creative advertising campaigns and media plans to react to different markets effectively.

Advertising communication must take cognizance of the underlying patterns of buyer behaviour in setting objectives so that strategies and messages may be accordingly devised. Needs and motivations of decision makers may be assessed through the use of various quantitative and qualitative marketing and advertising research methods.

Buyer behaviour—Buyer Behaviour is also reflected by the mode of advertising.

An insight into buyer behaviour is at the initial stage of communication objectives. Demographic, psychographic and cther relevant segmentation parameters provide the base for a sutdy of the myriad factors which go into the making of buying or acceptance inthe case of non-commercial goods and services decisions. In addition to a knowledge of attitudinal characteristics, it is necessary to acquire familiarity with individual, social and group alignments of decision makers and influencers. A nalve classification such as the following may be conceived :

Type of product	Dominant factor
Consumable products of frequent usages	Individual
Semi-durable and durable goods	Social configuration such as family, group of friends
Industrial products	Concerned departments and positions in the buying company.

Product personality and perception—It is the factor of advertising which supports it. It provides a distinct or unique form to a productand can gives the contribution is success of product and the brand in the minds of consumers or favourable emotional deposition towards the brand and easy recognition property of packing of product.

APPROACHES TO STRATEGIC PLANNING

There are various approaches to strategic planning.

Being clear about strategic goals and strategy of an organization that provides focus and helps managers to understand how to direct their resources and make decisions on daily basis. At this time, strategic plans do not necessarily result in a successfully implemented strategy.

There is no single best practice for how to do successful strategic planning. The timing and process will differ depending on marketing pressures, industry and size & status of business.

Strategic Planning is oriented to a particular circumstances of an organization at a particular time in its history.

There are number of proven and effective process that can be adopted for virtually and business.

There are many approaches to strategic planning but typically a three-step process may be used:

- Situation - evaluate the current situation and how it came about.
- Target - define goals and/or objectives (sometimes called ideal state)
- Path - map a possible route to the goals/objectives

One alternative approach is called *Draw-See-Think*

- Draw - what is the ideal image or the desired end state?
- See - what is today's situation? What is the gap from ideal and why?
- Think - what specific actions must be taken to close the gap between today's situation and the ideal state?
- Plan - what resources are required to execute the activities?

An alternative to the *Draw-See-Think* approach is called *See-Think-Draw*

- See - what is today's situation?
- Think - define goals/objectives
- Draw - map a route to achieving the goals/objectives

In other terms strategic planning can be as follows:

- Vision - Define the vision and set a mission statement with hierarchy of goals and objectives
- SWOT - Analysis conducted according to the desired goals
- Formulate - Formulate actions and processes to be taken to attain these goals
- Implement - Implementation of the agreed upon processes

- Control - Monitor and get feedback from implemented processes to fully control the operation

Strategy as Ecology

As a Environmental eco-system, business ecosystem can be a useful analogy when about strategic planning. This environment includes :-

Niche—If a business holds a lesser position in an erratic industry, a specific niche may be the best strategy. By focusing on a highly specialized industry function, a firm can develop the expertise to differentiate from competitors and fill a particular need in a volatile industry. For example, small "heart hospitals" providing focused cardiovascular care have recently sprung up all over the United States.

Commodity—In the case of a commodity business, strategy beyond efficiency may not be relevant to an ecosystem setting. However, certain actions may be necessary to ensure that the ecosystem (and client base) thrives. Corn syrup producers in the snack food industry supply a commodity.

Value Dominator—The business is at the center of a complex and dynamic ecosystem. It must manage available resources, respond to crises, and share wealth to get the best sustainable performance from the ecosystem. eBay, the keystone of a multibillion dollar online sales industry, is an example.

Physical Dominator—If a business is part of a complex network in a stable and mature industry, it can become a Physical Dominator, which absorbs and controls the ecosystem's components until it becomes its own self contained ecosystem. Though few true Physical Dominators exist in the modern business world, large oil companies, like Royal Dutch Shell and BP, are examples. They control products through drilling, refinement, and distribution.

SITUATIONAL ANALYSIS

When developing strategies, analysis of the organization and its environment as it is at the moment and how it may develop in the future, is important. The analysis has to be executed at an internal level as well as an external level to identify all opportunities and threats of the external environment as well as the strengths and weaknesses of the organizations.

There are several factors to assess in the external situation analysis:

- Markets (customers)
- Competition
- Technology
- Supplier markets
- Labor markets
- The economy
- The regulatory environment

It is rare to find all seven of these factors having critical importance. It is also uncommon to find that the first two - markets and competition - are not of critical importance.

Analysis of the external environment normally focuses on the customer. Management should be visionary in formulating customer strategy, and should do so by thinking about market environment shifts, how these could impact customer sets, and whether those customer sets are the ones the company wishes to serve. Analysis of the competitive environment is also performed, many times based on the framework suggested by Michael Porter. Situational analysis process is essential in determining the need of individuals and communities.

Factors conducting situational Analysis

- County or community demographics
- The economic structure of the county and its individual communities
- Topographical and other physical characteristics of the county or a specific area
- Governmental, public, private, community, and other support systems available
- Characteristics of the population, including:
- educational levels
- cultural characteristics
- life styles and living standards
- primary occupations

- income levels
- communities and their distinguishing characteristics
- mobility and rates on inflow and outflow of citizens
- services available
- any other aspect of society that may be useful in assessing factors such as attitudes, motivation, and other characteristics of individual learner groups.

Scope of Situational Analysis

A situational analysis may be broad based or highly specific, depending on the program in focus. In either case, the scope of the analysis should have a clear focus and purpose directed toward a specific subject, clientele, time, location, or other pertinent factors.

If boundaries are not defined, the analysis will lack the focus necessary for accurately assessing needs of targeted groups; as a result, developing successful educational programs to meet those needs will be difficult. For example, a home economics agent may conduct a situational analysis of the overall health of all citizens in the county if the program is on an “Eating Right for Life” nutrition education program intended to reach a broad spectrum of the county”s population. On the other hand, if prenatal nutrition is the intended focus, the situational analysis should be more specifically focused on obtaining information relevant to expectant mothers, such as their living standards, traditional eating habits, educational levels, and other factors that can be of value in identifying specific learning needs on the subject of proper prenatal nutrition.

Elements in Situational Analysis

Following are the elements that are used in situational Analysis:-

- Product situation includes what you sell
- Competitive situation includes what are their competitive advantages
- Distribution situation includes how are you getting your product to market.
- Opportunity and issue analysis

- Environmental factors

Planning Process in Situational Analysis

Development is a cyclical process. It starts with plan formulation; i.e., identifying a problem and a plan to solve this. The plan is then implemented and monitored. As a result of monitoring and evaluation, the plan is reviewed and adjusted. Adjustments are correspondingly made in the implementation. The iteration continues until the plan is declared as successfully completed (or abandoned).

There are several steps for planning process the first steps begins with situational Analysis, then it continues to formulation of goals, objectives and targets, it tends to the formulation of policies and strategies, this step then tends to identify the programs and projects, at last it tends to the Investment of the programs or budgets.

The first step in formulating a plan is to do a situational analysis, as shown in Figure 1 below.

Figure 1. Steps in plan formulation

Situational analysis	To identify and prioritize problem situations affecting the target population or specific segments of the population.
Formulation of goals, objectives and targets	To specify the desired outcomes to be achieved by addressing the priority problem identified in the situational analysis.
Formulation of policies and strategies	To provide a broad direction on how to achieve the stated goals, objectives and targets.
Identification of programs and projects	To translate the policies and strategies into specific implementable activities.
Investment programming or budgeting	To identify which programs and projects can be funded and implemented according to a definite schedule or time frame.

Problem Identification in Situational Analysis

Problem identification is a deductive process. This activity identifies the issues and problems that need to be addressed. It seeks to answer several questions :

- What is the problem?
- Why is there a problem?
  - o What are the probable causes of the problem?
  - o How serious is the problem?
- Who are affected by the problem?
  - o How many are they?
  - o Where are they located?
  - o What are their characteristics?
- What has been done to solve the problem?

There are five steps for analyzing the problem

These five steps are :-

- Outcomes
- Resources
- Services and facilities
- Access and utilization of services & facilities
- Environment
- the information

The information needed to answer these questions are both quantitative and qualitative. They could be categorized in the framework given below.

- Outcomes describe the effects of policy on area of concern. It can be described in order to status, participation or equity.
- Resources can be in order to human, financial and other material that are allocated for bringing about changes in the outcomes.
- All located resources i.e. services and facilities which are offered to produce the appropriate facilities in an organization
- services & facilities are expected to conclude in the outcomes only if there is access, retrieval and utilization is done by intended clicuts.
- Environment provides the context in which policy is expected to bring the changes. This is expected to bring about the

changes. This environment includes the physical, economic, social, cultural as well as political contexts.

Information requires for situational Analysis

The profile of the target population defines the context; i.e., the physical, economic, social, cultural, and political environment within which the population lives. At the same time, it includes a profile of the population in terms of the areas of concern that are the object of policy. This is done through the use of quantitative social and economic outcome indicators hand in hand with the descriptive analysis of the cultural and legal setting.

Table 1 below shows examples of information to be used in the profile.

Context	Type of information
Socio-demographic	Population composition and distribution Households and family formation Health and health services Learning and educational services Housing conditions Peace and order status
Economic activity	National accounts Labor force participation Wages Household income and expenditure patterns Poverty
Socio-cultural and political	Political structure Political participation Relevant laws, statutes, policies Predominant social structure Gender roles in the household Time use Decision- making patterns in the household

Above are the table that are shown as consisting the various contexts with their type of information.

Information on the outcomes are generally impact indicators from surveys and censuses. On the other hand, information on resources and use of services and facilities, are available from administrative records of concerned agencies. Statistical information on the environment from all three sources, while qualitative information are available from records review. The national statistical services of the region have varying degrees of capability to provide the necessary information. If the data needs cannot be met by secondary data, there may be a need to conduct other forms of data-gathering, such as focused group discussions and rapid appraisals.

Another set of information that would be needed in the analysis is the set of norms or standards against which the indicators on the actual situation is to be compared. These may be based on national planning standards or international commitments. Where standards have not been set, comparisons may be made on past data, data for similar localities, national average, or international averages.

Analysis of the information

The analysis of the outcomes would basically be gap analysis; i.e., comparing the actual situation with the planning standards or other norms. Analysis of the time series would show whether the situation is improving or deteriorating. Comparing the situation of various groups would

Analysis of information should answer the following question which to identify the problem, target population and other characteristics of the population as well as the immediate and underlying causes of problem.

A. Outcomes –Resources-

- What resources are needed to improve the outcomes?
- What resources are being provided?
- Are the allocated resources enough?

B. Resources – Services and Facilities-

- Are services and facilities produced efficiently?
- Are the right kind of services and facilities produced from the available resources?

C. Services and facilities – Access and Utilization of Services and Facilities

- Are the services and facilities located where they are needed?
- Do people know that the services and facilities are available?

- Are the services and facilities available to everyone who needs them?
- Are the services and facilities when needed?
- Are the services and facilities affordable?
- Do people actually use the services and facilities?

D. Access and Utilization of Services and Facilities – Outcomes-

- Do the services and facilities have an impact on the target population?
- Is the impact positive or negative?

E. Environment-

- What are the demographic, economic, social, political, and cultural conditions?
- How do the conditions affect the availability of resources, provision of services and facilities, access to and use of these, and the corresponding outcomes?

ADVERTISING SITUATION

Following are situations in which advertising may be required:-

- special offers
- competition
- product market variations
- Distribution and service
- seasonal
- Raising capital
- Recruitment
- Upgrading a product
- Membership and programme
- Institutional advertising
- Technology and other inputs
- change in brand name
- New application of a product

STRATEGIC PLANNING PROCESS

In today's highly competitive business environment, budget-oriented planning or forecast-based planning methods are insufficient for a large corporation to survive and prosper. The firm must engage in strategic planning that clearly defines objectives and assesses both the internal and external situation to formulate strategy, implement the strategy, evaluate the progress, and make adjustments as necessary to stay on track. This planning process begins with mission and ends with control.

The Strategic Planning Process

Mission

↓

Objectives

↓

Situational Analysis

↓

Strategy Formulation

↓

Implementation

↓

Control

Mission and Objectives

These are first two steps of planning process where, mission derives the business vision of the company and the leader of the firm can define the measures of financial and strategic objectives which are guided by business vision.

The mission statement describes the company's business vision, including the unchanging values and purpose of the firm and forward-looking visionary goals that guide the pursuit of future opportunities.

Guided by the business vision, the firm's leaders can define measurable financial and strategic objectives. Financial objectives involve measures such as sales targets and earnings growth. Strategic objectives are related to the firm's business position, and may include measures such as market share and reputation.

SITUATIONAL ANALYSIS

It is third step of planning process which includes their components such as Internal analysis of the firm, Analysis of firm's industry.

The internal analysis can identify the firm's strengths and weaknesses and the external analysis reveals opportunities and threats. A profile of the strengths, weaknesses, opportunities, and threats is generated by means of a SWOT analysis

An industry analysis can be performed using a framework developed by Michael Porter known as Porter's five forces. This framework evaluates entry barriers, suppliers, customers, substitute products, and industry rivalry.

Strategy Formulation

Given the information from the environmental scan, the firm should match its strengths to the opportunities that it has identified, while addressing its weaknesses and external threats.

To attain superior profitability, the firm seeks to develop a competitive advantage over its rivals. A competitive advantage can be based on cost or differentiation. Michael Porter identified three industry-independent generic strategies from which the firm can choose.

Strategy Implementation

The selected strategy is implemented by means of programs, budgets, and procedures. Implementation involves organization of the firm's resources and motivation of the staff to achieve objectives.

The way in which the strategy is implemented can have a significant impact on whether it will be successful. In a large company, those who implement the strategy likely will be different people from those who formulated it. For this reason, care must be taken to communicate the strategy and the reasoning behind it. Otherwise, the implementation might not succeed if the strategy is misunderstood or if lower-level managers resist its implementation because they do not understand why the particular strategy was selected.

Evaluation and Control

The implementation of the strategy must be monitored and adjustments that are made as needed.

Evaluation and control consists of the following steps:

- Define parameters to be measured
- Define target values for those parameters
- Perform measurements
- Compare measured results to the pre-defined standard
- Make necessary changes

ADVERTISING STRATEGY

An advertising strategy is a campaign developed to communicate ideas about products and services to potential consumers in the hopes of convincing them to buy those products and services. This strategy, when built in a rational and intelligent manner, will reflect other business considerations (overall budget, brand recognition efforts) and objectives (public image enhancement, market share growth) as well. As *Portable MBA in Marketing* authors Alexander Hiam and Charles D. Schewe stated, a business's advertising strategy "determines the character of the company's public face." Even though a small business has limited capital and is unable to devote as much money to advertising as a large corporation, it can still develop a highly effective advertising campaign. The key is creative and flexible planning, based on an indepth knowledge of the target consumer and the avenues that can be utilized to reach that consumer.

Strategy establishes the link between advertising objectives and plans for their implementation. There are five strategy alternatives for influencing attitudinal structures :-

- Increase or decrease the rating for a salient product class characteristics.
- Add characteristics. to those considered salient to the product class.
- Affect those forces which influence strongly the choice criteria for evaluating the brands belonging to the product class.
- change the perception of a competitive brand which regard to some particular salient product characteristics.
- change the perception of brand of the company with regard to some particular salient product characteristics.

Today, most advertising strategies focus on achieving three general goals, as the Small Business Administration indicated in *Advertising Your Business:* 1) promote awareness of a business and its product or services; 2) stimulate sales directly and "attract competitors' customers"; and 3) establish or modify a business' image. In other words, advertising seeks to *inform, persuade, and remind* the consumer. With these aims in mind, most businesses follow a general process which ties advertising into the other promotional efforts and overall marketing objectives of the business.

Stages of Advertising Strategy

As a business begins, one of the major goals of advertising must be to generate awareness of the business and its products. Once the business' reputation is established and its products are positioned within the market, the amount of resources used for advertising will decrease as the consumer develops a kind of loyalty to the product. Ideally, this established and ever-growing consumer base will eventually aid the company in its efforts to carry their advertising message out into the market, both through its purchasing actions and its testimonials on behalf of the product or service.

With these concrete objectives, the following elements of the advertising strategy need to be considered: target audience, product concept, communication media, and advertising message. These elements are at the core of an advertising strategy, and are often referred to as the "creative mix." Again, what most advertisers stress from the beginning is clear planning and flexibility. And key to these aims is creativity, and the ability to adapt to new market trends. A rigid advertising strategy often leads to a loss of market share.

So, that the core elements of the advertising strategy needs to mix in a way that allows the message to envelope the target consumer.

TARGET CONSUMER. The target consumer is a complex combination of persons. It includes the person who ultimately buys the product, as well as those who decide what product will be bought (but don't physically buy it), and those who influence product purchases, such as children, spouse, and friends. In order to identify the target consumer, and the forces acting upon any purchasing decision, it is important to define three general criteria in relation to that consumer, as discussed by the Small Business Administration:

Demographics—Age, gender, job, income, ethnicity, and hobbies.

Behaviors—When considering the consumers' behavior an advertiser needs to examine the consumers' awareness of the business and its competition, the type of vendors and services the consumer currently uses, and the types of appeals that are likely to convince the consumer to give the advertiser's product or service a chance.

Needs and Desires—Here an advertiser must determine the consumer needs—both in practical terms and in terms of self-image, etc.—and the kind of pitch/message that will convince the consumer that the advertiser's services or products can fulfill those needs.

Here, target consumer refers to the target audience which is the combination of person who purchase or buy the product. Target audience has some general criteria in relation to the consumer i.e. demographics, Behaviors of consumers, needs and desirer of target audience.

PRODUCT CONCEPT. The product concept grows out of the guidelines established in the "positioning statement." How the product is positioned within the market will dictate the kind of values the product represents, and thus how the target consumer will receive that product. Therefore, it is important to remember that no product is just itself.

COMMUNICATION MEDIA. The communication media is the means by which the advertising message is transmitted to the consumer. In addition to marketing objectives and budgetary restraints, the characteristics of the target consumer need to be considered as an advertiser decides what media to use. The types of media categories from which advertisers can choose include the following:

- Print—Primarily newspapers (both weekly and daily) and magazines.
- Audio—FM and AM radio.
- Video—Promotional videos, infomercials.
- World Wide Web.
- Direct mail.
- Outdoor advertising—Billboards, advertisements on public transportation (cabs, buses).

After deciding on the medium i.e. 1) financially in reach 2) most likely to reach the target audience, an advertiser needs to schedule the broadcasting of that advertising.

ADVERTISING MESSAGE. An advertising message is guided by the "advertising or copy platform," which is a combination of the marketing objectives, copy, art, and production values. This combination is best realized after the target consumer has been analyzed, the product concept has been established, and the media and vehicles have been chosen. At this point, the advertising message can be directed at a very concrete audience to achieve very specific goals. Hiam and Schewe listed three major areas that an advertiser should consider when endeavoring to develop an effective "advertising platform":

- What are the product's unique features?
- How do consumers evaluate the product? What is likely to persuade them to purchase the product?
- How do competitors rank in the eyes of the consumer? Are there any weaknesses in their positions? What are their strengths?

COPY. When composing advertising copy it is crucial to remember that the primary aim is to communicate information about the business and its products and services. The "selling proposal" can act as a blueprint here, ensuring that the advertising fits the overall marketing objectives. Many companies utilize a theme or a slogan as the centerpiece of such efforts, emphasizing major attributes of the business's products or services in the process.

The copy content needs to be clearly written, following conventional grammatical guidelines. Of course, effective headings allow the reader to get a sense of the advertisement's central theme without having to read much of the copy. An advertisement that has "50% Off" in bold black letters is not just easy to read, but it is also easy to understand.

ART WORK AND LAYOUT. Small business owners also need to consider the visual rhetoric of the advertisement, which simply means that the entire advertisement, including blank space, should have meaning and logic. Most industry experts recommend that advertisers use short paragraphs, lists, and catchy illustrations and graphics to break up and supplement the text and make the document both visually inviting and easy to understand. Remember, an advertisement has to capture the reader's attention quickly.

ADVERTISING BUDGET. The advertising budget can be written before or after a business owner has developed the advertising strategy. When to make a budget decision depends on the importance of advertising and the resources available to the business. If, for instance, a business knows that they only have a certain amount of money for advertising then the budget will tend to dictate what advertising is developed and what the overall marketing objectives will be. On the other hand, if a business has the resources available, the advertising strategy can be developed to meet predetermined marketing objectives. For small businesses, it is usually best to put together an advertising budget early in the advertising process.

Methods of Advertising

Small business owners can choose from two opposite philosophies when preparing their advertising strategy. The first of these, sometimes called the push method, is a stance wherein an advertiser targets retail establishments in order to establish or broaden a market presence. The second option, sometimes called the pull method, targets end-users (consumers), who are expected to ask retailers for the product and thus help "pull, it through the channel of distribution. There are two methods i.e. Push method and second is pull method.

PUSH METHOD. The aim of the push method is to convince retailers, salespersons, or dealers to carry and promote the advertiser's product. This relationship is achieved by offering inducements, such as providing advertising kits to help the retailer sell the product, offering incentives to carry stock, and developing trade promotions.

PULL METHOD. The aim of the pull method is to convince the target consumer to try, purchase, and ultimately repurchase the product. This process is achieved by directly appealing to the target consumer with coupons, in-store displays, and sweepstakes.

ADVERTISING PLANNING

Advertising planning takes a lot of work but the extra effort i.e. worth it.

The involvement of the advertising agency increases as we move from the stage of setting advertising objectives to that of evolving strategy and developing specific plans. At the stage of planning, it is necessary to provide for a flow system for various components of advertising, viz. creative strategy, message formulation and its presentation, budget, media plan and feedback from the target audience. It is also required to integrate the interations wih the advertising agency, which are required at all these stages.

Advertising planning starts with the campaign brief prepared by the advertising agency. The agency may have its plans board or a group of executives which may review the the outline of the campaign strategy prepared by the account group. The account group of the advertising agency would included the following :

- Account executive through whom the agency maintains liaison and coordination with the client.
- Creative department personnel such as creative/art director and copy writer
- Media department
- Production and research department personnel may also be included, if necessary.

An initial presentation of the plan of the campaign incorporating advertising objectives, creative and media strategies budget estimate and allocation to various advertising and sales promotion inputs is made to the advertising and sales promotion inputs is made to the advertiser. There may be reviews and revisions in any or all of these elements of the programme depending on the assessment of the client's marketing and Carryover from the era of a strong production orientation. In recent years there has been an increasing realisation of the contribution that advertising can make in the achievement of organizational goals and specific marketing objectives. Therefore, advertising is gradually assuming its proper interpretation of being an investment.

Why you need a Marketing Plan First

- Marketing is probably your company's only source of income, and as such your marketing plan is probably the most important document you have.
- Your marketing plan accurately describes your market, your customers, your products and services, and your competition.
- Your marketing plan calculates the size or potential of your market.

- Your marketing plan will help you to efficiently allocate money and resources.
- Your marketing plan provides focus, guidance, and direction for effective advertising and business practices.
- Your marketing plan positions your company in the marketplace.
- Your marketing plan will help with proper customer management and retention.
- Your marketing plan will define your communications strategy. It will help your entire company give a planned, clear, comprehensive, and consistent message to your customers, employees, investors, and business partners.

Why you need an Advertising plan

Going astray in advertising is all too easy. The most creative advertising in the world is worthless if it misses the target audience. The best offer in the world is worthless if it does not offer the benefits your clients want.

Even well planned and executed advertising has little value if you don't keep it in front of your customers. In today's world of information, it takes at least three exposures just to get your message through the first time. And then you face a huge rate of forgetfulness from your clients.

How defines your customers

The number one reason advertising fails is because it is poorly targeted. No advertising is going to be successful if its target audience is not well defined and understood. Talk to your customers and potential prospects. Listen to them. Understand them.

We have provided you with some excellent strategies for defining your customers. Please read the Market Targeting Strategy and the Generating Better Qualified Prospects chapters. These two chapters will give you insight into defining your customers, and knowing what they need, want, and desire.

There are three things about your customers:-

- First you target group doesn't include the whole world. If you try to advertise to the whole world, you will go out of business.

- Second, in many companies, 20% of the customers account for 80% of sales, and 100% of profits. These are high usage customers that you want to target.
- Third, one out of ten people strongly influence the other nine. They are the movers and shakers of the world. They are actively participate heavily in community and business activities.

Make no mistake – your advertising plan needs a clear, concise, written definition of who your customers are. Age, sex, marital status, economic status, geographic location, what they read, think, trust, value, desire, and any and all other relevant information should be included in your definition.

ORGANIZATIONAL APPROACH

It will be useful to develop an appreciation of the basic approach towards the organization of the advertising function rather than dwelling on details of structure. Once a company has recognized its advertising needs and identified those factors that influencing the area of its activity, the following issues will come up.

- Assigning advertising function a particular status relative to the various other other functions within the company.
- Developing the appropriate organization structure for the advertising division or department.
- Instituting a system of advertising decision making.

The relative status of advertising function in a company is governed by the general pattern of overall organization for the company, the environment in which it operates and the changes in which it oerates and the changes it anticipates. Accordingly, some of the possible organizational alternatives are as follows:

- Advertising can be a sub-function within the marketing department.
- Advertising can be separated as a major function directly under the top management.
- Functions such as sales promotion and public relations could be merged with the advertising function.

FACTORS INFLUENCING ORGANIZATIONAL FEATURES

It is hardly feasible to have a particular guidelines which may be used for organizing the advertising function. Many internal as well as external factors influence the organization of a company's effort. These are the following :

- Standing of the advertiser
- Nature of product
- Marketing environment
- Advertising environment
- Corporate philosophy

1. Standing of the advertisers refers to a firm operating for many years could have became established so well that its products may sell just by its name. When a new firm launches their products at that time it needs the support of advertising to encourage the target audience as well as market shores. This process consumes number of years that has been spent in operation and its stage of growth are some of the factor that go into determining the extent of effort.

2. Nature of product refers to those products that are consumed by consumer like food, cosmetics or garments are widely advertised.

3. Marketing Environment Until a few years ago, in India, manufacturers could sell what they produced because demand would usually exceed production. With the expansion of the industrial base, the supply of goods has been substantially augmented. At the same time, markets have also grown and expandexd in volume and diversity. There has been an increase in competition from a variety of products and brands. Thus, it has become imperative for advertisers to organize their advertising efforts efficiently in accordance with the changing needs of their market segments.

Business organizations in industrial countries have been better placed to organize their promotional efforts and implement their advertising plans because their marketing infrastucutre was more developed. However, in a country like India there are many constrains in this respect. Problems also arise owing to major differences in the nature and extent of marketing systems and operations between rural and urban markets and different types of urban centres.

Changes in the marketing environment have influenced the advertising environment to a considerable extent in two ways:

- More and more companies have resorted to advertising and
- the companies already making use of advertising have been putting in more money and effort.

4. Cooperate Philosophy It is not unlikely that despite the increasing receptivity of the environment to advertising, a conservative outlook of the top management may turn out to be an inhibiting factor. On the other hand, in a company with a professional orientation and a growth/and/or diversification perspective, organization of the advertising function is given considerable importance. This may be seen in the case of companies with a strong marketing orientation who have pioneered promotional efforts and have benefitted from it to a great extent.

5. Advertising Environment It is noticeable that the expectations of consumers and of channels of distribution also influence the advertising function. This ould apply to advertising the aimed at getting new buyers, inducing brand switching as well as maintining brand loyalty. Availability of advertising agencies, and ancillary facilities and services that creates favourable conditions for use of advertising and other forms of promotion. In this respect, considerable advance has been made in India. Not only has the number of advertising agencies increased substantially in recent years but qualitative improvements in techniques and creative approaches have become noticeble. Considerable development of the mass media has also taken place. Increased mobility of people has raised the chance of exposure to the various media and also increased receptivity to promotional messages. This as well as other factors have also affected social and cultural values. Consequently, the markets have become more responsive to advertising. Thus, advertisers have greater need to advertise in order to exploit the market porential to their advantage.

Case Study

Note : knowing more about "Advertising Strategy Planning" reader can study documentation process of Microsoft company by visiting their site : www.members.microsoft.com

http://www.overlandagency.com/branding_+strategic+ planning.aspx

http://harvardbusiness.org/search/advertising/4294934592/

8

Future of Advertising

This chapter includes the key concepts that are described below:-

- Introduction
- Future of Advertising
- Advertising Regulation
- Regulatory Authorities
- Regulation
- In United States
- In Canada
- In other countries
- Advertising and Constitutional Rights
- Stages of development
- Various aspects of International Advertising

INTRODUCTION

India has a mixed economy and large industrial enterprises in the public sector were set up to cope with the emerging needs of the economy which the private sector might not have been able to meet out of its resources.

Critics of advertising in India includes individuals and action groups such as associations of woman however, it is unfortunate that many a times much criticism, regardless of its merits. The image of advertising amount opinion leaders and decision makers as indicated by their personal opinions which is distinctly positive.

FUTURE OF ADVERTISING

Quality of advertising and its social acceptance are the two side of the common coin. Advertising agencies can justify their existence only if advertising produces results. Advertising has to reflect the social norms, values and aspirations or else it will be irrelevant and wasteful.

Global Advertising

It is aspects that includes in future of advertising.

Advertising has gone through five major stages of development: domestic, export, international, multi-national, and global. For global advertisers, there are four, potentially competing, business objectives that must be balanced when developing worldwide advertising: building a brand while speaking with one voice, developing economies of scale in the creative process, maximising local effectiveness of ads, and increasing the company's speed of implementation. Born from the evolutionary stages of global marketing are the three primary and fundamentally different approaches to the development of global advertising executions: exporting executions, producing local executions, and importing ideas that travel.

Advertising research is key to determining the success of an ad in any country or region. The ability to identify which elements and/or moments of an ad that contributes to its success is how economies of scale are maximised. Once one knows what works in an ad, that idea or ideas can be imported by any other market. Market research measures, such as Flow of Attention, Flow of Emotion and branding moments provide insight into what is working in an ad in any country or region because the measures are based on the visual, not verbal, elements of the ad.

Trends in Advertising

With the dawn of the Internet came many new advertising opportunities. Popup, Flash, banner, Popunder, advergaming, and e-mail advertisements (the last often being a form of spam) are now commonplace.

The ability to record shows on digital video recorders (such as TiVo) allow users to record the programs for later viewing, enabling them to fast forward through commercials. Additionally, as more seasons of pre-recorded box sets are offered for sale of television programs; fewer people watch the shows on TV. However, the fact that these sets are **sold**, means the company will receive additional profits from the sales of these sets. To counter this effect, many advertisers have opted for product placement on TV shows like Survivor.

Particularly since the rise of "entertaining" advertising, some people may like an advertisement enough to wish to watch it later or show a friend. In general, the advertising community has not yet made this easy, although some have used the Internet to widely distribute their ads to anyone willing to see or hear them.

Another significant trend regarding future of advertising is the growing importance of the niche market using niche or targeted ads. Also brought about by the Internet and the theory of The Long Tail, advertisers will have an increasing ability to reach specific audiences. In the past, the most efficient way to deliver a message was to blanket the largest mass market audience possible. However, usage tracking, customer profiles and the growing popularity of niche content brought about by everything from blogs to social networking sites, provide advertisers with audiences that are smaller but much better defined, leading to ads that are more relevant to viewers and more effective for companies' marketing products. Among others, Comcast Spotlight is one such advertiser employing this method in their video on demand menus. These advertisements are targeted to a specific group and can be viewed by anyone wishing to find out more about a particular business or practice at any time, right from their home. This causes the viewer to become proactive and actually choose what advertisements they want to view.

In the realm of advertising agencies, continued industry diversification has seen observers note that "big global clients don't need big global agencies any more". This trend is reflected by the growth of non-traditional agencies in various global markets, such as Canadian business TAXI and SMART in Australia and has been referred to as "a revolution in the ad world".

ADVERTISING REGULATION

Advertising is the topic including government regulation and industry self-regulation to prevent deceptive advertising or to limit the visibility of advertising. Advertising is regulated in United States, Canada and other European and Asian countries.

Advertising regulation refers to the laws and rules defining the ways in which products can be advertised in a particular region. Rules can define a wide number of different aspects, such as placement, timing, and content. In the United States, false advertising and health-related ads are regulated the most. Many communities have their own rules, particularly for outdoor advertising. Sweden and Norway prohibit domestic advertising that targets children. Some European countries don't allow sponsorship of children's programs, no advertisement can be aimed at children under the age of twelve, and there can be no advertisements five minutes before or after a children's program is aired. In the United Kingdom advertising of tobacco on television, billboards or at sporting events is banned. It is also prohibited to advertise cars on the basis of how fast they can move and the relationship which the event has with the sport seen as a healthy pursuit, unlike smoking. Similarly alcohol advertisers in the United Kingdom are not allowed to discuss in a campaign the relative benefits of drinking, in most instances therefore choosing to focus around the brand image and associative benefits instead of those aligned with consumption. There are many regulations throughout the rest of Europe as well. In many non-Western countries, a wide-variety of linguistic (Bhatia 2000, pp. 217-218) and non-linguistic strategies (e.g. religion; Bhatia 2000, pp 280-282) are used to mock and undermine regulations.

There are two most regulated form of advertising are tobacco advertising and alcohol advertising.

REGULATORY AUTHORITIES

It is the power that the legislature gives an agency to enforce the statues to develop the regulations that have the force of law and also to assist the public in complying with laws and regulation.

Regulatory authority is the power that the legislature gives an agency to enforce statutes, to develop regulations that have the force of law, and to assist the public in complying with laws and regulations. The power that can be delegated and the method of delegation are determined by the state or federal constitution. Some agencies are charged with enforcing specific statutes passed by a legislative body and given little discretion in their actions. Public health agencies are generally delegated broad authority and wide discretion to develop regulations and enforcement policies based on their expertise. When these regulations are published and adopted by the agency, they have the force of law unless they exceed the agency's statutory authority.

The most important regulatory authority delegated to public health agencies is the power to act quickly and flexibly—without promulgating formal regulations and without judicial hearings—when necessary to respond to exigent circumstances. To prevent abuse, hearings and other review proceedings are available after the action has been taken. More commonly, however, public health agencies promulgate specific regulations or adopt national codes as binding in their jurisdiction. These are enforced through licensing and other mechanisms that require regulated entities to adhere to the regulations. This provides clear guidance for the regulated entities and simplifies enforcement. Deviation from the standards is easily documented, preventing lengthy legal challenges to enforcement actions.

In United Kingdom, advertising content regulation is governed by the Advertising standards Authority whereas in the UK most forms of outdoor advertising such as the display of billboards that is regulated by the UK Town and Country Planning system.

REGULATION

There have been increasing efforts top protect the public interest by regulating the content and the influence of advertising.

In the US many communities believes that many forms of outdoor advertising blight the public realm. As long ago as the 1960s in the US there were attempts to ban billboard advertising in the open countryside. Cities such as Sao Paulo have introduced an outright ban with London also having specific legislation to control unlawful displays.

There have been incresing efforts to protect the public interest by regulating the content and the influence of advertising. Some examples are : the ban on television tobacco advertising imposed in many countries, and total ban of advertising to children under 12 imposed by the Swedish government in 1991. Though that regulation continues in effect for broadcasts that originating within the country, it has been weakened by the European Court of Justics, which had found that Sweden was obliged to accept foreign programming, including those from neighboring countries or via satellite.

In Europe and elsewhere, there is a vigorous debate on whether (or how much) advertising to children should be regulated.

This debate was exacerbated by report released by the Kaiser Family Foundation in February 2004 which suggested that food advertising, such as that for fast foods, targeting children was an important factor in the epidemic of childhood obesity in the United States.

In many countries—namely New Zealand, South Africa, Canada, and many European countries have the advertising industry that operates a system of self-regulation. Advertisers, advertising agencies and the media agree on a code of advertising standards that they attempt to uphold. The general purpose

There are general purposes of advertising that follows the general rules of advertising. All advertisement should be legal, decent, honest and truthful.

Legality: Advertisements should contain nothing which is neither a breach of the law nor omit anything which the law requires. It should not encourage or condone defiance of the law.

Decency: Advertisements should contain nothing which is likely in the light of the generally prevailing standards of decency and property to cause grave or offence.

Honesty: Advertisements should not be so framed as to abuse the trust of consumers or exploit their lack of experience or knowledge.

Truthful Presentation: Advertisements should not contain statements or visual presentation which directly or by implications, omissions, ambiguity are likely mislead the consumer about the product that are advertised, the advertiser or any other product or advertiser.

Advertisers and advertising agency are required to hold such substantiation that are ready for immediate production to the code of advertising standards authority.

Naturally, many advertisers view governmental regulation or even self-regulation as intrusion of their freedom of speech or a necessary evil. Therefore, they employ a wide-variety of linguistic devices to bypass regulatory laws (e.g. printing English words in bold and French translations in fine print to deal with the Article 120 of the 1994 Toubon Law limiting the use of English in French advertising). The advertisement of controversial products such as cigarettes and condoms is subject to government regulation in many countries. For instance, the tobacco industry is required by law in most countries to display warnings cautioning consumers about the health hazards of their products. Linguistic variation is often used by advertisers as a creative device to reduce the impact of such requirements.

IN UNITED STATES

In US, various regulations are passed either it is government regulation or industrial regulations, government regulation supports the regulatory agency i.e. Federal Trade Commissions (FTC).

Government Regulation

Federal, state, and city governments have all passed legislation restricting advertising in various ways in the United States. The Supreme Court of the United States has overturned some restrictions, however, ruling that advertising is protected under the free speech provisions of the First Amendment to the Constitution, although to a lesser extent than political speech. In a landmark 1976 ruling, *Virginia State Board of Pharmacy* v *Virginia Citizens Consumer Council,* the Court declared advertising to be a semiprivileged form of free expression, subject to some regulation. In the *Virginia* case the Supreme Court struck down a ban that prohibited pharmacists from advertising drug prices. The ruling removed bans that had applied to other professionals, such as physicians and lawyers, and enabled them to advertise their services.

In the United States the main government regulatory agency for advertising is the Federal Trade Commission (FTC). The FTC enforces a variety of consumer protection laws to eliminate ads that deceive the consumer. The FTC defines deceptive advertising as any ad containing a misrepresentation or omission harmful to the consumer. An advertisement does not have to be untrue to be deceptive. For example, ads for a certain bread product claimed that it had half as many calories per slice as its leading competitors. The advertiser failed to say, however, that each slice of its bread was also half as thick as the competitors. The ads were ruled to be deceptive.

The key purpose of FTC is its power to require that advertisers substantiate the accuracy of their claims. So, if advertisers apply the tests prove or physicians recommend, they must be able to show test results or afficlavits from doctors, companies cannot misuse evidence.

Products that can affect health receive special regulatory attention. The U.S. Congress banned cigarette advertising from radio and TV in 1971 under the Public Health Cigarette Smoking Act. In 1998 the tobacco industry and the attorneys general of 46 states agreed to ban outdoor cigarette advertising and the use of cartoon characters in advertising, a practice that many thought had encouraged young people to start smoking.

Advertising directed to children has received considerable scrutiny. In 1990 Congress passed the Children's Television Advertising Practice Act. Among other things, it set limits on the amount of advertising that could be included in children's television programming and barred hosts of children's shows from selling products.

State laws and enforcement bureaus impose additional regulations on certain types of advertising, particularly those involving contests. These regulations may differ from state to state. Consequently, advertisers planning a national contest through newspapers may have to prepare several different versions of an advertisement to comply with the varying laws. In some states the media are themselves regulated. For example, it is illegal in a number of states for radio and television stations to broadcast distilled-liquor advertising; outdoor billboard advertising is banned in certain other states.

Industrial Regulation

Industrial regulations are passed on various topics. The advertising industry has resorted to self-regulation in a serious effort to stop abuses before they occur. These self-imposed codes of ethics and procedures aim principally to curtail not only bad taste but also misrepresentation and deception in copy and illustrations, as well as derogatory and unfair representations of products of competitors.

Individual media and media groups often establish their own codes of ethics. Some newspapers and magazines refuse to publish advertising for tobacco and alcoholic beverages; most of them, in varying degree, investigate the reliability of advertisers before accepting their copy. Some publishers have strict rules about the presentation of advertising to prevent the publication of false or exaggerated claims and to preserve the aesthetic tone of their publications.

Radio and television stations generally try to investigate the company and its product before broadcasting advertising messages that might cause unfavorable reactions. The networks and the National Association of Broadcasters have established codes regulating the advertising of medical products and controlling contests, premiums, and other offers. All the networks maintain so-called acceptance departments, which screen both commercial and noncommercial scripts, either deleting or challenging for substantiation any questionable material. Most magazine publishers have their own strict rules on acceptance of advertising copy.

Several advertising trade associations are concerned with maintaining high standards. The associations believe it is good public relations to do so, inasmuch as advertising that weakens public confidence damages the impact and influence of all advertising.

The American Advertising Federation, an organization of leading national advertisers, has long campaigned for "truth in advertising." Other organizations that promote ethical standards are the American Association of Advertising Agencies and the Association of National Advertisers. The Institute of Outdoor Advertising encourages its members to improve the design of their advertising posters and signs and, more importantly, to make sure they do not erect advertising billboards in locations where they will mar the landscape or otherwise offend the public. The best-known and most active watchdogs in the advertising field are the Better Business Bureaus, which bring pressure to bear on unethical advertisers through persuasion, publicity, or, in extreme cases, legal action. The fact that local and national bureaus are subsidized by both advertisers and media reflects the conviction of modern business management that "good advertising is good business."

Industrial regulations supports by the American Advertising Federation in United States which acts as an organization of leading those advertisers who have long campaigned at national level.

IN CANADA

Canadian advertising regulations are even stricter than those in the United States. The Competition Act is the Canadian federal statute that seeks to prevent false and misleading advertising. The act is administered by the Bureau of Competition Policy which is part of Consumer and Corporate Affairs. If the bureau finds advertising to be misleading, it may simply ask the advertiser to stop running the ad or it may ask a company to take certain steps to correct the impression made by the false claims. The bureau may also take legal action against the advertiser in which case it will turn over its evidence to the Attorney General of Canada who will decide whether the evidence warrants a criminal prosecution.

Canadian Regulation is much stricter than in US. It is stricter because of their regulations and rules. This regulation is administered by the Bureau of competition policy. If bureau finds that if any advertisings are to be misleading, then bureau declares that this advertisement tends to be stop running or take steps to improve that ad.

Self-regulatory body, the Canadian Advertising Standards Council, has the right to take a commercial off the air if it offends taste and public decency. Moreover, in Canada ads that deal with products regulated by the government (for example, food, drugs, alcohol, and children's products) have to be approved before they air and can also be pulled if complaints arise after they run. In the United States, action can only be taken after the advertisement runs. Finally, beginning in 2001 tobacco advertising in Canada was limited to direct mail and to adults-only environments such as bars.

IN OTHER COUNTRIES

Advertising is often heavily regulated in other countries as well. But the regulations vary from country to country. For example, in Mexico advertising for tobacco and alcohol is limited to late evenings after children have gone to bed. France prohibits any reference to health in tobacco ads, and Italy allows alcohol advertising to promote the brand name but not product attributes such as 'cold filtered' or 'smooth tasting.' Each county has their own regulations which are always different from each other.

ADVERTISING AND CONSTITUTIONAL RIGHTS

Advertising is equated with constitutionally guaranteed freedom of opinion and speech. Therefore criticizing advertising or any attempt to restrict or ban advertising is almost always considered to be an attack on fundamental rights (First Amendment in the USA) and meets the combined and concentrated resistance of the business and especially the advertising community. "Currently or in the near future, any number of cases are and will be working their way through the court system that would seek to prohibit any government regulation of ... commercial speech (e. g. advertising or food labelling) on the grounds that such regulation would violate citizens' and corporations' First Amendment rights to free speech or free press." An example for this debate is advertising for tobacco or alcohol but also advertising by mail or fliers (clogged mail boxes), advertising on the phone, in the internet and advertising for children. Various legal restrictions concerning spanning, advertising on mobile phones, addressing children, tobacco, alcohol have been introduced by the US, the EU and various other countries. Not only the business community resists restrictions of advertising. Advertising as a means of free expression has firmly established itself in western society. Surveys e. g. reveal that advertising is generally seen as a welcome information and seldom as a nuisance. At worst it is seen as a necessary evil to be endured and most often its entertaining value is pointed out. Hardly any by-law restricting advertising fails to appease possible critics by pointing out the positive effects and the necessity of advertising in its foreword. McChesney argues, that the government deserves constant vigilance when it comes to such regulations, but that it is certainly not "the only antidemocratic force in our society. ...corporations and the wealthy enjoy a power every bit as immense as that enjoyed by the lords and royalty of feudal times" and "markets are not value-free or neutral; they not only tend to work to the advantage of those with the most money, but they also by their very nature emphasize profit over all else...Hence, today the debate is over whether advertising or food labelling, or campaign contributions are speech...if the rights to be protected by the First Amendment can only be effectively employed by a fraction of the citizenry, and their exercise of these rights gives them undue political power and undermines the ability of the balance of the citizenry to exercise the same rights and/or constitutional rights, then it is not necessarily legitimately protected by the First Amendment." In addition, "those with the capacity to engage in free press are in a position to determine who can speak to the great mass of citizens and who cannot". Critics in turn argue, that advertising invades privacy which is a constitutional right. For, on the one hand, advertising physically invades privacy, on the other, it increasingly uses relevant, information-based communication with private data assembled without the knowledge or consent of consumers or target groups.

STAGES OF DEVELOPMENT

There are five stages of development in advertising. These includes domestic, export, international, multination and last is Global marketing.

Domestic advertising

Domestic advertising refers to the local advertisement firms that will not be overjoyed, if more foreign owned advertising firms are apply to operate in any time soon. A marketing restricted to the political boundaries of a country, is called "Domestic Marketing". A company marketing only within its national boundaries only has to consider domestic competition. Even if that competition includes companies from foreign markets, it still only has to focus on the competition that exists in its home market. Products and services are developed for customers in the home market without thought of how the product or service could be used in other markets. All marketing decisions are made at headquarters.

The biggest obstacle these marketers face is being blind sided by emerging global marketers. Because domestic marketers do not generally focus on the changes in the global marketplace, they may not be aware of a potential competitor who is a market leader on three continents until they simultaneously open 20 stores in the Northeastern U.S. These marketers can be considered ethnocentric as they are most concerned with how they are perceived in their home country.

Export advertising

Generally, companies began exporting, reluctantly, to the occasional foreign customer who sought them out. At the beginning of this stage, filling these orders was considered a burden, not an opportunity. If there was enough interest, some companies became passive or secondary exporters by hiring an export management company to deal with all the customs paperwork and language barriers. Others became direct exporters, creating exporting departments at headquarters. Product development at this stage is still focused on the needs of domestic customers. Thus, these marketers are also considered ethnocentric.

International Advertising

International advertising entails dissemination of a commercial message to target audiences in more than one country. Target audiences differ from country to country in terms of how they perceive or interpret symbols or stimuli, respond to humor or emotional appeals, as well as in levels of literacy and languages spoken. How the advertising function is organized also varies. In some cases, multinational firms centralize advertising decisions and budgets and use the same or a limited number of agencies worldwide. In other cases, budgets are decentralized and placed in the hands of local subsidiaries, resulting in greater use of local advertising agencies.

International advertising can, therefore, be viewed as a communication process that takes place in multiple cultures that differ in terms of values, communication styles, and consumption patterns. International advertising is also a business activity involving advertisers and the advertising agencies that create ads and buy media in different countries. The sum total of these activities constitutes a worldwide industry that is growing in importance. International advertising is also a major force that both reflects social values, and propagates certain values worldwide.

International marketing is simply the application of marketing principles to more than one country. However, there is a crossover between what is commonly expressed as international marketing and global marketing, which is a similar term. For the purposes of this lesson on international marketing and those that follow it, international marketing and global marketing are interchangeable.

At its simplest level, international marketing involves the firm in making one or more marketing mix decisions across national boundaries. At its most complex level, it involves the firm in establishing manufacturing facilities overseas and coordinating marketing strategies across the globe.

VARIOUS ASPECTS OF INTERNATIONAL ADVERTISING

International advertising has various aspects including International Advertising as a communication process, as a business practice, as an industry and as a social force.

International Advertising as a Communication Process

In international markets the process of communicating to a target audience is more complex because communication takes place across multiple contexts, which differ in terms of language, literacy, and other cultural factors. In addition, media differ in their effectiveness in carrying different appeals. A message may, therefore, not get through to the audience because of people's inability to understand it (due to literacy problems), because they misinterpret the message by attaching different meanings to the words or symbols used, or because they do not respond to the message due to a lack of income to purchase the advertised product. Media limitations also play a role in the failure of a communication to reach its intended audience.

The process of communication in international markets involves a number of steps. First, the advertiser determines the appropriate message for the target audience. Next, the message is encoded so that it will be clearly understood in different cultural contexts. The message is then sent through media channels to the audience who then decodes and reacts to the message. At each stage in the process, cultural barriers may hamper effective transmission of the message and result in miscommunication.

International Advertising as aBusiness Practice

International advertising can also be viewed as a business activity through which a firm attempts to inform target audiences in multiple countries about itself and its product or service offerings. In some cases the advertising message relates to the firm and its activities, i.e. its corporate image. In other cases, the message relates to a specific product or service marketed by the firm. In either case, the firm will use the services of an advertising agency to determine the appropriate message, advertising copy and make the media placement.

An important issue in determining international advertising strategy is whether or not to develop a global or regional advertising campaign, or rather tailor communication to differences in local markets (Peebles and Ryans 1984). If the purpose of advertising is to develop a strong corporate or global image, a uniform global campaign is more likely to be used. When, on the other hand, the objective is to launch a new product or brand, or to more clearly differentiate the product or brand from other competing brands or products, local campaigns tailored to local markets are more typical.

A global campaign offers a number of advantages. In the first place, it can be an important means of building a strong and coherent global image for the firm and/or its products worldwide. Use of the same image in different countries builds familiarity and generates synergies across world markets. It allows utilization of good ideas and creative talent (both of which are scarce commodities) on a worldwide basis. In addition, use of a single campaign provides substantial cost savings in copy development and production costs. Conversely, development of multiple local campaigns can lead to duplication of effort, result in inconsistent brand images across countries and confusion in consumers' minds with regard to the benefits offered by the brand and corporate image.

While use of uniform advertising appeals offers a number of advantages, differences in customer perceptions and response patterns across countries and cultures, as well as media availability and government regulation are major barriers to use of a standardized campaign. Even though technological developments allow adaptation of advertising appeals to different languages (for example, TV can have audio channels in two languages, Internet messages can be automatically translated), development of visual and verbal copy that works effectively in multiple countries poses major creative challenges.

The organizational structure of the firm often plays a key role in the choice of global vs. locally adapted campaigns. If international operations are organized on a country-by- country or geographic basis and operate as local profit centers with local advertising budgets, pressures exist for use of local advertising campaigns. If, on the other hand, the company is organized by product divisions, with centralized advertising budgets at corporate or regional headquarters, use of regional or global advertising campaigns is more likely

International Advertising as an Industry

The world advertising industry is characterized by a large number of small and medium sized advertising agencies that operate primarily in one country and by a small number of very large advertising agencies with operations in many countries. These agencies have developed extensive networks of offices throughout the world in order to coordinate the advertising process in all the countries where their clients do business. These networks often include both wholly-owned subsidiaries and formal relationships with local advertising agencies to establish a presence in new markets, particularly in emerging markets.

Worldwide over $400 billion is spent on advertising. Approximately half of that amount is spent in the US and the other half outside the US. Information on advertising spending can be obtained from Advertising Age's web site and from McCann-Erickson's web site (www.mccann.com). The bulk of expenditure outside the US takes place in Europe and Japan, although Brazil, Canada, Mexico, and Australia are also important advertising markets. Outside of these markets, China is the next largest advertising market and is also growing rapidly.

The Table below shows advertising spending in the top ten global ad markets. The US and Japan account for 65 percent of the total advertising spending in these markets and the top four European markets an additional 25 percent. Apart from Brazil, no other market accounts for more than two percent of the total spending. The concentration of spending in the US in part explains the dominance of US-based advertising agencies. Not only do they work for US-based clients that continue to expand outside the US, but also they accumulate knowledge and experience in the practice of advertising that can be applied elsewhere.

Country	1997 Advertising Expenditures *(millions)*	Percent
U.S.	117.0	50
Japan	35.7	15
U.K.	20.8	9
Germany	20.3	9
France	9.7	4
Brazil	8.8	4
Italy	7.2	3
Australia	5	2.5
Canada	5.4	2
S. Korea	5.3	2
Total:	235.7	100

Note: The expenditures in this Table reflect only the 13 measured media tracked by Advertsing Age such as TV, magazines, radio, the Internet and yellow pages. The $400.billion figure cited above includes unmeasured spending such as direct mail, promotion, co-op advertising, and catalogues.

Once the advertising message has been created, a media plan that must be developed and specific media vehicles purchased to deliver the message to the target audience. Media is different from country in their availability, effectiveness and efficiency in delivering a message, these tends to be organized on a country-by-country basis.

International Advertising as a social force

In the view of the advertiser the primary objective of advertising is to sell products or services. In achieving this primary goal, there are often profound secondary consequences. Advertising exerts a formative influence whose character is both persuasive and pervasive. Through the selective reinforcement of certain social roles, language and values, it acts as an important force fashioning the cognitions and attitudes that underlie behavior not only in the market place, but also in all aspects of life. In an international setting, advertising has an important social influence in a number of ways. First, much international advertising is designed to promote and introduce new products from one society into another. Often this results in radical change in life-styles, behavior patterns of a society, stimulating for example the adoption of fast food, casual attire or hygiene and beauty products. International advertising also encourages desire for products from other countries, it creates expectations about " the good life", and establishes new models of consumption. Advertising is thus a potent force for change, while selectively reinforcing certain values, life-styles and role models.

Multinational Advertising

The word multinational refers to the brands and their advertising which span more than one country. 'Standardization' means to keep one or more of the three basic components of multinational advertising campaigns i.e. strategy, execution and language.

Here strategy means creative selling propositions, Executions refer to the actual elements and their structure in an ad and language considered as a separate element because there are situations when all executional elements of multinational ad are standardized except the language.

Global Marketing

When a company becomes a global marketer, it views the world as one market and creates products that will only require weeks to fit into any regional marketplace. Marketing decisions are made by consulting with marketers in all the countries that will be affected. The goal is to sell the same thing the same way everywhere.

Case Study

Note : knowing more about "Future of Advertising" reader can study documentation process of Microsoft company by visiting their site : www.members.microsoft.com

http://adverlab.blogspot.com/2008/10/case-study-burger-kings-advergames-part.html

http://www.slideshare.net/gamages/the-future-of-advertising-apa-170209

http://www.kff.org/entmedia/upload/7469.pdf

https://www.marketingprofs.com/login/join.asp?adref=rdblk&source=%2F7%2Fglimpse-advertising-future-japan-dentsu-tungate.asp

9

Industrial Advertising

This chapter includes the key concepts that are described below:-

- Introduction

INTRODUCTION

Industrial Advertising is defined as a form of business-to-business advertising, this is advertising which are aimed at manufacturers. This advertising typically promotes the parts, equipment, and raw materials which are used in the manufacturing process.

Modern Advertiser

Modern Advertiser appreciates the importance of industrial advertising even though it represents, in dollars, a relatively small percentage of the amount which are spent for all advertising. Studies differences between industrial and consumer advertising as to factors that make each effective. It becomes acquainted with the methods used by industrial advertisers to make the job of the salesman easier.

In modern advertising, industrial copy represents less than 10 per cent of all advertising expenditures. The total advertising volume estimated for 1960 is $8.5 billion. For industrial advertising the estimate is $845 million. This percentage is so small that some advertising practitioners tend to overlook its importance in our economy. One reason for this oversight is that consumer advertising has more attractiveness, uses more artistic, colorful illustrations in mass publications and appears in more glamorous television shows. Furthermore, the copywriters for consumer advertising prepare advertisements on which agency billings are relatively higher. The copy writer for the consumer advertisement can let his imagination go into clouds of ecstasy about the delights obtainable from the use of a soap or a soup; but the man who writes industrial advertising must stick closely to the cold facts-facts that will be read by technically trained men who buy on a logical rather than an emotional basis.

Functions of Industrial Advertising

The real importance of the industrial advertising man is in his behind-the-scenes contributing to your standard of living. He is one of the most important influences in educating and persuading manufacturers and processors to purchase more productive equipment and to adopt lower-cost technical processes. These in turn, help the producers to make better products at lower costs. As a result, consumers can buy more consumer goods, thus raising the standards of living for all. This role is, in a way, more significant but less glamorous than that of the consumer advertising man. One of the functions of industrial advertising is to reach the inaccessible purchasing influences.

Much industrial advertising is done to increase the effectiveness of the salesman. It costs money to have salesman that call on prospects. In the industrial field, the average cost of a salesman's call on a prospect was found to be $17.24, according to a survey conducted by the sales Executives Club of New York. Data was furnished by 223 representative manufacturers of industrial materials, equipment, and services. Of these companies, 81 per cent indicating upon the product or service being sold, its cost, and the amount of engineering and research necessary to meet customers' demands. The total range of costs per call was from a low of $1 to a high of $130.

The above figures are averages for some general classes. Each company must, of course, determine for its particular situation the appropriateness or inappropriateness of the marketing tools available. Advertising for many industrial firms becomes an effective, cost-reducing selling tool when rightly used. Generally, the greater the number of favorable contacts with the customer, the greater his recognition and preference for the brand or company.

A favorable contact may be in the form of use experience, a report from a pleased used, a demonstration, a news item, a catalog listing, a salesman's call, or a paid advertisement. Of these, the marketer has the greatest degree of control over the salesman's call and the paid advertisement. Studies of business and industrial buying practices show that the companies most likely to be considered in a purchasing decision are those that have made those two types of contact most frequently. In one test, 2,657 men (who indicated they had buying influence over unit air-conditioners) were asked to list in order of preference the brands of air-conditioners they would consider for purchase and to mention the names of companies that had recently contacted them through salesmen and advertising. Ranks in preference and contacts were almost identical.3

3 Howard G. Sawyer, "Can Ads Sell as Well as salesmen?" Printer's Ink, July 16 1954. Copyright, 1954, by Printer's Ink Publishing Company, Inc., New York

The salesman is limited in his scope of activity. This is indicated by the percentage of buyers in four manufacturing industries who remembered to seeing salesmen from five leading oil companies. The percentages ranged from 7 to 30.

Salesmen have problems in keeping contact with the many rapid changes in personnel of industrial firms. McGraw-Hill circulation records show that out of any 1,000 industrial buyers during a 12-month period, 148 will change their addresses while still holding the same or similar jobs; 65 will change their titles (due to promotions, etc.) within the same company 326 will die, retire, or move to another company.

United States Steel Company asked 11 of its subsidiary companies to furnish names of all the people their salesmen contact in 33 prospect and customer plants; 105 names came back. Yet a check of those plants revealed that in addition to those 105 individuals, there were 1,850 buyers with titles indicating buying influence for U.S. Steel products. The 1,850 buyers were not seen by salesmen, but they were subscribers to publications in which U.S. Steel advertises.

Advertising – it must be said cannot button hold a prospect, cannot adjust its message to each individual case, carrot answer on a waver-but-not-yet sold order, and it does not possess in anywhere nearly so great a degree the unquestionable advantage of selling through individual personality. However, it can be more truly and permanently representative of the company's personality. And this is an advantage that should not be underestimated.

Many industrial advertisers whose products are sold to consumers through distributors and dealers have to furnish merchandise aids: store displays direct mail services, and attractive packaging that meet their needs in the same way that the consumer advertisers have to provide merchandising aids. These selling tools are developed by industrial advertising men in much the same manner as they are prepared in companies that sell consumer products only. However, Advertising for industrial publications requires special knowledge that meets the needs of the technically trained reader.

Special Requirements of Technical Advertising

Many of the products advertised to industry are ingredients or parts of equipment whose identities are lost when the product reaches the ultimate user. Chemicals and metals are common examples. Textiles, such as cloth for automobile seats and insulating materials for refrigerators are sold to other manufacturers who utilize them in end products. The manufacturers' purchasing experts must be given the kinds of product information that they want highly technical. They want formulas, physical properties, and technical descriptions.

The advertising copy writer for basic raw materials cannot be expected to know all the technical details that apply to all of perhaps fifty products which are made by his materials manufacturer. The copywriter must ask the experts for help. Of course, they are likely to provide technical information, which the copy writer may not understand or be able to interpret to the readers. Frequent consultations between the experts and the copywriter are essential until an advertisable idea and a plan are developed.

Sometimes the problem can be solved by publishing an advertisement in a many industry magazine that describes the product in a way that is understandable to a wide range of technical men, each of whom will be able to see possible applications to his industry.

There are some advertisers to whom technical advertising is vitally important because acceptance and use of their products begin with technical people. These people may be engineers- chemical, research, design, mechanical or they may be technicians- chemists, metallurgists, and the like. At any rate, they are specialists in their work.

The men who scan, with interest and understanding, the algebraic formulas that are involving differential equations, which are concerned with the deflections of perpendicularly loaded split circular rings, or the prediction of reaction equilibrium, but they're people with pride of intellect – and with a lot to say about what goes into things chemical or mechanical.

Sure, these people may read the comic strips in the daily paper. They may buy neckties as irrationally as the next guy. But in their professions and sheer specialities within their professions, they can be cold in their judgments while intense in their professional interests, and likely to dismiss as "just advertising that is flamboyant,, general, inaccurate, overstates the case, or reveals no familiarity with their field.

They will read long copy and think nothing of it, if it's right for them. And paradoxically, a degree of favourable emotional reaction can be won from them – in the profitable form of product loyalty – by advertising that adheres to high standards of honesty and that leans toward understatement.

A leading industrial advertising manager, one who is an advertising manager for Crucible Steel Co., has summarized some basic principles about industrial copy:

Factual product information is without doubt the most helpful kind of copy. The industrial advertising man, in the majority, will list the following as his guide for a good ad:

- Application of the product (actual use)
- Technical data to support his claim
- Cost and economy
- Availability of the product
- Offer of more technical information and or field engineering service and
- Company name and sales department address

The copy must be as clear and precise as a purchase order. Industrial advertising, unlike much consumer advertising, is so basic a part of the editorial content of a trade publication, that it should take the tenor of the editorial itself. Survey after survey has shown that where an industrial advertiser patterns his copy after the style of editorial, he will gain greater readership and more believability...

Industrial Advertising copy can be long

If the copy applies to the reader's interests, it can be as long as necessary to explain the facts. McGraw-Hill Research made a survey of 1,069 single-page advertisements in one publication, and found that industrial copy is more widely read and remembered longer if the advertisement is detailed and informative. This finding indicates that the people who read industrial publications want the facts fully explained. They want detailed information in the advertising they read.

In order to evaluate readability of advertisements by the amount of information, full-page advertisements in five issues were studied and grouped into three classes on the basis of their length of text. The classes were divided into short (120 words or less), medium (121 to 200 words), and long 201 to 500 words). There were 426 cases in the short class, 430 in the medium, and 213 in the long.

The use of an index system permitted the making of comparisons without bias due to color or bleed. "Remembered seeing" and "readership" classifications were compared in short copy, in medium copy, ad in long copy. The medium-length advertisements were remembered by 10 per cent more people and the long text ads by 34 per cent more people than the short copy advertisements.

The comparison in "readership' followed the same general pattern. Medium-length advertisements measured 9 per cent more readership and long text advertisements measured 23 per cent more readership than short text advertisement.

Further analysis was necessary to determine whether the findings were related to the length of the advertisement rather than to the product or service advertised. After cross tabulating the data, it was found that the advertisements using the same techniques of size of space, color and bleed were better remembered and more widely read when the information in the advertisement was detailed and full. The results of this survey clearly indicate that long-text industrial advertisements are recalled better and read more widely.

However, it should be recognized that the mere use of long copy or big illustrations does not force readers to read the advertisement. The advertisement must earn readers by offering copy that is worth reading. Successful advertising men keep their management, informed about the company's advertising and make themselves accepted as members of management, thus setting up a basis for trust and confidence.

If long copy is helpful to the reader, it gets better reading than short copy. In an issue of a technical magazine, two brass and bronze companies happened to have facing pages. They had equal opportunity to win readers. The short-copy advertisement, less than 100 words, gave general information about the items available. The 801 word advertisement had technical copy that gave specific, helpful information. The latter got 70 per cent higher reading.

Position in the publication is relatively unimportant. Generally, consumer advertisements that are placed opposite or near related editorial matter are more likely to be noticed and read than those placed at the back of the publication or "buried in the middle. Therefore, advantageous positioning is frequently important in the consumer advertising. This is not the case in industrial advertisements. If they have reader interest, they will be read regardless of their position in the publication.

Industrial advertisements are selective. Audience selection plays an important part in industrial advertising. The reader should quickly identify the subject of an industrial advertisement and the company sponsoring the product or service. The industrial advertiser does not aim to achieve universal appeal. He is interested only in qualified prospects.

Industrial advertising may have hidden objectives. In the case of industrial advertising, many objectives other than immediate sales may be sought. Getting the product accepted as the leader in its field and assuring the reader of its availability at all times are examples of these hidden objectives whose success cannot be measured statically. To produce effective advertising, advertising men and management must cooperate fully.

Management often has objectives in advertising, which are never actually voiced. Good advertising campaigns have clear out objectives, so it is virtually impossible for adverting to be effective unless management has confidence in the advertising man and states fully and frankly just what these objectives are.

Industrial advertising usually stresses the manufacturer as well as the product. The manufacturer, his facilities, and his reputation are important aspects of industrial advertising. Consumer advertising relies on brand names rather than corporate names. The brand name is often advertised to the extent that the public has no idea whatsoever of the manufacturer's name. Industrial advertising endeavors to pre sell products by associating the public with corporate names.

What Readership studies show about Industrial Advertising

Number of surveys are being made of the extent to which readers of industrial publications read the advertising. The nature of the product is, of course, one important factor in readership. Obviously, an advertisement for a lubricant is likely to have a greater number of reader prospects than one for railroad bridges. There are more technical people who buy oil than bridges. In spite of this and other differences related to product interest, readership surveys do elicit significant finding for the advertising man such as the following:

- Cartoon and humor treatments get less attention than "how to" or reader benefits. One industrial advertiser, for example, ran a double spread in Power Magazine. The left-hand page was in two colors and had a cartoon; the right-hand page was in black and white and offered "how to" information. Only 5 per cent of the publication's readers noted the left-hand page and 4 percent read most of the copy. The right-hand page, in contrast, got 20 percent Noted and 10 percent Read Most scores.

- Technical men like to read about technical problems. They even read direct questions such as "How would you insulate this valve?" They like to solve problems and read about the ways other men solve problems.

Three manufacturers of water conditioning equipment used three different types of advertisements. One had an illustration of an owl with the headline "Whose expert advice should you follow?" and argued for the advertiser.

A Second advertisement had a cartoon illustration and posed the question of "Sludge" versus "Scale" and explained the differences.

The third asked an important technical question, "Which chemicals is best for your plant?" It included a checklist to enable the engineer to answer the technical questions himself according to his own best judgment.

The first advertisement was one of the lowest scoring advertisements in the issue, the second average, and the third was one of the very best.

• Technical men like illustrations that show how a device really works. In one issue of Machinery Magazine, four grinder manufacturers had illustrated advertisements: two let the reader see the grinding workings of the apparatus and two did not. The two that let the reader see the inwards of the machine and how it worked got two and one-half times as much attention as the others. Brief, numbered copy points often help to set up readership.

• Catalog formats do better than generalized copy. Catalog formats that contain detailed information about a product's use, effectiveness, or construction is likely to have better reading than general institutional copy. Institutional advertisements with copy such as "our nationwide staff of engineers will welcome the opportunity of discussing this important subject with you" get very little attention or reading. Technical readers needs particular information about improvements that cut waste, records that show increased production at lower cost, longer life for equipment, case histories that are genuine, and similar solutions to engineering problems. Today's best-read advertisements provide technical information that rivals in value and accuracy the editorial content of the best industrial magazines.

Some Industrial Advertisers find consumer media helpful in selling their technical products

Consumer media are at times used by industrial firms, and the advertisements are adapted to the consumer reader. They are more generalized and less technical. This may be done to get the attention of wholesalers and retailers or it may be part of a planned campaign to make the company name a generic one for that company's products. It may be done by the manufacturer of a technical product who wants to widen his market. A good example is furnished by a manufacturer of steam generators for the garment trade. The manufacturer decided to expand his operations into other industries in order to even out his production schedule.

Catalogs

Catalogs are widely used as advertising by manufactures, wholesalers house in selling to merchants and industrial buyers. Their usefulness as advertising is increased due to their relatively greater length of life when compared to other forms of advertising.

In most cases, Catalogs serve a definite marketing function because they are the buyer's first-used source of information for comparing competing products and deciding which companies should be asked to have a salesman call. Indeed, some industrial advertisers think of the catalog as a marketing tool for buying rather then a selling.

In a good catalog, every word sells, and the pictures as well as the headline give necessary information to the reader. Ti is obviously advantageous to the wholesaler, manufacturer, and mail-order house that catalogs containing comprehensive information and technical data in the hands of all important potential buyers, readily accessible for instant use whenever buying needs arise.

The National Industrial Advertisers Association made a survey of its members and found that nearly one third of the companies let from four to ten years go by before redesigning their catalogs, that 41 per cent of the fourth of the companies distribute their catalogs mainly on the basis of requests for them. Men in industrial field who do marketing is any of the areas in which sweet's specializes are likely to consult them or use their services at sometime.

Compiling such catalogs is a laborious and time-consuming job and requires specialized knowledge. For this reason, there are various business services in the industrial and institutional field that arrange to develop catalogs for their clients and circulate them to customers.

Sweet's Catalog Service is an organization of catalog specialists. Founded in 1907, Sweet's, in a recent year, handled more catalogs then any other organization – over 40 million copies for 1,353 manufacturers. Sweet's endeavors to help clients find the answers to their individual catalog problems. It services fall into three categories:

- catalog design,
- catalog production, and
- catalog distribution.

In the area of catalog design, Sweet's maintains that good design starts with an analysis of the client's products and markets. The most effective catalogs are market specialized to meet the different product-information needs of each buying group. Market specialized catalogs defines only products of possible interest to the prospect and interpret them in order to his special requirements. Moreover, market-specialised catalogs are economical to produce and distribute, and to replace when they become obsolete.

Manufacturers' catalogs, distributed by Sweet's, are delivered to selected organizations and individuals representing the bulk of the buying power in each market served. Sweet's maintains an up-to-date record of the most important concerns and of the individuals in each concern who have real buying power for the following markets: product engineering, plant engineering, general building, industrial construction, and light construction.

To increase the proportion of calls are made after prospects have read the catalog, it follows that a sales executive must increase the use of his catalog. Here are a number of points to keep in mind which are based on techniques used by Sweet's catalog Service:

Design your catalog from the prospect's point of view. Good design doesn't mean window dressing. Your prospect has an application. Your catalog should give him the facts he needs, quickly, to decide whether your product might fit.

Aside from organization of facts, the catalog should induce the prospect to call in your representative. After he has made a tentative decision, tell him what he should do next. Send the catalog to all important potential customers within your distribution network. It is dangerous to assume that hordes of potential customers will ask for the catalog and wait for the mailing when they want production information – they may have your competitor's catalog handy.

Maintain your catalog. How many prospects have lost it or thrown it out? How many have failed to add recent mailings to their loose-leaf catalogs?

Your catalog procedures should be integrated into your basic marketing plan. Your basic tools are advertising, direct mail, point-of-sale displays, personal selling, and catalogs. Is your catalog coordinated with your advertising, for example? Do you devote any ad space to catalog promotion? Do your salesmen often talk from the prospect's catalog, rather than bring their own? If your products are bought in more than one market, do you have several catalogs, each geared to a market's requirements?

Case Study

Note : knowing more about "Industrial Advertising" reader can study documentation process of Microsoft company by visiting their site : www.members.microsoft.com

http://advertising.microsoft.com/advertising-case-studies?Search=1&Tag_VerticalID=1&Tag_TopicID=0&Tag_PropertySubpropertyID=&DocType=casestudy

http://www.ibscdc.org/Case_Studies/Strategy/Innovation%20Management/INM0100C.htm

http://www.postersonwheels.com/testimonials.asp

http://www.dynamiclogic.com/na/research/casestudies/

10

Decision and Methods in Media

This chapter includes the key concepts that are described below:-

- Print Media
- Features of Commercial Broadcasting
- Europe
- TV advertisements around the world
- Consumer Promotion
- Role of Media

PRINT MEDIA

Before partition, Lahore was the hub of print media and almost all the newspapers of the United Punjab were being published from there. After the holocast of partition, the press shifted to Jalandhar and started afresh with limited means. In a very short span of period the press stood on its feet and has now become very influential organ of public opinion.

Jalandhar City is the centre of print media. Many dailies and weeklies are published in various languages. Some of them are fine manifestation of journalism. The daily Ajit is a leading newspaper which has wider circulation and readership especially in the rural areas. Hind Samachar Group publishes Jag Bani in Punjabi, Punjab Kesari in Hindi and Hind Samachar in Urdu. These newspapers are also read by a large number of people. Amar Ujala and Dainik Jagran are published in Hindi. These two newspapers have included several interesting sections thus arousing the curiosity of public.

National newspapers like Times of India, Hindustan Times, The Tribune, Indian Express have posted their reporters here for collecting all local news. Akali Patrika, Aj Di Awaj and Lehar are other dailies which are published in Punjabi Milap in Hindi and Urdu, Vir Partap in Hindi are also published from Jalandhar.

These newspapers are disseminating news and information to the people and are a great source of media to educate the people in the method of performing their civic duty. They are also playing a very positive role in strengthening the bonds of communal harmony and adopt an attitude of restraint in projecting views involving communal tension and disturbance.

Commercial Broadcasting

Commercial broadcasting is defined as the practice of broadcasting for profit. This is usually achieve by interrupting normal programming to air advertisement which are also commonly called commercials in this context.

Private television as called in all neolatin countries or commercial broadcasting is the United States first model of television born in 1920 decade, antithetical to the "public television" model born in Europe in 1930, 1940 and 1950 decads and dominant worldwide except America up until the 1980 decade. Today it is the historically global and dominant model of television.

The difference between *private television* and *public television* are state and private ownership and not "commercials", because in some public television, as the french and german model, scheduled programming are not interrupted by commercials, while in other public television, as Italian and Spanish model, they are.

When broadcasting is done at commercial level, i.e., to earn profit then, this type of broadcasting is termed as commercial Broadcasting. Commercial broadcasting is the practice of broadcasting for profit. This is normally achieved by interrupting normal programming to air advertisements, also commonly called "commercials" in this context. This is the dominant type of broadcasting in the United States and a large number of other countries such as most of Latin America. It is also common elsewhere, but usually exists alongside public broadcasting where programming is largely funded by broadcast receiver licences, public donations, or government grants.

In an hour of broadcast time on a commercial broadcast outlet, typically ten to twenty minutes are devoted to advertising.

Advertisers pay a certain amount of money to air their commercials, usually based upon the popularity or ratings of a station or network. This effectively makes commercial broadcasters more answerable to advertisers than the public, which is a major criticism of commercial radio and television. Programming on commercial stations is often more sensationalistic ; particularly during ratings periods such as sweeps in the U.S.

Commercial broadcasting also has considerable overlap with pay services such as cable television, cable radio, satellite television and satellite radio; though such services are generally partially or wholly paid for by local subscribers, much of the programming, particularly on cable television, is produced by companies operating in much the same manner as commercial broadcasters, and both they and often the local cable provider will sell commercial time in the same manner. There does exist, however, completely advertisement-free commercial television and radio; premium cable services such as HBO and Showtime generally operate solely on subscriber fees with no need to sell ad space, as do the parts of the two major satellite radio systems that are produced in-house (mostly music material).

Role of commercial broadcasting can be controversial sometimes. This controversies involves due to some reasons like low quality programming high ratio of advertising during program time, server failure, etc. Commercial radio in particular is often attacked for perceived homogeneity in programming, covert politicized censorship of content, and a desire to cut costs at the expense of giving the station an identifiable personality. Politics is a major force in media criticism, with an ongoing battle (especially in the United States) as to what moral standards, if any, are to be applied to the airwaves.

In much of the world, analog broadcasting is giving way to digital, a process effectively complete some time ago for many satellite television providers and some cable systems. Standards such as DVB and ATSC promise to provide vastly enhanced picture quality and bandwidth usage, allowing the practical use of HDTV (which did not catch on anywhere until the arrival of digital technology) and multiple channels from the same broadcaster. The same transition is happening with radio transmissions but is unlikely to be complete for some time if ever; Digital Audio Broadcasting, HD Radio, and Digital Radio Mondiale are all rising formats for radio broadcasts.

Perhaps the best known commercial broadcasters are the venerable ABC, CBS, Fox and NBC television networks, as well as radio giant Clear Channel Communications, based in the United States. Major US commercial cable operators include Comcast, Adelphia, Time Warner Cable, and Cox Communications; satellite services include DirecTV, Dish Network, the UK's BSkyB, and the radio services Sirius, WorldSpace, and XM. In Asia the best known Commercial Service was with the oldest radio station in the region, Radio Ceylon.

FEATURES OF COMMERCIAL BROADCASTING

Massive practice of advertisement

Commercial broadcasting is based on massive practice of broadcasting advertisements for profit, in contrast to public media which eschews most or all paid advertisements. It is also elsewhere, but usually exists alongside public broadcasting where programming is largely funded by broadcast receive licenses, public donations or government grants.

However. In United States does exist completely advertisement-free commercial television and radio; premium cable services such as HBO and Showtime generally operate solely on subscriber fees with no need to sell ad space, as do the parts of the two major satellite radio systems that are produced in-house (mostly music material).

Pay services in Commercial Broadcasting

Commercial broadcasting also has considerable overlap with pay services such as cable television, cable radio, satellite television and satellite radio; though such services are usually partially or wholly paid for by local subscribers, much of the programming, specifically on cable television, is produced by companies operating in much the same manner as commercial broadcasters, and both they and often the local cable provider will sell commercial time in the same manner.

Sensationalism in Commercial Broadcasting

Programming on commercial stations is frequently more sensationalistic—particularly during ratings periods such as sweeps in the U.S. and also in some Latin American countries.

Other features of Commercial Broadcasting

Commercial broadcasting (especially over-the-air) is often controversial for a great many reasons. Chief among them is a perceived lack of quality and risk in the programming to which more conservative elements respond that it is too risky much of the time, an excessively high ratio of advertising to program time especially on children's television, and a perceived failure to serve the local interest due to media consolidation. Commercial radio in specifically attacked for perceived homogeneity in programming, covert politicized censorship of content, and a desire to cut costs at the expense of giving the station an identifiable personality. Politics is a major force in media criticism, with an ongoing battle especially in the United States as to what moral standards, if any, are to be applied to the airwaves.

In the United States, commercial broadcasting is the dominant type of broadcasting and a large number of other countries such as most of Latin America.

Perhaps the best known commercial broadcasters are the venerable ABC, CBS, Fox and NBC television networks, as well as radio giant Clear Channel Communications, based in the United States. Major US commercial cable operators include Comcast, Adelphia, Time Warner Cable, and Cox Communications; satellite services include DirecTV, Dish Network, the UK's BSkyB, and the radio services Sirius, WorldSpace, and XM. In Asia the best known Commercial Service was with the oldest radio station in the region, Radio Ceylon.

In much of the world analog broadcasting is giving a way to digital, a process effectively complete sometime ago for many satellite television providers and some cable systems.

In an hour of broadcast time on a commercial broadcast outlet, typically ten to twenty minutes are devoted to advertising. Advertisers pay a certain amount of money to air their commercials, usually based upon the popularity or ratings of a station or network. This effectively makes commercial broadcasters more answerable to advertisers than the public, which is a major criticism of commercial radio and television. Standards like DVB and ATSC promise to provide vastly enhanced picture quality and bandwidth usage, allowing the practical use of HDTV which did not catch or anywhere until the arrival of digital technology and multiple channels from the some broadcaster the same transition is happening with radio transmission but is unlikely to be complete for some time if ever.

EUROPE

Today in Europe, Commercial broadcasting coexist alongside public broadcasting, where programming is largely funded by broadcast receiver licences, public donations, or government grants.

Television advertisement

A **television advertisement** or **television commercial** it is often just known as **commercial** in US or **advert** or **ad** in UK or **ad-film** in India, it is defined as a span of television programming produced and paid for by an organization that conveys a message. Advertisement revenue provides a significant portion of the funding for most privately owned television networks. The vast majority of television advertisements today consist of brief advertising spots, ranging in length from a few seconds to several minutes as well as program-length infomercials. Advertisements of this sort have been used to sell every product imaginable over the years, from household products to goods and services, to political campaigns.

The effect of television advertisements upon the viewing public has been so successful and so pervasive that in some countries, like the United States, it is considered impossible for a politician to wage a successful election campaign without the purchase of television advertising. In other countries, such as France, political advertising is strictly limited on television, and some, like Norway, even completely ban it.

Characteristics of Television Advertisement

Many television advertisements feature catchy jingles (songs or melodies) or catch-phrases slogan that generate sustained appeal, which may remain in the minds of television viewers long after the span of the advertising campaign. Some of these ad jingles or catch-phrases may take on lives of their own, spawning gags or "riffs" that may appear in other forms of media, such as comedy movies or television variety shows, or in written media, such as magazine comics or literature. These long-lasting advertising elements may therefore be said to have taken a place in the pop culture history of the demographic to which they have appeared.

Television is changing a lot and television advertising is changing with it. Internet are changing the way content and advertising is consumed. It changes they see on the horizon.

Advertising agencies frequently use humor as a tool in their creative marketing campaigns. In fact, many psychological studies tried to demonstrate the effect of humour and indicate the manner to empower advertising persuasion.

Animation is often used in advertisements. The pictures can changes from hand-drawn traditional animation to computer animation. By using animated characters, an advertisement may have a certain appeal that is difficult to achieve with actors or mere product displays. For this reason, an animated advertisement (or a series of such advertisements) can be very long-running, several decades in many instances.

TV ADVERTISEMENTS AROUND THE WORLD

United States of America

Frequency: Television is advertisements appear between shows, but also interrupt the shows at intervals. This method of screening advertisements is intended to capture or grab the attention of the audience, keeping the viewers focused on the television show so that they will not want to change the channel; instead, they will (hopefully) watch the advertisements while waiting for the next segment of the show. However, remote controls have now made it easier for audiences to "tune out" advertisements simply by allowing them to turn down the volume or even switch channels when the advertisement comes on.

Entire industries exist that focus solely on the task of keeping the viewing audience interested enough to sit through advertisements. The Nielsen ratings system exists as a way for stations to determine how successful their television shows are, so that they can decide what rates to charge advertisers for their advertisements. TIVO, DVRS and the internet are changing the way content and advertising in consumed.

Advertisements take airtime away from programs. In the 1960s a typical hour-long American show would run for 51 minutes excluding advertisements. Today, a similar program would only be 42 minutes long; a typical 30-minute block of time now includes 22 minutes of programming with 6 minutes of national advertising and 2 minutes of local.

In other words, over the course of 10 hours, American viewers will see approximately 3 hours of advertisements, twice what they would have seen in the sixties. Furthermore, if that sixties show is rerun today it may be cut by 9 minutes to make room for the extra advertisements.

Back in the 1950s and 1960s, the average advertisement was one minute. As the years passed, the average length shrank to 30 seconds (and often 10 seconds, depending on the television station's purchase of ad time), but more of them are now shown during the break, while in the '60's, only one or two advertisements would be shown at each break. However, today a majority of advertisements run in 15-second increments are often known as "hooks". TV advertisements are identified by an ISCI code.

Popularity: In the United States, the TV advertisement is usually considered the most effective mass-market advertising format, and this is reflected by the high prices TV networks charge for commercial airtime during popular TV events. The annual Super Bowl American football game is known as much for its commercial advertisements as for the game itself, and the average cost of a single 30-second TV spot during this game which are seen by 90 million viewers has reached US$2.7 million as of February 2008s.

In general, advertisers covet the 18-49 age demographic; older viewers are of almost no interest to most advertisers. The number of viewers within the target demographic is more important to ad revenues than total viewers. According to *Advertising Age*, during the 2007-08 season, *Grey's Anatomy* was able to charge $419,000 per commercial, compared to only $248,000 for a commercial during *CSI*, despite CSI having almost five million more viewers on average. Due to its demo strength, *Friends* was able to charge almost three times for a commercial as *Murder, She Wrote*, even though the two series had similar total viewer numbers during the seasons they were on the air together. Broadcast networks are concerned by the increasing use of DVRs by young viewers, resulting in aging of the live viewing audience and consequently, lower ad rates.

The major reason is people find advertisements annoying is that the advertisement's offer is not of interest at that moment or the presentation is unclear.

Because a single television advertisement can be broadcast repeatedly over the course of weeks, months, and even years television advertisement production studios often spend enormous sums of money in the production of one single thirty-second television spot. This vast expenditure has resulted in a number of high-quality advertisements, ones which boast of the best production values, the latest in special effects technology, the most popular personalities, and the best music. A number of television advertisements are so elaborately produced that they can be considered miniature thirty-second movies; indeed, many film directors have directed television advertisements both as a way to gain exposure and to earn a paycheck.

Despite the popularity of some advertisements, many consider them to be an annoyance for a number of reasons. The main reason may be that the sound volume of advertisements that tends to be higher and in some cases much higher than that of regular programming. The increasing number of advertisements, as well as overplaying of the same advertisement, are secondary annoyance factors. A third might be the increasing ability to advertise on television, prompting ad campaigns by everyone from cell-phone companies and fast food restaurants to local businesses and small businesses.

Restrictions on Television Advertising : Beginning on January 2, 1971, advertisements featuring cigarettes have been banned from American TV. Advertisements for alcohol products are allowed, but the consumption of any alcohol product is not allowed in a television advertisement. Since the late 1990s TV advertisements have become far more diverse, and in addition household products and foods that are not new are no longer usually advertised as they were in the mid to late 20th century.

In Europe : In many European countries television advertisements appear in longer, but less frequent advertising breaks. For example, instead of 3 minutes every 8 minutes, there might be around 6 minutes every half hour. European Union legislation limits the time taken by commercial breaks to 12 minutes per hour (20%), with a minimum segment length of 20 or 30 minutes, depending on the programme content. However, these are maximum limits and so specific regulations which differ widely from both within and outside the EU, and indeed from network to network. Unlike in the United States, in Europe the advertising agency name may appear at the beginning or at the end of the advert.

In United Kingdom : In the UK, the British Broadcasting Corporation which is abbreviated as (BBC) is funded by a licence fee and does not screen adverts in the conventional sense of the term but it frequently advertises its commercially available products, programmes and 'personalities', increasingly in a way which are identical to the commercial channels' adverts. Nevertheless, on the commercial channels, the amount of airtime allowed by the UK broadcasting regulator Ofcom for advertising is an overall average of 7 minutes per hour, with limits of 12 minutes for any particular clock hour including 8 minutes per hour between 6pm and 11pm

The first advert which to be shown in the UK was an advert for S.R. Toothpaste in 1955. Freeview has provided a cheap entry level which are alternative to satellite and cable subscription services and has taken the penetration of digital television to well over 80%.

The growth of multi-channel television has changed the face of TV advertising making the medium which are effective for companies with niche products and a targeted audience. 30-second advertisements on digital channels such as Sky News, MTV or E4 that can be bought for less than £50000 and adverts on more targeted channels like the Business Channel, Motors TV or Real Estate TV for less than £500 per 30 seconds.

In 2008, Ofcom announced a Review of television advertising and teleshopping regulation, with a view to possibly changing their code, *Rules on the Amount and Distribution of Advertising* (RADA), which regulates the duration, frequency and restriction of adverts on television. New Tv channels are launching every week in the UK and advertising opportunities are plentiful.

In Germany : As in Britain, in Germany, public television stations own a major share of the market. Their programming is funded by a licence fee as well as advertisements on particular hours of the day (5 p.m. to 8 p.m.), except on Sundays and holidays. Private stations are allowed to show up to 12 minutes of ads per hour with a minimum of 20 minutes of programming in between interruptions.

In Ireland : In the Republic of Ireland, the Broadcasting Commission of Ireland allows up to a maximum of 10 minutes of advertising minutage per hour for all broadcasters. Regarding overall advertising minutes there is a difference between the public funded TV broadcasters and commercial TV broadcasters. Broadcasters funded by a television licence fee, RTÉ and TG4, are permitted to allocate 10% of their broadcast minutage to advertising. Commercial broadcasters, TV3 and 3e (formerly Channel 6) and Setanta Ireland are permitted a maximum of 15% advertising time vs. overall broadcast time. This effectively gives an average of either 6 minutes or 9 minutes an hour depending on the type of broadcaster.

Russia : The Russian advertising break constitutes of 2 parts: federal adverts and regional adverts. The duration for each is 4 minutes and 15 minutes per hour respectively. The Russian government intends to decrease TV advertisements because of a drop in TV channels' ratings.

CONSUMER PROMOTION

Consumer Promotion is a set of related actions directed at stimulating sales by influencing the end customer. One of the best manner of ensuring effectiveness and stimulating sales is to use a well thought out and solid approach that responds to all aspects of the task at hand. It's important to remember that in today's conditions of intense competition and a market saturated with identical goods and services, companies must be original and memorable to potential customers. We are able to offer non-standard and high-tech solutions for any good or service. A sales promote are used to designed to stimulate the consumer purchasing. It way offer samples, coupons, rebates, price reductions, premiums, patronage, rewards, displays, contests, etc.

Consumer promotion All those sales promotion techniques which are made to attract customers and increase customer purchasing, these are known as consumer promotion. It may offer samples, coupons, rebates, price reductions, premiums, patronage rewards, displays, contests, sweepstakes, etc.

The objective of company into when it comes to Consumer Promotion is to take an individually oriented approach to the good or service, designing and implementing detailed BTL techniques to make a strong impression on the end customer.

Meeting Client Demands

Consumer Promotion allows you to get a significant increment in turnover, market share, and profit by completing the following tasks:

- Increasing consumer familiarity with the product and product recognizability
- Stimulating sales
- Increasing product demand
- Getting consumers to switch from the competition to the promoted brand
- Being effective by conducting promotions in a diverse group of points of purchase (in chains and non-chains, open markets, clubs, restaurants and bars, train and bus stations, airports, fitness and business centers, and other places people go to relax and spend time).

BeeTL has implemented the following basic types of Consumer Promotions:

Consultations : This method is recommended for promoting complex products and services or those possessing special, unique traits, which is done by promotes.

These promotes make the customers aware about the special features and the benefits of the product.

Non-Standard Techniques : Flash Mob. The appearance of promoters in places where the customers congregates who attract attention due to their unusual appearance or actions.

Sales Animation. This methods includes organizing special activities for the target audience; involving the TA in a game. It is mainly used by HoReCa sector.

Gift with Purchase/Drawings : In order to encourage customers to buy a specific product, use of gifts is the most widely used tactics while promotion on of a product. Gifts with purchase/ drawings are recommended for new product launches, product repositioning, and seasonal sales or other price reductions. The particularities of the promoted product and the client's goals are taken into careful consideration in the development of these campaigns.

Tastings : This method is most frequently used in the food segment. The customer can try the product before deciding whether to buy it. Tastings is the term which are especially recommended for the market that are launch for new brands or when expanding the product line within a single brand.

Sampling : Sampling is the methods which includes the target audience with the product by distributing samples. This method is most effective when combined with the distribution of informational advertising materials about the promoted product.

Sampling is recommended for stimulating sales, reclaiming customer interest and, when essential, encouraging customers to switch from a competing brand, as well as for informing customers of changes in the product's formula and for launching new products.

BeeTL Technologies and Advantages

Proposal Development:

- We adhere closely to the tasks at hand and focus on the result.
- Combo of several methods are used to get good results.
- We apply a creative approach to any task.

Bringing your Ideas to Life :

- We can give life to any idea of any scale.
- In order to promote our product we design essential things.
- We have vast experience in conducting promotions for producers and suppliers of the most varied goods and services.

Quality Control :

- A unique system of working with promotional personnel that removes the chance the promoter will show up late or not at all
- High quality work ensures the encouraging promoters.
- With online casting, our clients can choose promoters without ever leaving the office.
- With online accounting, clients can access all information about the campaign in real time.
- ISO 9000 certification

Our Team :

- Highly professional specialists
- Highly experienced personnel in several methods of promotions for motivating
- Quality client service

Our Experience, Knowledge, and Abilities:

- We develop and introduce non-standard techniques.
- We can appraise the effectiveness of sales of both your advertised product and that of the main competitors.
- We have the highest quality projects.
- We achieve effective promotions by conducting them in a diverse group of points of purchase (in chains and non-chains, open markets, clubs, restaurants and bars, train and bus stations, airports, fitness and business centers, and other places people go to relax and spend time).

ROLE OF MEDIA

Media and Advertising

Today, is the world of information and communication and several new technologies have been evolved in this aspect. In this cut throat competition where information and immediate reasonable and proactive action or decision decides the fate of a company, product, person or system it becomes prerequisite to be informed and knowledgeable. Media works as a mediator or platform to exchange information, knowledge and make people as (consumers) aware of all if about of the market .Thus media serves as a catalyst, transformer and a information support system to disseminate , filter and collect feedback or response about all events thus spreading awareness and thus making things happen.

Right management approach and effective leadership style are the two major success indicator and determiner which can be judiciously used only if a right medium is selected. Reverence of media acts as the widest platform and most accessible medium for expanding horizon for information dissemination.

Role of Media in the Society

In order to make fast money channels are utilizing their usage in a wrong manner. The channels of media have crossed their limits and have broken all the barriers for the benefit of the society. They have no respect for the sentiments and ethics of the people and land whom they serve to, with their immense power to influence the masses they just make judgment like a true dictator rather than a good advice of a true friend as they previously used to do. If it will be going in the future then we people have to think about the role of media in our life.

Defining Advertising: - Advertising is the most widely used method of sales promotion used by the companies. It is used by the promoters to make the consumer aware about their products and services. Many advertisements are also designed to generate increased consumption of those products and services through the creation and reinforcement of brand image and brand loyalty. For these purposes advertisements often contain both factual information and persuasive messages. Every major medium is used to deliver these messages, including: television, radio, movies, magazines, newspapers, video games, the Internet , and billboards. Advertising is often placed by an advertising agency on behalf of a company.

Advertisements are usually placed anywhere an audience can easily and/or frequently access visuals and/or audio and print like the walls of walkways, sides of buses, seats of grocery cart etc.

Thus the role of media in advertising becomes very crucial and significant where it acts as lifeblood in increasing chances of success. Organizations which frequently spend large sums of money on advertising but do not strictly sell a product or service to the general public include: political parties, interest groups, religion-supporting organizations, and militaries looking for new recruits. Additionally, some non-profit organizations are not typical advertising clients and rely upon free channels, such as public service announcements.

Investment in advertising sector has lead to a drastic increase. In the United States alone in 2006, spending on advertising reached $155 billion, reported TNS Media Intelligence. That same year, according to a report titled Global Entertainment and Media Outlook:

2006-2010 issued by global accounting firm PricewaterhouseCoopers, worldwide advertising spending was $385 billion. The accounting firm's report projected worldwide advertisement spending to exceed half-a-trillion dollars by 2010.

Advertising essential in every field for economy growth of our sectors but this should not be on the social cost, advertising should be done considery the society at first. Unsolicited Commercial E-mail and other forms of span have become so prevalent as to have become a major nuisance to users of these services, as well as being a financial burden on internet service providers. Advertising is increasingly invading public spaces, such as schools, which some critics argue is a form of child exploitation.

Multi- usage of media in varied type of advertising :- Different forms of media are been widely used for advertising different product , services to make it customer friendly and useful. The different types of advertising can be–

Sponsorship - Sponsorship is advertising that seeks to establish a deeper association and integration between an advertiser and a publisher. The most common forms of sponsorship are content sponsorship, such as sponsored supplements, columns, micro sites, and event sponsorship.

Recruitment advertising - All jobs advertising are termed as requirement advertising, it appears in the range of Guardian recruitment supplements and on guardian.co.uk/jobs.

Inserts advertising -Insert advertising is brand, product or service advertising that, rather than appearing on the page of the newspaper, takes the form of loose inserts, bound-in inserts, tip-ons, product inserts such as chocolate bars, or sponsored polybags containing an onset such as CD, DVD or special booklet.

Display advertising -Display advertising is brand, product or service advertising that appears in various sizes and positions throughout all sections of the newspapers and on all channels of the website.

Internet advertising - Guardian Unlimited offers a wide range of online advertising solutions from established formats, such as banners, buttons, skyscrapers and overlays, to micro site sponsorship and innovative targeting techniques such as surround sessions and behavioral targeting.

Classified advertising - Classified advertising is product or service advertising that appears in specific sections of the newspapers under headings classifying the product or service being offered i.e. travel, lifestyle, and entertainment.

Role of media in advertising: - The involvement of media is of great relevance in advertising it help the companies to approach a maximum number consumers and make them aware about cation products and services, It help in not only market expansion and leadership but also in making products services or systems to be popularized and known. It works as a profitability indicator and the feedback received helps in further decision making, forecasting and in making business strategies for future promotion.

Media helps in gaining and retaining attention of people as prospective customers thus creating a relationship and a bond by touching the emotional or the need front through alluring commercials and above all it is the strongest medium for mass marketing

It serves as a Global tool for accessing people throughout the globe and making the chances of profitability fast and minimizes the risk factor.

Regime of good advertisement:-

- It should be able to draw attention
- Demonstrate an advantage
- Prove an advantage

Social Media Marketing :- An added advantage

Social media marketing is the process of promoting your site or business through social media channels and it is a powerful strategy that will get you links, attention and massive amounts of traffic. Social media marketing termed as social influence marketing is the act of using social influencers, social media platforms, online communities for marketing, public relations and customer service. Common social media marketing tools include Twitter, blogs, LinkedIn, Facebook, Flickr and YouTube.

There is no other low-cost promotional method out there that will easily give you large numbers of visitors, some of whom may come back to your website again and again.

If you are selling products/services or just publishing content for ad revenue, social media marketing is a potent method that will make your site profitable over time.

Those who ignore the efficacy of social media usually fall into three categories; the ones who don't know much or anything about social media, the ones who are interested but don't know how to use it and those who don't believe in the value that a social media strategy can bring to any site or business.

Regime of Media Planning

In marketing strategy media planning played a vital role. That is why marketing strategy move further after considering the important prospects of media planning. Media planning on the whole answers a lot of questions like "How many prospects do I need to Reach?". "In which medium should I place the Ads?", etc.

The target customers or audience must be specifically stated while deciding a media strategy.

- Target audience and advertisement must be compatible each other.
  - Kind of argumentation, esthetics, used language etc.
  - Appropriate prominent endorsers (e.g., Shah Rukh Khan for Pepsi)
- Through advertising a large scale of customers audience can be approached by the company, e.g., Increase product sales in group 14-29, Increase brand awareness and the image in group 30+
- Reaching target audiences by mass media advertising means: matching.
  - Target audience of advertisement and]
  - (Factual) audience of vehicle

To increase the value derived by the advertiser, the intersection 'B' should be increased by identifying the target audience of the brand and the audience reached by the brand.

The Value of Marketing through Social News Websites

Social media websites played a vital role in advertising but still some of the people don't agree with this view, so in order to make them understand lets consider the advantages of essence social media websites in advertising.

Developing link baits and successfully getting it popular on various social media websites like Digg and Stumble Upon will lead to multiple benefits for any website:

* **Primary and Secondary Traffic**. Primary traffic is the large amount of visitors who come directly from social media websites. Secondary traffic is referral traffic from websites which link to and send you visitors, after they come across your content through the social sites.

* **High Quality Links.** Becoming popular on social news websites like Digg or Reddit will get you a large number of links, some of which may be topically relevant, some not. A good story can realistically acquire a large number of high quality editorial links, most of which cannot be easily bought.

Benefits of Social Media Marketing

There are some reasons why one should consider using social media:

a. Natural. Not only do we get natural links without any discernible pattern, website is exposed to large groups of people in a spontaneous fashion. This differs from paid advertising which has overt commercial overtones.

b. Higher returns on lower cost. If done by yourself, costs are limited to only time and perhaps the expenses involved in hiring a freelance programmer/designer. The benefits will often exceed the cost. It would take you thousands of dollars to buy many links; social media has the ability to give you that for free.

c. Defensible. Once successfully mastered, social communities can be a great source of web traffic on top of any traffic you are already receiving from search engines. While you can't easily increase your search engine traffic, social media traffic can be very easily controlled through strategic marketing.

d. Complements other efforts. Social media optimization and marketing is usually community-specific. It doesn't interfere with any other methods of getting traffic to your website. It can and will fit perfectly with an advertising campaign targeting other websites or search engines.

Channels of Media in Advertising

The several kinds of media used in Advertising can be categorized in following:

Niche Media: Cable TV, Direct mail, etc. Reach the target audience with specific demographics, narrowly defined target audience.

Non-Conventional Media: Internet.

Traditional Mass Media: The traditional mass media based on the idea of approaching a vast audience or consumers. This includes channels of media includes Tv, Radio, etc.

Regime of Media Planning

One of the most important aspect for any organization in its marketing strategies is the media planning, i.e., through which medium it will advertise its product and approach its customers. Therefore, marketing considerations must precede Media Planning. Media planning on the whole answers a lot of questions like "How many prospects do I need to Reach?". "In which medium should I place the Ads?", etc.

In the media strategy the target audience must be defined more clearly and thoroughly.

- Target audience and advertisement must be compatible each other.
  - — Kind of argumentation, esthetics, used language etc.
  - — Appropriate prominent endorsers (e.g., Shah Rukh Khan for Pepsi)
- Advertising might communicate to different target audiences with different objectives, e.g., Increase product sales in group 14-29, Increase brand awareness and image in group 30+
- Reaching target audiences
  - — Target audience of advertisement and
  - — (Factual) audience of vehicle

Other essentials where media helps are –

1) Reach 2) Frequency 3) Continuity

The two most basic words in Media Planning are:

* **Medium**: A medium is of great relevance in advertising, its because only through these medium advertising can be a large scale. It is a broad general category of carries such as Newspapers, Television, Radio, Internet, Outdoor, Direct Mail, etc.

* **Vehicle**: It is a specific carrier within a Media category. So a Zee TV would be the vehicle in the category of TV. Many a time a specific programs or sections within a medium may be termed as a vehicle. For example, a "Kyunki saas bhi.." on Star Plus would be the vehicle in the Television category.

Consequences of Advertising

Advertising should not be done by the organization or companies in the social cost. Sometime it might have happen that these advertisement convey negative information or wrong impression on the something like this happen, then the company must withdraw from such information block these displayed.

This behavior makes the editors of the media self-censor content that might upset their ad payers. The bigger the companies are, the bigger their relation becomes, maximizing control over a single piece of information.

Advertisers may try to minimize information about or from consumer groups, consumer-controlled purchasing initiatives (as joint purchase systems), or consumer-controlled quality information systems.

Another indirect effect of advertising is to modify the nature of the communication media where it is shown. Media that get most of their revenues from publicity try to make their medium a good place for communicating ads before anything else. The clearest example is television, where broadcasters try to make the public stay for a long time in a mental state that encourages spectators not to switch the channel during advertisements. Programs that are low in mental stimulus require light concentration and are varied best for long sitting times. These also make for much easier emotional transition to ads, which are occasionally more entertaining than the regular shows. A simple way to understand objectives in television programming is to compare the content of programs paid for and chosen by the viewer with those on channels that get their income mainly from advertisements.

Role of usage of Media: -Advertising is expanding its legs over all the sectors of the economy. On the same way role and is also increasing in advertising. Companies are using media for effective advertising of their products. In the US many communities believe that many forms of outdoor advertising blight the public realm As long ago as the 1960s in the US there were attempts to ban billboard advertising in the open countryside. Cities such as São Paulo have introduced an outright ban with the UK capital also having specific legislation to control unlawful displays.

There have been increasing efforts to protect the public interest by regulating the content and the influence of advertising. Some examples are: the ban on television tobacco advertising imposed in many countries, and the total ban of advertising to children under twelve imposed by the Swedish government in 1991. Though that regulation continues in effect for broadcasts originating within the country, it has been weakened by the European Court of Justice, which had found that Sweden was obliged to accept foreign programming, including those from neighboring countries or via satellite.

Children got much influenced by the advertising so, recently in this view point, a vigorous discussion was made in Europe that how advertising for children should be regulated. This debate was exacerbated by a report released by the Kaiser Family Foundation in February 2004 which suggested that food advertising targeting children was an important factor in the epidemic of childhood obesity in the United States of America.

In many countries - namely New Zealand, South Africa, Canada, and many European countries - the advertising industry operates a system of self-regulation. Advertisers, advertising agencies and the media agree on a code of advertising standards that they attempt to uphold. The general aim of such codes is to ensure that any advertising is 'legal, decent, honest and truthful'. Some self-regulatory organizations are funded by the industry, but remain independent, with the intent of upholding the standards or codes (like the Advertising Standards Authority in the UK).

Naturally, many advertisers view governmental regulation or even self-regulation as intrusion of their freedom of speech or a necessary evil. Therefore, they employ a wide-variety of linguistic devices to bypass regulatory laws (e.g. printing English words in bold and French translations in fine print to deal with the Article 12 of the 1994 Toubon Law limiting the use of English in French advertising); see Bhatia and Ritchie 2006:542. The advertisement of controversial products such as cigarettes and condoms is subject to government regulation in many countries. For instance, the tobacco industry is required by law in most countries to display warnings cautioning consumers about the health hazards of their products. Linguistic variation is often used by advertisers as a creative device to reduce the impact of such requirements

Conclusion - After going through a long discussion over role of media in advertising, one can easily conclude that media helps to approach a huge target audience. It also help in developing an emotional bonding between the producer and consumer of a product or service. It helps in making people as consumers informative and knowledgeable about the diversity in product availability or in making them the right choosers. But what is important is to regulate and to have proper checks on the right usage of media in promoting the filtered and the authentic information so as the right purpose of media in making people aware and judicious can be achieved.

Role of Media

Step 1—In order to understand the market plan of any organization or a company one should preferably understand the four important role of media advertising..

Step 2—Role number 1: To help your business build market equity. This is the front of mind awareness or dominance in the marketplace. An example is thinking about the term "pizza"...doesn't Dominoes come to mind first?

Step 3—Role number 2: Through media advertising company can rate itself after in the market place. This is how your consumer perceives your product (i.e. high priced, highest quality, etc...).

Step 4—Role number 3: Advertising can create a sense of immediacy and urgency in attracting people to your business. This gives them a reason to visit today, but not necessarily a reason to buy today.

Step 5—Role number 4: Media Advertising can help educate your consumer to the benefits of your product or service. However most advertising is "institutional" in nature, and therefor unproductive in an overall marketing plan unless combined with other marketing strategies.

Step 6—Several channels of media advertising includes newspaper, television, radio, magazines, etc., but now it can also be done through online, i.e., internet advertising.

Case Study

Note : knowing more about "Decision and Methods in Media" reader can study documentation process of Microsoft company by visiting their site : www.members.microsoft.com

11

Advertising in Marketing Mix

This chapter includes the key concepts that are described below:-

- Marketing Concept
- Marketing Strategy
- Marketing in Practice
- Marketing Plan
- Role of Advertising in Marketing Mix
- Marketing Public Relation (MPR)
- Marketing Effectiveness
- Marketing Situation Analysis

MARKETING CONCEPT

Marketing was defined by the American Marketing Association as "thde performation of business activities that direct the flow of goods and services from producer to consumer or user." However, marketing is much more than the mere physical movement of goods from the points of production to consumer outlets. The key marketing functions include distribution, promotion, selling and standardisation, financing of marketing inputs, risk bearing and also gathering of market information. These activities blended together constitue marketing as it is practised in a competitive marketing environment.

A more recent definition of the term probably better reflects the broad-ranging scope of marketing :

Merketing is a total system of interacting business activities designed to plan, price, promote and distribute want-sattisfying products and services to present and potential customers.

MARKETING STRATEGY

The concept of marketing in an organization around the profitable satisfaction of customer needs has helped firms to get success in high-growth. A marketing strategy is a process that can allow an organization to concentrate its limited resources on the greatest opportunities to increase sales and achieve a sustainable competitive advantage. A marketing strategy should be centered around the key concept that customer satisfaction is the main goal. Marketing has a great role in advertising.

Key part of the general Corporate Strategy

If an organization wants to be successful in markets in which economic growth has leveled and in which there exist many competitors who follow the marketing concept, a well-developed marketing strategy is required. A marketing strategy is a written plan which combines product development, promotion, distribution, and pricing approach, identifies the firm's marketing goals, and explains how they will be achieved within a stated timeframe. Marketing strategy determines the choice of target market segment, positioning, marketing mix, and allocation of resources. It is most effective when it is an integral component of firm strategy, defining how the organization will successfully engage customers, prospects, and competitors in the market arena. Corporate strategies, corporate missions, and corporate goals. As the customer constitutes the source of a company's revenue, marketing strategy is closely linked with sales. A key component of marketing strategy is often to keep marketing in line with a company's overarching mission statement.

Following are the basic theory of marketing strategy:

- Target Audience
- Proposition/Key Element
- Implementation

Methods and Tricks in Marketing strategy

A marketing strategy can serve as the foundation of a marketing plan. A marketing plan contains a set of specific actions required to successfully implement a marketing strategy. Such a strategy considers a portfolio of products and takes into account the anticipated moves of competitors in the market.

A strategy consists of a well thought out series of tricks and tactics to make a marketing plan more effective. Marketing strategies serve as the fundamental underpinning of marketing plans which are designed to fill market needs and reach marketing objectives. Plans and objectives are usually tested for measurable results.

A marketing strategy frequently integrates goals, policies, and action sequences (tactics) of an organization's marketing into a cohesive whole. Similarly, the various strands of the strategy , which might include advertising, channel marketing, internet marketing, promotion and public relations can be orchestrated. Many companies cascade a strategy throughout an organization, by creating strategy tactics that then become strategy goals for the next level or group. Each one group is expected to take that strategy goal and develop a set of tactics to achieve that goal. This is why it is important to make each strategy goal measurable. Marketing strategies are dynamic and interactive. They are partially planned and partially unplanned. There are always some tricks which helps an organization to get benefited. There is also a trick including the use of low cost product which are needed to attract the customers and once an organization has established a relationship with consumers through the low cost product, then an organization will sell additional higher margin products and services.

Types of Strategies

Marketing strategies may differ depending on the unique situation of the individual business. However there are numerous methods of categorizing some generic strategies. A brief description of the most common categorizing schemes is presented below:

- Strategies based on market dominance - In this scheme, firms are classified on the basis of their market share or dominance of an industry. Typically there are three types of market dominance strategies:
    - Leader
    - Challenger
    - Follower
- Porter generic strategies – Porter generic strategy are defined as strategy on the dimensions of strategic scope and strategic strength. Strategic scope generally refers to the market

penetration while strategic strength refers to sustainable competitive advantage of the firm. The generic strategy framework (porter 1984) consists of two alternatives each with two alternative scopes. These are *Differentiation* and *low-cost leadership* each with a dimension of *Focus*-broad or narrow.

- o Product differentiation
- o Market segmentation

- Innovation strategies - Innovation strategies deals with rate of the new product development of the firm and business model innovation. It asks whether the company is on the cutting edge of technology and business innovation. There are three types of Innovation strategies:
  - o Pioneers
  - o Close followers
  - o Late followers
- Growth strategies - In this scheme we ask the question, "How should the firm grow?". There are a number of several methods of answering that question, but the most common gives four answers:
  - o Horizontal integration
  - o Vertical integration
  - o Diversification
  - o Intensification

  A more detailed scheme uses the categories:
- Prospector
- Analyzer
- Defender
- Reactor
- Marketing warfare strategies - This scheme draws parallels between marketing strategies and military strategies.

There is not only particular of project strategic planning model for each organization. Each organization ends up the developing it own nature and model of strategic manning frequently selecting a model and modifying it as they go along in developing their own planning process.

Several marketing strategy concepts:

- Competitors have certain strengths and abilities. To succeed, a firm must leverage its own unique abilities.
- Price / Selling Effort Strategies: A firm that follows a skimming strategy seeks to be the first to introduce a product with very good performance, selling it to the innovator market segment and charging a premium price for it. It makes as much profit as possible, then moves on when the competition arrives. The price is likely to fall over time as competition is encountered. Such a skimming strategy contrasts with a penetrating strategy, which seeks to gain market share by sacrificing short-term profits, and increasing the price over time as market share is gained.
- The probable response to actions of a firm's should be considered carefully.
- A firm should prepare defensive strategies before potential threats arrive. If the competition surprises a firm with the introduction of a vastly superior product, the firm should resist the temptation to proceed with its mediocre product. A firm never should introduce a product that is obsolete when it hits the market.

Strategic Models

Marketing participants employs strategic models and tools to analyze marketing decisions. When beginning a strategic analysis, the 3Cs can be employed to get a broad understanding of the strategic environment. An Ansoff Matrix is also often used to convey an organization's strategic positioning of their marketing mix. The 4Ps can then be utilized to form a marketing plan to pursue a defined strategy.

The following models provide a range of alternatives from which organizations might select an approach and begin to develop their own strategic planning process. Note that an organization might choose to integrate the models, e.g., using a scenario model to creatively identify strategic issues and goals, and then an issues-based model to carefully strategize to address the issues and reach the goals.

The following models include: "basic" strategic planning, issue-based (or goal-based), alignment, scenario, and organic planning.

Model One - "Basic" Strategic Planning

The first model includes in strategic models are basic strategic planning. This is very basic process is typically followed by organizations that are extremely small, busy, and have not done much strategic planning before. The process might be implemented in year one of the nonprofit to get a sense of how planning is conducted, and then embellished in later years with more planning phases and activities to ensure well-rounded direction for the nonprofit. Planning is usually carried out by top-level management. The basic strategic planning process includes some steps which are following below:

Step 1. Identify your purpose (mission statement) - This is called as mission statement, it is the statement(s) that describes why your organization exists, i.e., its basic purpose. The statement should describe what client needs are intended to be met and with what services, the type of communities are sometimes mentioned. The top-level management should develop and agree on the mission statement. The statements will change somewhat over the years.

Step 2. Select the goals your organization must reach if it is to accomplish your mission – This is the second step basic strategic planning model. Goals are general statements about what you need to accomplish to meet your purpose, or mission, and address major issues facing the organization.

Step 3. Identify specific approaches or strategies that must be implemented to reach each goal - The strategies are often what change the most as the organization eventually conducts more robust strategic planning, specifically by more closely examining the external and internal environments of the organization.

Step 4. Identify specific action plans to implement each strategy - These are the specific activities that each major function (for example, department, etc.) must undertake to ensure it's effectively implementing each strategy. Objectives should be clearly worded to the extent that people can assess if the objectives have been met or not. Ideally, the top management develops specific committees that each have a work plan, or set of objectives.

Step 5. Monitor and update the plan - Planners regularly reflect on the extent to which the goals are being met and whether action plans are being implemented. Perhaps the most important indicator of success of the organization is positive feedback from the organization's customers.

Note that organizations following this planning approach that may want to further conduct step 3 above to the extent that additional goals are identified to further developing the central operations or administration of the organization, e.g., strengthen financial management.

Model Two - Issue-Based Planning

Second model is issue based planning, it is also known as goal based planning. Organizations that begin with the "basic" planning approach described above, that frequently evolve to using this more comprehensive and more effective type of planning. The following table depicts a rather straightforward view of this type of planning process. That an organization may not do all of the following activities every year.

- External/internal assessment is used to identify "SWOT" (Strengths and Weaknesses and Opportunities and Threats)
- Strategic analysis is used to identify and prioritize all major issues/goals
- Design major strategies or programs to address issues/goals
- Design/update vision, mission and values that some organizations may do this first in planning
- Establish action plans including objectives, resource needs, roles and responsibilities for implementation
- Record issues, goals, strategies/programs, updated mission and vision, and action plans in a Strategic Plan document, and attach SWOT, etc.
- Develop the yearly Operating Plan document from year one of the multi-year strategic plan
- Develop and authorize Budget for year one includes the allocation of funds which are needed to fund year one
- Conduct the organization's year-one operations
- Monitor/review/evaluate/update Strategic Plan document

Model Three - Alignment Model

Third model of strategic model is Alignment model which is used to ensure strong alignment among the mission of an organization.

The major objective of the model is to ensure strong alignment among the organization's mission and its resources to effectively operate the organization. This model is useful for organizations that need to fine-tune strategies or find out why they are not working. An organization might also choose this model if it is experiencing a large number of issues around internal efficiencies. Alignment model includes some steps which are following:

- The planning group outlines the organization's mission, programs, resources, and needed support.
- Identify what's working well and what needs adjustment.
- Identify how these adjustments should be made.
- Include the adjustments as strategies in the strategic plan.

Model Four-Scenario Planning

Fourth strategic model is scenario planning. This approach might be used in conjunction with other models to ensure planners truly undertake strategic thinking. The model may be useful, specifically in identifying strategic issues and goals.

Select various external forces and imagine related changes which might influence the organization, e.g., change in regulations, demographic changes, etc. Scanning the newspaper for key headlines frequently suggests potential changes that might effect the organization.

For each change in a force, discuss three distinct future organizational scenarios including best case, worst case, and OK/ reasonable case which might arise with the organization as a conclusion of each change. Reviewing the worst-case scenario often provokes strong motivation to change the organization.

Suggest what the organization might do, or potential strategies, in each of the three scenarios to respond to each change.

Planners soon detect common considerations or strategies that must be addressed to respond to possible external changes.

Select the most likely external changes to effect the organization, e.g., over the next three to five years, and identify the most reasonable strategies the organization can undertake to respond to the change.

Model Five-Organic Planning

Fifth strategic model is organic planning which is also called

Self-organizing process. Traditional strategic planning processes are sometimes considered as "mechanistic" or "linear," i.e., they're rather general-to-specific or cause-and-effect in nature. For example, the processes often begin by conducting a broad assessment of the external and internal environments of the organization, conducting a strategic analysis ("SWOT" analysis), narrowing down to identifying and prioritizing issues, and then developing specific strategies to address the specific issues.

Another view of planning is similar to the development of an organism, i.e., an "organic," self-organizing process. some cultures, e.g., Native American Indians, might prefer unfolding and naturalistic "organic" planning processes more than the traditional mechanistic, linear processes. Self-organizing needs continual reference to common values, dialoguing around these values, and continued shared reflection around the systems current processes. Following are the general steps of marketing organic planning model of:-

Step 1. Clarify and articulate the organization's cultural values. Use dialogue and story-boarding techniques.

Step 2. Articulate the group's vision for the organization. Use dialogue and story-boarding techniques.

Step 3. On an ongoing basis, e.g., once every quarter, dialogue about what processes are needed to arrive at the vision and what the group is going to do now about those processes.

Step 4. Continually remind yourself and others that this type of naturalistic planning is never really "over with," and that, rather, the group requires to learn to conduct its own values clarification, dialogue/reflection, and process updates.

Step 5. Be very and very patient.

Step 6. Focus on learning and less on method.

Step 7. Ask the group to reflect on how the organization will portray its strategic plans to stakeholders, etc., who often expect the "mechanistic, linear" plan formats.

Porter's Generic Strategies

Their strategies was proposed by Michaal porter who gives the concept that ultimately fall into two categories neurely cost advantage and differentiation.

If the primary determinant of a firm's profitability is the attractiveness of the industry in which it operates, an important secondary determinant is its position within that industry. Even though an industry may have below-average profitability, a firm that is optimally positioned can generate superior returns.

A firm positions itself by leveraging its strengths. Michael Porter has argued that a firm's strengths ultimately fall into one of two headings: cost advantage and differentiation. By applying these strengths in either a broad or narrow scope, three generic strategies result: *cost leadership*, *differentiation*, and *focus*. These strategies are applied at the business unit level. They are called generic strategies because they are not firm or industry dependent. There exists a view point that a generic strategy is not always best because within the same product customers of seek multi dimensionional satisfaction like a combination of quality, style, convenience and price.

Cost Leadership Strategy—This generic strategy calls for being the low cost producer in an industry for a given level of quality. The firm sells its products either at average industry prices to earn a profit higher than that of rivals, or below the average industry prices to gain market share. In the event of a price war, the firm can maintain some profitability while the competition suffers losses. Even without a price war, as the industry matures and prices decline, the firms that can produce more cheaply will remain profitable for a longer period of time. The cost leadership strategy usually targets a broad market.

Some of the ways that firms acquire cost advantages are by improving process efficiencies, gaining unique access to a large source of lower cost materials, making optimal outsourcing and vertical integration decisions, or avoiding some costs altogether. If competing firms are unable to lower their costs by a similar amount, the firm may be able to sustain a competitive advantage based on cost leadership. Numerous firms follows market which may be able to achieve lower cost product including in their segments.

Firms that succeed in cost leadership frequently have the following internal strengths:

- Access to the capital required to make a significant investment in production assets; this investment represents a barrier to entry that many firms may not overcome.
- Efficient distribution channels.

- High level of expertise in manufacturing process engineering.
- Skill in designing products for efficient manufacturing, for example, having a small component count to shorten the assembly process.

Differentiation Strategy—A differentiation strategy calls for the development of a product or service that offers unique attributes that are valued by customers and that customers perceive to be better than or different from the products of the competition. The value added by the uniqueness of the product may allow the firm to charge a premium price for it. The firm hopes that the higher price will more than cover the extra costs incurred in offering the unique product. Because of the product's unique attributes, if suppliers increase their prices the firm may be able to pass along the costs to its customers who cannot find substitute products easily.

Firms that succeed in a differentiation strategy often have the following internal strengths:

- Access to leading scientific research.
- Highly skilled and creative product development team.
- Strong sales team with the ability to successfully communicate the perceived strengths of the product.
- Corporate reputation for quality and innovation.

The risks which are associated with a differentiation strategy include imitation by competitors and changes in customer tastes. Additionally, several firms pursuing focus strategies may be able to achieve even greater differentiation in their market segments.

Focus Strategy—The focus strategy concentrates on a narrow segment and within that segment which attempts to get either a cost advantage or differentiation. The premise is that the needs of the group can be better serviced by focusing entirely on it. A firm using a focus strategy frequently enjoys a high degree of customer loyalty, and this entrenched loyalty discourages other firms from competing directly.

Due to their narrow market focus, firms pursuing a focus strategy which have lower volumes and therefore less bargaining power with their suppliers. However, firms pursuing a differentiation-focused strategy which may be able to pass higher costs on to customers since close substitute products do not exist. Perter argued that firms that are to proceed at multiple strategies to do so by creating separate business units for each strategy. Firms that succeed in a focus strategy are able to tailor a broad range of product development strengths to a relatively narrow market segment that they know very well.

Some risks of focus strategies include imitation and changes in the target segments. Furthermore, it may be fairly easy for a broad-market cost leader to adapt its product in order to compete directly. Finally, other focusers may be able to carve out sub-segments that they can serve even better.

MARKETING IN PRACTICE

The Consumer-Centric Business

There are a many companies especially those in the Consumer Package Goods (CPG) market that adopt the theory of running their business centered around Consumer, Shopper & Retailer needs. Their Marketing departments spend quality time looking for "Growth Opportunities" in their categories by identifying relevant insights (both mindsets and behaviors) on their target Consumers, Shoppers and retail partners. These Growth Opportunities emerge from changes in market trends, segment dynamics changing and also internal brand or operational business challenges.The Marketing team can then prioritize these Growth Opportunities and begin to develop strategies to exploit the opportunities that could include new or adapted products, services as well as changes to the 7Ps.

Real-life marketing initially revolves around the application of a great deal of common-sense; dealing with a limited number of factors, in an environment of imperfect information and limited resources complicated by uncertainty and tight timescales. Use of classical marketing techniques, in these circumstances, is inevitably partial and uneven.

MARKETING PLAN

A Marketing plan is a written document that details the necessary actions to achieve one or more marketing objectives. It can be for a product or service, a brand, or a product line. Marketing plans cover between one and five years.

A Marketing plan may be part of an overall business plan. Factors such as market penetrate, market share, profits margins, budgets, financial analysis, capital investment, government actions, demography changes and cultural trends are also addressed. Solid marketing strategy is the foundation of a well-written marketing plan. While a marketing plan contains a list of actions, a marketing plan without a sound strategic foundation is of little use. Concept of marketing planning addressed sometasks including generic strategic and strategies for pricing, distribution, promotion, advertising and segmented.

Marketing Planning Process

Mrketing process model was proposed by Philip kotler. It consists of five steps, beginning with the market and environment research. After fixing the targets and setting the strategies, they will be realised by the marketing mix in step 4. The last step in the process is the marketing controlling.

In most organizations, "strategic planning" is an annual process that typically covering just the year ahead. Occasionally, a few organizations may look at a practical plan which stretches three or more years ahead.

To be most effective, the plan has to be formalized, which commonly in written form, as a formal "marketing plan." The essence of the process is that it moves from the general to the specific; from the overall purposes of the organization down to the individual action plan for a part of one marketing program. It is also an interactive process, therefore, so that the draft output of each stage is checked to see what impact it has on the earlier stages - and is amended.

Components of Marketing Strategy

There are two major components to marketing strategy:

- how an enterprise will address the competitive marketplace
- how an will implement and support the day to day operations in an organization.

In today's very competitive market place a strategy that insures a consistent approach to offering your product or service in a way that will outsell the competition is critical. However, in concert with defining the marketing strategy you must also have a well defined methodology for the day to day process of implementing it. It is of little value to have a strategy if you lack either the resources or the expertise to implement it.

The marketing objectives commonly be based on financial objectives of an organization and converting these financial measurements into the related marketing measurement.

In the process of creating a marketing strategy you must consider many factors. Of those many factors, some are more important than others. Because each strategy must address some unique considerations, it is not reasonable to identify 'every' important factor at a generic level. However, many are common to all marketing strategies.

To begin the creation of strategy by deciding what are the overall objective of your enterprise should be. In general this falls into one of four categories:

- If the market is very attractive but your enterprise is one of the weaker ones in the industry you must concentrate on strengthening the enterprise, using your offering as a stepping stone toward this objective
- If the market is very attractive and your enterprise is one of the strongest in the industry you will want to invest your best resources in support of your offering.
- If the market is not especially attractive and your enterprise is one of the weaker ones in the industry you should promote this offering only if it supports a more profitable part of your business (for instance, if this segment completes a product line range) or if it absorbs some of the overhead costs of a more profitable segment. Otherwise, you should determine the most cost effective way to divest your enterprise of this offering.
- If the market is not especially attractive, but your enterprise is one of the strongest in the industry then an effective marketing and sales effort for your offering will be good for generating near term profits.

The financial step of any marketing planning process is to establish targets or standards so that progress can be monitored. Having selected the direction most advantages for the overall interests of the enterprise, the next step is to choose a strategy for the offering that will be most effective in the market.

A COST LEADERSHIP STRATEGY is based on the concept that you can produce and market a good quality product or service at a lower cost than your competitors. Cost leadership strategy commonly targets a broad market. These low costs should translate to profit margins that are higher than the industry average. Some of the conditions that should exist to support a cost leadership strategy include an on-going availability of operating capital, good process engineering skills, close management of labor, products designed for ease of manufacturing and low cost distribution. This is already discussed in this chapter previously.

A DIFFERENTIATION STRATEGY is one of creating a product or service that is perceived as being unique "throughout the industry". Differentiation strategy calls for the development of a product or service that offers unique attributes which are valued by customers. The emphasis can be on brand image, proprietary technology, special features, superior service, a strong distributor network or other aspects that might be particular to your industry. This uniqueness should also translate to profit margins that are higher than the industry average. In addition, some of the situations that should exist to support a differentiation strategy include strong marketing abilities, effective product engineering, creative personnel, the ability to perform basic research and a good reputation. This strategy is already discussed in this chapter previously.

A FOCUS STRATEGY may be the most sophisticated of the generic strategies, in that it is a more 'intense' form of either the cost leadership or differentiation strategy. Focus strategy is used in a firm to enjoy the high degree of customer loyalty and their loyalty discourages other firms. It is designed to address a "focused" segment of the marketplace, product form or cost management process and is commonly employed when it isn't appropriate to attempt an 'across the board' application of cost leadership or differentiation. It is based on the concept of serving a particular target in such an exceptional manner, that others cannot compete. Usually this means addressing a substantially smaller market segment than others in the industry, but due to minimal competition, profit margins can be very high.

ROLE OF ADVERTISING IN MARKETING MIX

B2B Branding

B2B Branding is different from B2C in some crucial ways, including the need to closely align corporate brands, divisional brands and product/service brands and to apply your brand standards to material often considered "informal" such as email and other electronic correspondence.

Product or Service

You should be thoroughly familiar with the factors that establish products/services as strong contenders in the marketplace. Because business customers are focused on creating shareholder value for themselves, the cost-saving or revenue-producing benefits of products and services are important to factor in throughout the product development and marketing cycles. Benefits the prospect will derive from use of offering. Factors to consider Product/service include:

- Impact on customer's business as measured by costs of trying out your offering, how quickly the customer can realize a return from their investment in your offering, how disruptive the introduction of your offering is to the customer's operations and the costs to switch to your offering.
- The extent to which common introduction problems can be avoided such as lack of adherence to industry standards, unavailability of materials, poor quality control, regulatory problems and the inability to explain the benefits of the offering to the prospect.
- Whether some or all of the technology for the offering is proprietary to the enterprise.
- The complexity of your offering as measured by the existence of standard interfaces, difficulty of installation, number of options, requirement for support devices, training and technical support and the requirement for complementary product interface.
- The extent to which the offering is differentiated from the competition.
- The potential for product obsolescence as affected by the enterprise's commitment to product development, the product's proximity to physical limits, the ongoing potential for product improvements, the ability of the enterprise to react to technological change and the likelihood of substitute solutions to the prospect's needs.

People (Target Market)

Quite often People refers to the target market for a business product or service is smaller and has more specialized needs reflective of a specific industry or niche. Regardless of the size of the target market, the business customer is making an organizational purchase decision and the dynamics of this, both procedurally and in terms of how they value what they are buying from you, differ dramatically from the consumer market. There may be multiple influencers on the purchase decision, which may also have to be marketed to, though they may not be members of the decision making unit.

Pricing

The business market can be convinced to pay premium prices more often than the consumer market if you know how to structure your pricing and payment terms well. This price premium is particularly achievable if you support it with a strong brand.

The overall offering goals and selecting the generic strategy that you must then decide on range of closely related operational strategies. One of these is how you will price the offering. A pricing strategy is mostly influenced by your requirement for net income and your objectives for long term market control. There are three basic strategies you can consider.

- A *Skimming Strategy* includes the concept that if your offering has enough differentiation to justify a high price and you desire quick cash and have minimal desires for significant market penetration and control, then you set your prices very high.
- A *Market Penetration Strategy* includes the concept that if near term income is not so critical and rapid market penetration for eventual market control is desired, then you set your prices very low.
- A *Comparable Pricing Strategy* includes the concept that if you are not the market leader in your industry then the leaders will most likely have created a 'price expectation' in the minds of the marketplace. In this case you can price your offering comparably to those of your competitors.

Promotion

To sell an offering you must effectively promote and advertise it. Promotion planning is relatively easy when you know the media, information seeking and decision making habits of your customer base, not to mention the vocabulary unique to their segment. Specific trade shows, analysts, publications, blogs and retail/wholesale outlets tend to be fairly common to each industry/product area. What this means is that once you figure it out for your industry/ product, the promotion plan almost writes itself (depending on your budget) but figuring it out can be a special skill and it takes time to build up experience in your specific field. Promotion techniques really heavily on marketing communications strategies.There are two basic promotion strategies, PUSH and PULL.

- The PUSH STRATEGY is used to maximizes the use of all available channels of distribution to "push" the offering into the marketplace. This commonly needs generous discounts to achieve the objective of giving the channels incentive to promote the offering, thus minimizing the need for advertising.
- The PULL STRATEGY needs direct interface with the end user of the offering. Use of channels of distribution is minimized during the first stages of promotion and a major commitment to advertising is needed. The major goal is to "pull" the prospects into the various channel outlets creating a demand the channels cannot ignore. There are many strategies for advertising an offering. These strategies includes:
- *Corporate advertising* When you have a range of offerings and your audience is fairly broad, it is frequently beneficial to promote your enterprise identity rather than a specific offering.
- *Product Benefits advertising* When you want to promote your offering without comparison to competitors, the product benefits ad is the correct approach. This is especially advantageous when you have introduced a new approach to solving a user need and comparison to the old approaches is not suitable.
- *Product Comparison advertising* In a market where your offering is one of several providing similar capabilities, if your offering stacks up well when comparing features then a product comparison ad can be advantageous.
- *Product Family advertising* If your offering is part of a group or family of offerings that can be of benefit to the customer as a set, then the product family ad can be of benefit.

Place (Sales and Distribution)

Place including sales and distribution. The importance of a

knowledgeable, experienced and effective direct (inside or outside) sales force is often critical in the business market. If you sell through distribution channels also, the number and type of sales forces can vary tremendously and your success as a marketer is highly dependent on their success. You must also select the distribution method(s) you will use to get the offering into the hands of the customer. These include:

- On-premise Sales includes the sale of your offering using a field sales organization that visits the facilities of prospect to make the sale.
- Direct Sales includes the sale of your offering using a direct, in-house sales organization that does all selling through the Internet, telephone or mail order contact.
- Wholesale Sales involves the sale of your offering using intermediaries or "middle-men" to distribute your product or service to the retailers.
- Self-service Retail Sales involves the sale of your offering using self service retail methods of distribution.
- Full-service Retail Sales involves the sale of your offering through a full service retail distribution channel.

Of course, making a decision about pricing, promotion and distribution is heavily influenced by some key factors in the industry and marketplace. These factors should be analyzed primarily to develop the strategy and then regularly monitored for changes. If any of them change substantially the strategy should be reevaluated.

Profit Potential

This is an analysis of the factors that could influence the potential for generating and maintaining profits over an extended period. Following are the factors to consider including:

- The intensity of competitive rivalry as measured by the size and number of competitors, limitations on exiting the market, differentiation between offerings and the rapidity of market growth.
- The availability of substitute solutions to the prospect's need.
- The freedom of the enterprise to make critical business decisions without undue influence from distributors, suppliers, unions, investors and other outside influences.

- The enterprise's ability to sustain its market position is determined by the potential for competitive imitation, resistance to inflation, ability to maintain high prices, the potential for product obsolescence and the 'learning curve' faced by the prospect.
- The prospect's bargaining power as measured by the ease of switching to an alternative, the cost to look at alternatives, the cost of the offering, the differentiation between your offering and the competition and the degree of the prospect's need.
- The ability of the enterprise to limit suppliers bargaining power.
- The enterprise's ability to construct entry barriers to competition such as the creation of high switching costs, gaining substantial benefit from economies of scale, exclusive access to or clogging of distribution channels and the ability to clearly differentiate your offering from the competition.
- Potential for competitive retaliation is based on the competitors resources, commitment to the industry, cash position and predictability as well as the status of the market.
- Market potential for new products considering market growth, prospect's need for your offering, the benefits of the offering, the number of barriers to immediate use, the credibility of the offering and the impact on the customer's daily operations

Cost To Enter Market

This is an analysis of the factors that will influence your costs to achieve significant market penetration. Factors to consider include:

- Access to low cost materials and effective production.
- Distribution effectiveness as measured by history of relations, the extent of channel utilization, financial stability, reputation, access to prospects and familiarity with your offering.
- Technological efforts likely to be successful as measured by the strength of the development organization.
- The complexity of introduction problems such as lack of adherence to industry standards, unavailability of materials, poor quality control, regulatory problems and the inability to explain the benefits of the offering to the prospect.

- The experience of your enterprise.
- The effectiveness of the enterprise infrastructure in terms of organization, recruiting capabilities, employee benefit programs, customer support facilities and logistical capabilities.
- The availability of adequate operating capital.
- Your marketing strength.

Customer Services—The strength of the customer service function has a strong influence on long term market success. Factors to consider include:

- Accessibility of service outlets for the customer.
- Experience of the Customer Service manager in the areas of similar offerings and customers, quality control, technical support, product documentation, sales and marketing.
- One or more factors that causes your customer support to stand out as unique in the eyes of the customer.
- The availability of technical support to service your offering after it is purchased.
- The reputation of the enterprise for customer service.

Environment

Environmental factors positively or negatively impact the industry and the market growth potential of your product/service. Following factors are including:

- Cultural trends includes cultural changes such as fashion trends and life style trends may or may not support your offering's penetration of the market
- Demographic changes are defined as Anticipated demographic changes may support or negatively impact the growth potential of your industry and market. This includes factors such as education, age, income and geographic location.
- Emerging technology includes various Technological changes that are occurring may or may not favor the actions of your enterprise.
- Government actions - Government actions (current or undeı consideration) can support or detract from your strategy. Consider subsidies, safety, efficacy and operational regulations,

licensing requirements, materials access restrictions and price controls.

Prospect

It is essential to understand the market segment(s) as defined by the prospect characteristics you have selected as the target for your offering. Factors to consider prospect include:

- Likelihood of adoption by the prospect is based on the criticality of the prospect's need, their attitude about change, the significance of the benefits, barriers that exist to incorporating the offering into daily usage and the credibility of the offering.
- The potential for market penetration involves whether you are selling to past customers or a new prospect, how aware the prospects are of what you are offering, competition, growth rate of the industry and demographics.
- The amount of time it will take the prospect to make a purchase decision is affected by the prospects confidence in your offering, the number and quality of competitive offerings, the number of people involved in the decision, the urgency of the need for your offering and the risk involved in making the purchase decision.
- The prospect's willingness to pay higher price because your offering provides a better solution to their problem.
- The prospect's willingness to pay for product value is determined by their knowledge of competitive pricing, their ability to pay and their need for characteristics such as quality, durability, reliability, ease of use, uniformity and dependability.

Strength of Enterprise

An honest appraisal of the strength of your enterprise is a critical factor in the development of your strategy. Following are factors to consider include:

- Freedom from having to deal with legal problems.
- The freedom of the enterprise to make critical business decisions without undue influence from distributors, suppliers, unions, creditors, investors and other outside influences.
- The adequacy of the enterprise's infrastructure in terms of organization, recruiting capabilities, employee benefit programs, customer support facilities and logistical capabilities.

- The enterprise's ability to construct entry barriers to competition such as the creation of high switching costs, gaining substantial benefit from economies of scale, exclusive access to or clogging of distribution channels and the ability to clearly differentiate your offering from the competition.
- The enterprise's ability to sustain its market position is determined by the potential for competitive imitation, resistance to inflation, ability to maintain high prices, the potential for product obsolescence and the 'learning curve' faced by the prospect.
- The prominence of the enterprise.
- The competence of the management team
- Enterprise capacity to be leader in low-cost production considering cost control infrastructure, cost of materials, economies of scale, management skills, availability of personnel and compatibility of manufacturing resources with offering requirements.

Development

A review of the strength and viability of the product/service development program will heavily influence the direction of your strategy. Factors to consider include:

- Adequacy and appropriateness of the development tools and equipment.
- Design specifications that are manageable.
- Personnel who understand the relevant technologies and are able to perform the tasks necessary to meet the development objectives.
- The strength of the development manager including experience with personnel management, current and new technologies, complex projects and the equipment and tools used by the development personnel.
- The necessary funding to achieve the development objectives.

Production

You should review your enterprise's production organization with respect to their ability to cost effectively produce products/ services. The following factors are considered:

- The necessary production personnel skill level and/or the enterprise's ability to hire or train qualified personnel.
- The ability of the enterprise to limit suppliers bargaining power.
- Adequate access to raw materials and sub-assembly production.
- The ability of the enterprise to control the quality of raw materials and production.
- Technology and production experience
- Economies of scale allowing the sharing of operations, sharing of production and the potential for vertical integration.
- The strength of production manager including experience with personnel management, current and new technologies, complex projects and the equipment and tools used by the manufacturing personnel.

Marketing/Sales

The marketing and sales organization is analyzed for its strengths and current activities. Factors to consider include:

- Sales capabilities including availability of personnel, quality of personnel, location of sales outlets, ability to generate sales leads, relationship with distributors, ability to demonstrate the benefits of the offering and necessary sales support capabilities.
- Sales promotion techniques such as trade allowances, special pricing and contests.
- The ability to generate good publicity as measured by past successes, contacts in the press, quality of promotional literature and market education capabilities.
- The appropriateness of the pricing of your offering as it relates to competition, price sensitivity of the prospect, prospect's familiarity with the offering and the current market life cycle stage.
- The effectiveness of your distribution channels as measured by history of relations, the extent of channel utilization, financial stability, reputation, access to prospects and familiarity with your offering.
- Advertising capabilities including media relationships,

advertising budget, past experience, how easily the offering can be advertised and commitment to advertising.

- Experience of Marketing/Sales manager including contacts in the industry (prospects, distribution channels, media), familiarity with advertising and promotion, personal selling capabilities, general management skills and a history of profit and loss responsibilities.

Performance Analysis

We describes three basic steps in the performance analysis process. These three steps are: data collection, data transformation, and data visualization. *Data collection* is the phenomenon by which data about program performance are obtained from an executing program. Data are generally collected in a file, either during or after execution, although in some situations it may be presented to the user in real time. Three basic data collection techniques can be following below:

- *Profiles* record the amount of time spent in different parts of a program. This information, though minimal, is often invaluable for highlighting performance problems. Profiles typically are gathered automatically.
- *Counters* record either frequencies of events or cumulative times. The insertion of counters may require some programmer intervention.
- *Event traces* record each occurrence of various specified events, thus typically producing a large amount of data. Traces can be produced either automatically or with programmer intervention.

The raw data produced by profiles, counters, or traces are rarely in the form required to answer performance questions. Hence, *data transformations* are applied, frequently with the goal of reducing total data volume. Transformations can be used to determine mean values or other higher-order statistics or to extract profile and counter data from traces. For example, a profile recording the time spent in each subroutine on each processor might be transformed to determine the mean time spent in each subroutine on each processor, and the standard deviation from this mean. Similarly, a trace can be processed to produce a histogram giving the distribution of message sizes. Each of the various performance tools described in subsequent sections incorporates some set of built-in transformations; more specialized transformation can also be coded by the programmer.

Parallel performance data are inherently multidimensional, consisting of execution times, communication costs, and so on, for multiple program components, on different processors, and for different problem sizes. Although data reduction techniques can be used in some situations to compress performance data to scalar values, it is often necessary to be able to explore the raw multidimensional data. As is well known in computational science and engineering, this process can benefit enormously from the use of *data visualization* techniques. Both conventional and more specialized display techniques can be applied to performance data.

Issues in Performance Analysis

A wide variety of data collection, transformation, and visualization tools are available. When selecting a tool for a specific task, the following issues should be considered:

Accuracy. In general, performance data obtained using sampling techniques are less accurate than data obtained by using counters or timers. In the case of timers, the accuracy of the clock must be taken into account.

Abstraction. A good performance tool allows data to be examined at a level of abstraction appropriate for the programming model of the parallel program. For example, when analyzing an execution trace from a message-passing program, we probably wish to see individual messages, particularly if they can be related to send and receive statements in the source program. However, this presentation is probably *not* appropriate when studying a data-parallel program, even if compilation generates a message-passing program. Instead, we would like to see communication costs related to data-parallel program statements.

Flexibility. A flexible tool can be extended easily to collect additional performance data or to provide different views of the same data. Flexibility and simplicity are often opposing requirements.

Intrusiveness. Unless a computer provides hardware support, performance data collection inevitably introduces some overhead. We need to be aware of this overhead and account for it when analyzing data.

Simplicity. The best tools in many circumstances are those that collect data automatically, with little or no programmer intervention, and that provide convenient analysis capabilities.

Sales Analysis—Most organizations track their sales results; or, in non-profit organizations for example, the number of clients. The more sophisticated track them in terms of 'sales variance' - the deviation from the target figures - which allows a more immediate picture of deviations to become evident.

'Micro-analysis', which is a nicely pseudo-scientific term for the normal management process of investigating detailed problems, then investigates the individual elements (individual products, sales territories, customers and so on) which are failing to meet targets.

Market Share Analysis—Few organizations track market share though it is often an important metric. Though absolute sales might grow in an expanding market, a firm's share of the market can decrease which bodes ill for future sales when the market starts to drop. Where such market share is tracked, there may be a number of aspects which will be followed:

- overall market share
- segment share - that in the specific, targeted segment
- relative share -in relation to the market leaders
- annual fluctuation rate of market share

Financial Analysis—The "bottom line" of marketing activities should at least in theory, be the net profit for all except non-profit organizations, where the comparable emphasis may be on remaining within budgeted costs. There are a number of separate performance figures and key ratios which need to be tracked:

- gross contribution<>net profit
- gross profit<>return on investment
- net contribution<>profit on sales

The above performance analyses concentrate on the quantitative measures which are directly related to short-term performance. But there are a number of indirect measures, essentially tracking customer attitudes, which can also indicate the organization's performance in terms of its longer-term marketing strengths and may accordingly be even more important indicators. Some useful measures are:

- market research - including customer panels (which are used to track changes over time)
- lost business - the orders which were lost because, for example, the stock was not available or the product did not meet the customer's exact requirements
- customer complaints - how many customers complain about the products or services, or the organization itself, and about what

Use of Marketing Plans

A formal written marketing plan is essential; in that it provides an unambiguous reference point for activities throughout the planning period. However, perhaps the most important benefit of these plans is the planning process itself. This typically offers a unique opportunity, a forum, for information-rich and productively focused discussions between the various managers involved. The plan, together with the associated discussions, then provides an agreed context for their subsequent management activities, even for those not described in the plan itself.

Budgets as Managerial Tools

The classic quantification of a marketing plan appears in the form of budgets. Because these are so rigorously quantified, they are particularly important. They should, thus, represent an unequivocal projection of actions and expected results. What is more, they should be capable of being monitored accurately; and, indeed, performance against budget is the main (regular) management review process.

The purpose of a marketing budget is, thus, to pull together all the revenues and costs involved in marketing into one comprehensive document. It is a managerial tool that balances what is needed to be spent against what can be afforded, and helps make choices about priorities. It is then used in monitoring performance in practice.

The marketing budget is usually the most powerful tool by which you think through the relationship between desired results and available means. Its starting point should be the marketing strategies and plans, which have already been formulated in the marketing plan itself; although, in practice, the two will run in parallel and will interact. At the very least, the rigorous, highly quantified, budgets may cause a rethink of some of the more optimistic elements of the plans.

MARKETING PUBLIC RELATION (MPR)

MPR is used to let the people who know about a product and a company. Of the four promotional mix options available to marketers public relations (PR) is probably the least understood and, consequently, often receives the least amount of attention. Many marketers see public relations as only handling rudimentary communication activities, such as issuing press releases and responding to questions from the news media.

But in reality, in a time when customers are inundated with thousands of promotional messages everyday, public relations offers powerful methods for cutting through the clutter.

Public relations involves the cultivation of favorable relations for organizations and products with its key publics through the use of a variety of communications channels and tools. Traditionally, this meant public relations professionals would work with members of the news media to build a favorable image by publicizing the organization or product through stories in print and broadcast media. But today the role of public relations is much broader and includes:

- building awareness and a favorable image for a company or client within stories and articles found in relevant media outlets
- closely monitoring numerous media channels for public comment about a company and its products
- managing crises that threaten company or product image
- building goodwill among an organization's target market through community, philanthropic and special programs and events

In this tutorial most of our focus is on how public relations supports marketing by building product and company image It is sometimes referred to as publicity. Yet, it should be noted that there are other stakeholders companies reached via the public relations function, such as employees and non-target market groups. Favorable media coverage about a company or product often reaches these audiences as well and may offer potential benefit to the marketer.

Finally, in most large companies, investor relations (IR) or financial public relations is a specialty in itself guided by specific disclosure regulations. However, coverage of this type of PR will not be provided here.

Marketing public relations is used to let people know about a product and a company. It is like advertising in that it pushes and promotes a product but it isn't done through traditional ways. Advertising is done through television, newspapers, billboards, and the mail. Marketing public relations is done through press releases and events like parties and basketball games.

Often times companies will issue statements to the press or public about a certain product or issue in the company. If the publicity is negative or positive from the public the statement will be about the good parts of the company and how it is trying to become a better company, through better waste management or not outsourcing to other countries.

Marketing public relations is often considered more credible than normal advertising. Sometimes advertisements can be misleading. They can't lie by law, but they are often misunderstood by the public or a product is made to seem better than it really is. Consumers tend to believe the news or the statements that come from high up in the company, rather than actors who are paid to tell how great a product is.

Going on a news broadcast is a way of MPR. By talking with a host, like on an early morning news show helps to promote the company. The audience sees the company representative up there and is told about the company directly from them. The representative is advertising the company and sometimes the product by being there and just talking with the host. It helps to familiarize a consumer with the company so they will either go check out the company or look around for more information. It also helps to make the image of the company better.

Marketing public relations is a way for companies to get their message out about a product or service, without having to pay for it. It is free for the companies and lets people know about the company and what they do.

Advantages of Public Relations

Public Relation is a management function that involves monitoring and evaluating public attitudes and maintaining mutual relations and understanding between an organization and its public. There are many advantages of Public Relations which help business in many ways. They are.

Avoidance of Clutter

Because they are typically perceived, as news items, PR messages are not subject to the clutter of ads. A story regarding a new product, introduction of break through is treated as a news item and is likely to receive attention.

Ability to reach specific groups

Because some products appeal to only small market segments, it is not feasible to engage in advertising and / or promotions to reach them. If the firm does not have the financial capabilities, to engage in promotional expenditures, the best way to communicate to these groups is through PR. Language barriers in different parts of India.

Cost

In both absolute and relative terms, the cost of PR is very low, especially when the possible effects are considered. While a firm can employ AD agencies and spend millions of dollars on AD, for smaller companies, this form of communication may be the most affordable alternative available.

Credibility

Because PR communications are not perceived in the same light as advertising – that is, the public does not realize the organization either directly or indirectly paid for them – they tend to have more credibility. The fact that the media are not being compensated for providing the information may lead receivers to consider the news more truthful and credible. For example, an article in newspapers or magazines discussing the virtues of aspirin may be perceived very much as more credible than an ad for a particular brand of aspirin.

Image Building

Effective PR helps to develop positive image for the organization. A strong image is insurance against later misfortunes.

Lead Generation

Information about the technological innovations, medical break-throughs and the like results almost immediately in a multitude of inquiries. These inquiries may give the firm some quality sales lead.

Finally, in many cases public relations objectives can be achieved at very low cost when compared to other promotional efforts. This is not to suggest public relations is not costly, it may be, especially when a marketer hires PR professionals to handle the work.

Disadvantages of PR systems

Most of the criticisms of PR in general are based around the tendency of PR systems to give rise to coalition governments and a fragmented party system. While PR holds many advantages for marketers, there are also concerns when using this promotional methods. Following are the disadvantages of PR systems:

- A destabilizing fragmentation of the party system. PR can reflect and facilitate a fragmentation of the party system. It is possible that extreme pluralism can allow tiny minority parties to hold larger parties to ransom in coalition negotiations. In this respect, the inclusiveness of PR is cited as a drawback of the system. In Israel, for example, extremist religious parties are often crucial to the formation of a government, while Italy endured many years of unstable shifting coalition governments. Democratizing countries are often fearful that PR will allow personality-based and ethnic-cleavage parties to proliferate in their undeveloped party systems.
- A platform for extremist parties. In a related argument, PR systems are often criticized for giving a stage in the legislature to extremist parties of the left or the right. It has been argued that the collapse of Weimar Germany was in part due to the way in which its PR electoral system gave a toehold to extremist groups of the extreme left and right.
- Coalition governments, which in turn lead to legislative gridlock and consequent inability to carry out coherent policies. There are particularly high risks during an immediate post-conflict transition period, when popular expectations of new governments are high. Quick and coherent decision making can be impeded by coalition cabinets and governments of national unity which are split by factions.

• Difficulties either for voters to understand or for the electoral administration to implement the sometimes complex rules of the system. Some PR systems are considered to be more difficult than non-PR systems and may require more voter education and training of poll workers to work successfully.

• The inability of the voter to enforce accountability by throwing a party out of power or a particular candidate out of office. Under a PR system, it may be very difficult to remove a reasonably-sized centre party from power. When governments are usually coalitions, some political parties are everpresent in government, despite weak electoral performances from time to time.

• Governing coalitions which have insufficient common ground in terms of either their policies or their support base. These coalitions of convenience are sometimes contrasted with coalitions of commitment produced by other systems (e.g. through the use of AV), in which parties tend to be reciprocally dependent on the votes of supporters of other parties for their election, and the coalition may thus be stronger.

• Small parties getting a disproportionately large amount of power. Large parties may be forced to form coalitions with much smaller parties, giving a party that has the support of only a small percentage of the votes the power to veto any proposal that comes from the larger parties.

Finally, in some areas of the world the impact of traditional news outlets is fading forcing public relations professionals to scramble to find new ways to reach their target markets.

Objectives of Public Relations

The objectives of public relations communications are usually designed by Public Relations planners. There are three basic dimensions in which these objectives are divided, consisting mainly of creating a strong sense of credibility, the effective delivery of information and the proper establishment of positive image of the organization. These dimensions contain further smaller goals that focus on prospects like creating a sound and concrete corporate brand, chiselling or repositioning the reputation of a corporation, redefining the positioning of an organization or any of its brands.

In addition to that, public relations also aims at shifting any specific brand of the organization to a new consumer market or even to a global market and even the launch of a product or brand is also provided aegis by public relations. Also when it comes to the prospect of giving and conveying news about the organization or any of its brand, public relations is a suitable tool to accomplish the respective goal.

Like other aspects of marketing promotion, public relations is used to address several broad objectives including:

- Building Product Awareness – When introducing a new product or relaunching an existing product, marketers can use a PR element that generates consumer attention and awareness through media placements and special events.
- Creating Interest – Whether a PR placement is a short product article or is included with other products in "round up" article, stories in the media can help entice a targeted audience to try the product.
- Providing Information – PR can be used to provide customers with more in depth information about products and services. Through articles, collateral materials, newsletters and websites, PR delivers information to customers that can help them gain understanding of the product.
- Stimulating Demand – A positive article in a newspaper, on a TV news show or mentioned on the Internet, often results in a discernable increase in product sales.
- Reinforcing the Brand – In many companies the public relations function is also involved with brand reinforcement by maintaining positive relationships with key audiences, and thereby aiding in building a strong image. Today it is ever more important for companies and brands to build a good image. A strong image helps the company build its business and it can help the company in times of crises as well.

Marketers should be aware of the tools used in the public relations function. While some marketers may prefer to handle their own PR tasks, many others will seek the assistance of outside PR professionals rather than attempt to handle these activities themselves. Skilled PR professionals offer many advantages for marketers with their two most important being:

1) their ability to understand and unearth good stories about a company and its product, and

2) their knowledge of the media market may place them in a better position to match stories to the news angles media reporters look for.

Most of the efforts chapters make in public relations are through forms of print media, primarily newspapers. These are usually the most visible outlets on college campuses, especially school newspapers, and in the local community.

Photographs is also the key tool for PR. They are generally two types of photographs in publicity portrait shots, where people pose for the camera and smile, and candids, where the subjects are doing something.

Whether handling PR internally or hiring professionals, marketers should be familiar with the tools available for public relations: Before choosing among the various tools marketers should begin by identifying their targeted audiences (e.g., target markets) and key messages they wish to send. These should align with the messages and audiences identified for the product being promoted or corporate goals for non-specific product promotions, such as corporate image promotions.

The key messages are used in the development of public relations materials and supporting programs described below. The purpose of key messages is to provide a consistent point of view over time and across numerous PR methods that reinforce product positioning (i.e., customer's perceptions) and reach the desired target audience.

MARKETING EFFECTIVENESS

Marketing effectiveness is defined as the quality of how marketers go to market with the goal of optimizing their spending to achieve good results for both the short-term and long-term. It is also related to Marketing ROI and Return on Marketing Investment (ROMI).

Dimensions of Marketing Effectiveness

Marketing effectiveness has four dimensions:

Corporate – Each company operates within certain bounds. These are determined by their size, their budget and their ability to make organizational change. Within these bounds marketers operate along the five factors described below.

Competitive – Each company in a category operates within a similar framework as described below. In an ideal world, marketers would have perfect information on how they act as well as how their competitors act. In reality, in many categories have reasonably good information through sources, such as, IRI or Nielsen. In many industries, competitive marketing information is hard to come by.

Customers/Consumers – Understanding and taking advantage of how customers make purchasing decisions can help marketers improve their marketing effectiveness. Groups of consumers act in similar ways leading to the need to segment them. Based on these segments, they make choices based on how they value the attributes of a product and the brand, in return for price paid for the product. Consumers build brand value through information. Information is received through many sources, such as, advertising, word-of-mouth and in the distribution channel often characterized with the purchase funnel, McKinsey & Company concept. Lastly, consumers consume and make purchase decisions in certain ways.

Exogenous Factors – There are many factors outside of our immediate control that can impact the effectiveness of our marketing activities. These can include the weather, interest rates, government regulations and many others. Understanding the impact these factors can have on our consumers can help us to design programs that can take advantage of these factors or mitigate the risk of these factors if they take place in the middle of our marketing campaigns.

Factors Affecting Marketing Effectiveness

There are five factors driving the level of marketing effectiveness that marketers can achieve:

1. Marketing Creative – Even without a change in strategy, better creative can improve results. Without a change in strategy, AFLAC was able to achieve stunning results with its introduction of the Duck (AFLAC) campaign. With the introduction of this new creative concept, the company growth rate soared from 12% prior to the campaign to 28% following it.

2. Marketing Execution – By improving how marketers go to market, they can achieve significantly greater results without changing their strategy or their creative execution. At the marketing mix level, marketers can improve their execution by making small changes in any or all of the 4-Ps (Product, Price, Place and

Promotion) (Marketing) without making changes to the strategic position or the creative execution marketers can improve their effectiveness and deliver increased revenue. At the program level marketers can improve their effectiveness by managing and executing each of their marketing campaigns better. It's commonly known that consistency of a Marketing Creative strategy across various media (e.g. TV, Radio, Print and Online), not just within each individual media message, can amplify and enhance impact of the overall marketing campaign effort. Additional examples would be improving direct mail through a better call-to-action or editing web site content to improve its organic search results, marketers can improve their marketing effectiveness for each type of program. A growing area of interest within Marketing Strategy and Execution are the more recent interaction dynamics of traditional marketing (e.g. TV or Events) with online consumer activity (e.g. Social Media).

3. Marketing Strategy – Improving marketing effectiveness can be achieved by employing a superior marketing strategy. By positioning the product or brand correctly, the product/brand will be more successful in the market than competitors' products/brands. Even with the best strategy, marketers must execute their programs properly to achieve extraordinary results.

4. Marketing Infrastructure–This is also known as Marketing Management) – Improving the business of marketing can lead to significant gains for the company. Management of agencies, budgeting, motivation and coordination of marketing activities can lead to improved competitiveness and improved results. The overall accountability for brand leadership and business results is often reflected in an organization under a title within a Brand management department.

5. Exogenous Factors - Generally out of the control of marketers external or exogenous factors also influence how marketers can improve their results. Taking advantage of seasonality, interests or the regulatory environment can help marketers improve their marketing effectiveness.

Criticism and defense of Marketing Effectiveness

The practice of marketing effectiveness is often criticized because it allegedly only focuses on short term revenue gains. When, in fact, by definition, it concentrates on marketing actions that can be taken to improve both short and long term results. Short term results improvements are measured in terms of revenue gains. Long term improvements are typically measured in terms of gains in brand equity in the minds of a company's customers.

MARKETING SITUATION ANALYSIS

The Marketing Situation Analysis requires significant investigation of the organizationýÿs products and services in relations to the current market, sales viability and opportunities to market company products or services, competitive considerations, success and failure of past marketing efforts, SWOT analysis, key resources available, etc. This investigation will require significant research, including utilizing interviews from key individuals inside and outside the company, online research, and, if budget permits, customer/ prospect surveys.

12

Mediums of Advertisement

This chapter includes various key concept which are described below:-

- The Newspapers
- Magazines
- Advantages of Magazines
- Mass Coverage
- Radio and TV
- Tabloids
- Point of Purchase
- Home Journals
- Postal Publicity
- Screen Advertising
- Transportation
- The Directory
- Standards of Advertising
- Rules and regulations
- Code of Ethics
- Committee Report in Advertising

THE NEWSPAPERS

The one of the major source or medium of advertising is newspaper. At this time, so many newspaper are published in various language. These are included in category of point media.

A newspaper is any material or document other than a book containing words printed or written. It is a daily or weekly publication which are containing news or comments on public news, also feature articles. Advertisers can make use of newspapers to deliver their product message to a large cross sections of the people. One of the forms of the print media is the newspaper, the oldest, largest and leading mass medium. It is a local as well as national advertising medium, having the ability to reach a some percentage of homes or prospects in a given area. In India newspapers are published both in English as well as in many regional languages. *The Times of India. Hindustan Times, Indian Express. Hindu* etc., have national circulations. Advertising messages in these papers reach a qualitatively selective audience composed largely of executives, employees, and educational institutions.

Like an advertising medium, various regional newspaper reach at large sections of the people. Regional language newspaper appeal to various special groups of scope rather than a national coverage.

The importance of a newspaper as an advertising medium is indicated by the number of publications registered by the Registrar of newspapers and by the amount of money invested in newspaper advertising. Today there are about 31,957 newspaper publications registered and more than 70 rupees out of every 100 rupees is spent on newspapers and magazine advertising. Newspapers may be classified as metropolitan comprising daily morning, evening, Sunday supplements, weekly newspapers, shopping news and specialized newspapers. Town and suburban weekly papers are more localized in circulation which contain largely local and personal news of the communities. The supplement is the hybrid medium within the newspaper. A variant form of Sunday supplement is the Sunday magazine supplement delivered to newspaper readers without collecting extra money.

Advantages of Newspaper

There are number of newspaper which have some advantages that are mention below:-

- A best medium for the local and retail advertiser.
- As many papers are in regional languages a target audience can be reached effectively.
- Inexpensive medium.
- They reach all classes of people.
- The advantage of selectivity is also there in newspapers.

- They combine news and advertisements.
- To test campaigns and check results newspapers can be effectively used.
- The best medium in cooperative advertising efforts.
- Newspaper advertising has another advantage, the advantage of flexibility to the advertiser.
- Newspapers are most suitable for tabloid inserts.
- Sunday supplements serve as a Sunday magazine.

Disadvantages of Newspaper

As there are some advantage, so there are also have some disadvantages which are mention below:-

- Newspapers have a very short life. Today's newspaper is a stale newspaper tomorrow.
- In a country like India where the percentage of illiteracy is high a newspaper is not an effective medium compared to broadcast media.
- More than 60 per cent of paper space is full of advertisements. A particular message may not attract the attention of the prospects hence the very purpose of a newspaper advertisement is buried.
- Newspapers are read hurriedly and the advertisements may not attract the readers.
- Newspapers are read usually once in a day and there is no memorizing value.
- There is considerable waste in circulation.
- Nowadays a newspaper has become expensive and many people are not purchasing.
- Special qualities of product or service which require use of special colors and mechanical treatments for which a newspaper is not suitable.
- Today broadcast media comprising a radio and television are more popular and attractive than print media.
- Selection of specific newspaper for the target audience is a difficult task. Sometimes three or more newspapers may have

to be used to publish the advertisements. Then it becomes expensive and wasteful.

- Newspaper is not placed at the first medium of advertising because of illiteracy and the advertisement in newspaper not attracts the readers.

MAGAZINES

Magazines are also known as Periodicals, it is the second form of advertising which has many advantages over newspaper. It is also a type of print media.

Periodicals differ widely from newspapers in quality as well as mechanical characteristics. They include dailies, weeklies, semi-monthlies, by-weeklies, by-monthlies, quarterlies, semi-annuals, seasonal, periodicals, annuals and any publications issued with definite periodicity. Periodicals sell space for commercial advertising which is generally sold in units such as full page, half page, quarter page and by the column, half column, quarter column etc. Advertisers who want to transmit a message to all kinds of communities prefer magazines. They have to pay advertising rates for space. The magazine appeals to specific kinds of people in all types of communities. Unlike a newspaper which has a short life, a magazine advertising may have more life and produce results for a week, fortnight, month, quarter, half year or year depending on the periodicity. The quality of the paper, volume, printing process, color appeal and in other respects magazines are superior to newspapers. Periodicals have national circulations commanding a general readership to a highly specialized audience. Magazines are a second publication medium. They provide both entertainment, education and information and meet the needs of several cross sections of society. There are several methods for classifying magazines. Classification can be made on the basis of size, type of readership, frequency of publication and generally in relation to special interest magazines. Consumer magazines, form publications, business publications, industrial publications, institutional magazines are some examples. The Magazine Publisher Association marketing division, U.S.A., is the advertising promotional arm of the industry.

Why Magazines Sell

There are some reasons by which magazines sell:

- *Authority:* Magazine authority dates back to man's very acceptance of the printed word as dependable.
- *Believability:* Magazine believability builds reader confidence. Its influence affects ideas.
- *Color:* Magazine color spreads before the reader a spectrum of exciting visual pleasure.
- *Efficiency:* The ability of magazines to offer the widest range of incorporable values which can be translated into dollar sales makes magazines the choice of leading advertisers.
- *Flexibility:* Magazines offer a full range of prospects.
- *Permanence:* Magazines last. People save them.
- *Selectivity:* Magazine selectivity targets places and people. It reaches your best prospects.

ADVANTAGES OF MAGAZINES

There are numerous advantages of magazines which are mention below:-

- A magazine is read in several sittings, advertisements get the attention of the readers.
- Magazines offer high selectivity.
- Magazines are attractive to the advertisers.
- High quality of paper is used, which permits application of colors and mechanical techniques.
- National coverage as well as local coverage are possible.
- English magazines have national coverage, local coverage is achieved through regional magazines and editions.
- Comparing newspapers, magazines have a longer life.
- They are supporting agents, prevail on local dealers.
- There are different magazines to suit different classes of people like women, farmers, students, etc., the message reaches wide cross sections.

Disadvantages of Magazines

If there are some advantages, so there also have some disadvantages which are described below:-

- Magazines do not appeal to all kinds of people, like newspapers.
- Advertisements take a long time that are depending upon the periodicity of the magazine, before appearance to the reader. Timely value is very limited.
- Magazine advertising is suitable only for a big concern but not appropriate for a local retailer.
- Waste circulation is bound to be there, in the absence of national distribution or lack of uniformity in the demand for the product.
- It serves geographical area which is limited.
- In one way, it is costly to advertise, due to copyright for different markets.
- They are not an instantaneous medium like radio and television.

MASS COVERAGE

A mass medium which provides a mass coverage. One of the media which effectively carries the product or service message to the mass audience. The budget on outdoor advertising is considerable. It includes transit advertising also. But for clarity both are studied here separately. Outdoor advertising may be defined as any advertisement message carried on an out of door structure which includes sky writing. There are wide range of outdoor media available such as hoardings, bulletin boards, information panels, bill boards, sign posters, directional maps and puppet shows. Also loud-speaker vans called mobile advertising, huge hand painted portraits, slide projections, state and national highways advertising, rail, bus and air terminals, painted boards and building walls, electric spectaculars, illuminated sky writing and wall displays. Outdoor advertising is the oldest and an important form of advertising medium. It serves the needs of both local and national advertisers.

Mass coverage is the type of outdoor advertising. Outdoor advertising is defined as any advertisement message which are carried on out of door structure that includes sky writing.

Increase in the numerous of vehicles, trains, buses, mobility of people, crowded centres, gatherings etc., have given rise to the importance of outdoor advertising. It is well suited as national medium. The advertiser has to buy space to advertise his product or service. The passer-by is easily attracted to took at it and read. It has a universal value and is a vastly used medium by the manufacturer. It consists of any message, models, sign, signboard, notice etc., used for the purpose of advertisement or announcement. Outdoor advertising is an effective communication medium specifically in India where the percentage of illiteracy is higher. It creates interest and awareness because it is accompanied by slogans, drawings and cartoons. It has widespread popular appeal and quality because posters and paintings are very catching owing to their size and color combination. The other advantages are durability, mass coverage, flexibility with regard to market copy, time etc.

RADIO AND TV

Radio: An Introduction

Radio is kind of advertising medium. Radio is also known as frequency modulation (FM). Radio is the transmission of signals by modulation of electromagnetic waves with frequencies below those of visible light. Electromagnetic radiation travels by means of oscillating electromagnetic fields that pass through the air and the vacuum of space. Information is carried by systematically changing (modulating) some property of the radiated waves, such as amplitude, frequency, or phase. When radio waves pass an electrical conductor, the oscillating fields induce an alternating current in the conductor. This can be detected and transformed into sound or other signals that carry information.

Radio is frequently refers to the actual transceiver device or chip, where as wireless refers to the system or method which are used for radio communication.

Processes of Radio : Radio systems are mostly used for communication. This type of communication will done with the help of elements. Each process is implemented by a variety of methods specialized for different communication purposes.

Each system contains a transmitter. This constitutes of a source of electrical energy, generating, alternating current of a desired frequency of oscillation. The transmitter contains a system to modulate (change) some property of the energy produced to impress a signal on it. This modulation might be as simple as turning the energy on and off, or altering more subtle properties such as amplitude, frequency, phase, or combinations of these properties.

The transmitter sends the modulated electrical energy to an antenna; this structure transforms the rapidly-changing alternating current into an electromagnetic wave that can move through free space.

Electromagnetic waves travel either directly or their path which are altered by refection, refraction or diffraction through space. Noise will usually alter the desired signal, this electromagnetic interference directly comes from natural sources as well as from artificial sources such as other transmitters and accidental radiators. Noise is also generated at every step due to the inherent properties of the devices used.

The electromagnetic wave is intercepted by a receiving the signals of antenna; this structure captures some of the energy of the wave and returns it to the form of oscillating electrical currents. At the receiver, these currents are demodulated, which is conversion to a usable signal form by a detector sub-system. The receiver is "tuned" to respond preferentially to the desired signals, and reject undesired signals.

Early radio systems which are relied entirely on the energy that are collected by an antenna to produce signals for the operator. Radio became more useful after the invention of electronic devices such as the vacuum tube and later the transistor, which made it possible to amplify weak signals. Today, radio systems are used for applications from walkie-talkie children's toys to the control of space vehicles, as well as for broadcasting, and many other applications.

Uses of Radio : Today, radio takes many forms which includes wireless networks and mobile communications of all types, as well as radio broadcasting. Before the invent of television, commercial radio broadcasts included not only news and music, but dramas, comedies, variety shows, and many other kinds of entertainment. Radio was unique among methods of dramatic presentation in that it used only sound. Radio was used to pass on entire orders and communication between armies and navies on both side, at the time of war.

Audio : Audio refers to AM radio Amplitude Modulation, in which the amplitude of the transmitted signal is made proportional to the sound amplitude captured by the microphone, while transmitted frequency remains constant.

FM broadcast radio sends music and voice with higher fidelity than AM radio. In frequency modulation, amplitude variation at the microphone causes the transmitter frequency to fluctuate. FM signal is not subject to static and interference in the same way as AM signals, because audio signal modulates the frequency and not the amplitude, due to its need for a wider bandwidth, FM is transmitted in the Very High Frequency (VHF, 30 MHz to 300 MHz) radio spectrum. VHF radio waves act more like light, traveling in straight lines; hence the reception range is generally limited to about 50-100 miles. During unusual upper atmospheric conditions, FM signals are occasionally reflected back towards the Earth by the ionosphere, resulting in long distance FM reception. FM receivers are subject to the capture effect, which causes the radio to only receive the strongest signal when multiple signals appear on the same frequency. FM receivers are relatively immune to lightning and spark interference.

Government area, police and commercial voice services also use narrowband FM on special frequencies. Early police radios used AM receivers to get one way dispatches.

Amateur Radio Service : Amateur radio are also known as "ham radio", is a hobby in which enthusiasts are licensed to communicate on numerous of bands in the radio frequency spectrum non-commercially and for their own enjoyment. They may also provide emergency and public service assistance. This has been very advantages in emergencies, saving lives in many instances Radio amateurs use a variety of modes, including nostalgic ones like Morse code and experimental ones like Low-Frequency Experimental Radio. Several forms of radio were pioneered by radio amateurs and later became commercially important including FM, single-sideband (SSB), AM, digital packet radio and satellite repeaters. Some amateur frequencies may be disrupted by power-line internet service.

Data or Digital Radio : Most new radio system are digital. The oldest form of digital broadcast was spark gap telegraphy which are used by pioneers. By pressing the key, the operator could send messages in particular code by energizing a rotating commutating spark gap.

Systems that require reliability, or that share their frequency with other services, may use "coded orthogonal frequency-division multiplexing" or COFDM. COFDM breaks a digital signal into as many as several hundred slower subchannels. The digital signal is often sent as QAM on the subchannels. Modern COFDM systems use a small computer to make and decode the signal with digital signal processing, which is more flexible and far less expensive than older systems that implemented separate electronic channels. COFDM resists fading and ghosting because the narrow-channel QAM signals can be sent slowly. An adaptive system, or the system that sends error-correction codes which can also resist interference, because most interference can affect only a few of the QAM channels. COFDM is used for Wi-Fi, some cell phones, Digital Radio Mondiale, Eureka 147, and many other local area network, digital TV and radio standards.

Heating : Radio-frequency energy generated for heating of objects is usually not intended to radiate outside of the generating equipment, to prevent interference with other radio signals. Microwave ovens use intense radio waves to heat food. Diathermy equipment is used in surgery for sealing of blood vessels. Induction furnaces are generally used for melting metal for casting.

Navigation : Navigation are used in satellite which refers to satellite navigation system that use the satellite with precision clocks. All satellite navigation systems use satellites with precision clocks. The satellite transmits its position, and the time of the transmission. The receiver listens to four satellites, and can figure its position as being on a line that is tangent to a spherical shell around each satellite, determined by the time-of-flight of the radio signals from the satellite. A computer in the receiver does the math.

Direction finding process in radio is the oldest form of radio navigation. Before 1960 navigations used movable loop antennas to locate commercial AM station near cities.

Radio Remote Control : These are used the radio waves to transmit the control data to a remote object as in some early kinds of guided missile, some early TV remotes and a range of model, cars as well as airplanes. The remote controlled equipment which are used in large industries includes cranes and switching co motives which commonly use digital radio methods to ensure safety and reliability.

Radar : Here Radar stands for radio detection and ranging which detects the objects at a distance by bouncing radio waves of them. These radars are also used for searching which scan a wide area with pulses of short radio waves.

Radar (Radio Detection And Ranging) detects objects at a distance by bouncing radio waves off them. The delay caused by the echo measures the distance. The direction of the beam determines the direction of the reflection. The polarization and frequency of the return can sense the type of surface. Navigational radars scan a wide area two to four times per minute. They use very short waves that reflect from earth and stone. They are common on commercial ships and long-distance commercial aircraft.

General purpose radars commonly use navigational radar frequencies, but modulate and polarize the pulse so the receiver can determine the type of surface of the reflector. The best general-purpose radars distinguish the rain of heavy storms, as well as land and vehicles. Some can superimpose sonar data and map data from GPS position.

Search radars scan a wide area with pulses of short radio waves. They usually scan the area two to four times a minute. Sometimes search radars use the Doppler effect to separate moving vehicles from clutter. Targeting radars use the same principle as search radar but scan a much smaller area far more often, usually several times a second or more. Weather radars resemble search radars, but use radio waves with circular polarization and a wavelength to reflect from water droplets. Some weather radar use the Doppler effect to measure wind speeds.

Television : An Introduction

Television is abbreviated as TV which are widely used telecommunication medium for transmitting and retrieving moving images. TV set has become a general communications receiver in home, businesses and institutions.

Broadcast TV is typically disseminated via radio transmissions on designated channels in the 54-890 megahertz frequency band. Signals are now frequently transmitted with stereo and/or surround sound in many countries. Until the 2000s broadcast TV programs were generally recorded and transmitted as an analog signal, but in recent years public and commercial broadcasters have been progressively introducing digital television broadcasting technology.

A standard television set consists of multiple internal electronic circuits, including those for receiving and decoding broadcast signals. A visual display device which lacks a tuner is properly called a monitor, rather than a television. A television system may use different technical standards such as digital television (DTV) and high-definition television (HDTV). Television systems are also used for surveillance, industrial process control, and guiding of weapons, in places where direct observation is difficult or dangerous.

Amateur television (HAM TV or ATV) is also used for experimentation, pleasure and public service events by amateur radio operators. HAM TV stations were on the air in many cities before commercial TV stations came on the air.

Wide range of television makes it a powerful and attractive medium for advertisers. Many television networks and their stations sell blocks of broadcast time to advertisers in terms to fund their programming.

Broadcast television is trounced by government, licensing which is in form of tax, advertising, subscription or any combination of these. To protect revenues, subscription TV channels are commonly encrypted to ensure that only subscription payers receive the declaration codes to see the signal. The channels which are non-encrypted is known as free to air (FTA).

Taxation or License : In some countries, television services may be funded by a television license which is a form of television that means an advertising plays a lesser rote or no rote at all.

Psychological Effects of TV : Some studies suggest that, when a person plays video games or watches TV, the basal ganglia portion of the brain becomes very active and dopamine is released. Some scientists believe that release of high amounts of dopamine reduces the amount of the neurotransmitter available for other purposes, although this remains a controversial conclusion.

Physical Effects of TV : Studies in both children and adults have found an association between the number of hours of television watched and obesity. A study found that watching television decreases the metabolic rate in children to below that found in children at rest.

Propaganda : Television is used to promote commercial, social and political agendas. Use of public service announcements (including those paid for by governing bodies or politicians), news and current affairs, commercial advertising, advertorials and talk shows are used to influence public opinion. The Cultivation Hypothesis suggests that some viewers may begin to repeat questionable or even blatantly fictitious information gleaned from the media as if it were factual. Considerable debate remains, however, whether the Cultivation Hypothesis is well supported by scientific literature, however, the effectiveness of television for propaganda (including commercial advertising) is unsurpassed. The US military and State Department often turn to media to broadcast into hostile territory or nation.

THE TABLOIDS

Tabloids is another medium of advertising. Tabloids use the term tab inserts which are more common. Tabloid inserts commonly called tab inserts are more common and popular are included in the media and delivered in the usual manner. It is the responsibility of the advertiser to print the tabloid advertising sections. Tabloid inserts are a more dependable and efficient methods of transmitting product messages. Newspapers earn revenue from classified advertising which is placed in a special section of the paper and arranged by specific products and services classifications for easy reference. There is another way which are known as display advertising that includes all advertising matter which are not included in the classified special section of the paper. Display advertising is placed on news and feature pages throughout the paper. Display advertising need not necessarily be in the classified advertising section. This appears in several pages of the paper that uses various space sizes, layout designs, type faces ad sizes etc. Display may again be classified as national display or general display, retail or local display.

POINT OF PURCHASE

For this medium, there are other terms which are used like dealer aids, dealer displays, point of sale, etc. It emphasizes greatly the consumer rather than the dealer. It is an advertising method inside, outside and around a retail store. The messages are directly transmitted to the customers. Messages and visuals all appear in or adjacent to the retail outlets where the goods are actually sold. The method which is to attract the people who are passing by to enter into the place of business such as retail stores, departmental stores, super markets, cooperative stores and other points of outlet where advertising takes place.

However, point of purchase advertising materials do not include the labels, packages and containers. The store itself or the manufacturer whose merchandise is put for sale in the store may create advertising at the point of sale. Many devices at the store have a message potential and communicate effectively with the buyer or customer. There are various kinds of point of purchase advertisements such as posters, playcards, displays, banners, samples, premium, window display, floor displays, counter and wall displays. These are all generally followed to promote the sale at the store. A good display may attract the interest of the passer-by. Sometimes the manufacturer may supply various kinds of display materials. It is the responsibility of the retailer to install these attractively or use the materials. The point of sale has increasing importance in these days. The advertising materials at point of sale must be attractive, create interest, confidence, impression, and have educative and information value. Point of purchase is the last stage to remind the buyer to buy.

HOME JOURNALS

The employees, dealers, and customers are also essentially to be informed, educated and pursued to promote goodwill and public opinion with the ultimate object of increasing sales. For this moto, a company uses a house organ. This is another medium like a magazine or bulletin published and circulated among the employees, dealers and partly customers. They are distributed free of charge. Many of the companies in India publish a house journal. The house organ is versatile and can render a real service. Properly viewed the house publication is a direct channel to a specific public. Frequency format, number of pages, color, black and white, method of distribution, editorial cost, art and photography are the various factors considered in issues of a house organ. A house organ has editorial matter and properly edited a house organ can attract the customers and establishes a contact with the people working in the organisation. But its publication is a costly matter. Only a few big organisations can do so. The publication is generally made out to be interesting and informative to the customers.

Home journals are distributed free of charge at home to home service. This the alternative medium lice a magazine or bulletin published.

POSTAL PUBLICITY

One mass medium of advertising may be called direct advertising or direct mail advertising or postal publicity. Under this medium the advertiser himself can transit the advertising communication to the prospective buyers. It is a direct communication involving a process of sending advertisements direct to prospective customers by the advertiser himself by means of the postal services. The services like hand delivery or mail drop and door to door distribution of advertising messages or materials are excluded from direct mail advertising. This medium has four basic types. Such as direct method: seeks immediate response; informative: product message or literature is sent to educate the addressee; reminder: reminder direct mail reminds the prospective customers and utility direct mail: distributing samples, calendars, charts etc. Thus different advertisers may follow various methods to meet their particular needs. Direct advertising is not a new method. Messages may be directly communicated when an advertiser sends a handbill to a customer's home or a booklet or a catalogue.

Postal publicity is also known as direct mail advertising as well as direct advertising. The size of audience is to be ascertained by the advertiser and the advertising process is to be undertaken solely by the advertiser.

The objectives of direct mail advertising are to creating good will, developing a product image to secure leads for the sales force, promote consumers interest, dealer promotion as well as obtaining direct sales to have personnel touch for prospects in leisurely way. For example, letters, postcards, folders, leaflets. Handouts, catalogues as well as portfolios, etc. There are numerous sources from which to prepare a mailing list such as past customers' names from various companies.

SCREEN ADVERTISING

It is also known as films. With the help of screen advertising or film. Advertising is much easier. These advertising includes commercial film, whose duration is to minute to 40 minutes. Screen advertising is also represents as Films. Commercial films are used in theatres. Motion picture theatres sell time for screening advertisement films as well as slide projections. Theatre advertising commercial films are short films that are shown before the main feature film, intermission, or be fore newsreels. Also between the feature film and newsreels. As a mass medium, many advertisers use short motion films shown in regular cinema houses.

In India theatre screen advertising is an important and popular medium; it is a major medium. Both local and national advertisers can use screen advertising. Retailers may merely use slides rather than films. They are more flexible than any other medium. They have great influence, demonstrate, use color, action and voice, and have the advantage of selectivity. There is a compulsion on the part of the audience to sit in the theatre, as they have paid to view the picture and the audience is certain to see and hear the message.

These advertising held by the company or an organization when they launch popular, these films are host by some specific celebrity.

TRANSPORTATION

Transportation may be referred as spending the advertising budget on public transportation. It involves various transportation systems, goods on or by land, air, railway, alighting point, premises and terminals. Public transportation vehicles includes trains, buses, taxies and auto rickshaws. A range of sites are available covering advertisements on city buses, city buss transports, outside suburban coaches, railway station areas or premises, bus stations, and air terminals. Also trams, over-rails, under bridges, coaches of inter-city express trains, bus terminals or alighting points, back and side roof panels on city and mofussil buses, inside front panels in city and mofussil buses, paper posters and advertising on rickshaws. Also stickers on cars, advertising carriers, trolleys, goods delivery vehicles, and passenger ships.

All these are constitute of overall transit advertising. Here, this transportation refers to transit advertising. Transit or transportation advertising acts as a mass medium and usually an outdoor medium or part of an outdoor medium. There are some similarities in their operations but the only difference is transit media are commonly moving from one place to another, and the way in which transportation advertisements are seen and observed. However, it is a good medium of mass communication. It reaches and catches the crowds, the frequently changing and accumulated audience. Double crowns on double deck bus sides, overall painted buses and car cards are the most important sites in cities. Millions of people travel everyday from place to place, from the suburbs to their work place and back home, thousand of trains and buses ply everyday and thousand of railway, road transportation and airline employees are exposed to transit advertising.

THE DIRECTORY

A directory is a type of book which are containing names and addresses such as a telephone directory, industrial directory, product directory etc. It is another medium that are used by the advertisers. Directories are published by directory publishers, magazines, trade associations, chambers of commerce, institutions and government agencies. Many directories are concerned with trade, business, industry, manufacturers etc. The advertisers can use this medium to transmit their product message. There are several users of a product or service looking for the source of certain products or services. For example, the yellow pages of a telephone directory serve this purpose. Potential consumers interested in a certain product or service can find it in directories. There is a classification for the convenience of the consumer. So it is an effective tool for the advertiser. Directory contains entire manners and addresses. These are always published by directory publishers, institutions and government agencies.

STANDARDS OF ADVERTISING

There are large variety of standards in advertising which are mention below:-Standards of Advertising

- Advertisements asking the reader to send money to a Post Office box number or a Detroit News box number.
- Fraudulent advertisements or those that contain statements of doubtful honesty.
- All advertising that can be misinterpreted by the reader and which makes dubious and exaggerated claims or is likely to cause injury to the health or morals of the reader.
- Attacks on a person or company or on the goods or services of another person or company.
- Advertisements that offer work to be done in the home for pay.
- Advertisements in bad taste or offensive to any group on moral, religious or discriminatory grounds. Suggestive captions or illustrations are not permitted. No copy, headline or illustration can be employed which states or implies conduct which by normal standards is considered morally or socially unacceptable.
- Advertisements proposing marriage.
- Advertisements describing goods not available and not intended to be sold on request but used as bait to lure customers are not acceptable.
- Advertisements that seek introductions to members of the opposite sex will be judged by the Detroit News Advertising Acceptance Committee.

- Advertisements of fortune tellers and similar practitioners.
- Help wanted advertisements that make extravagant or misleading offers of salary or reward are not acceptable. It is illegal for an advertiser offering employment to advertise his own race, color, creed, or nationality or to indicate any such preference in his prospective employee.
- This list is not intended to include all the types of advertisements unacceptable to the News. Generally speaking, any other advertising that may cause financial loss to the reader, or loss of his confidence in reputable advertising and ethical business practices is likewise unacceptable.

RULES AND REGULATIONS

Advertising has some rules and regulation which are always followed by all companies those who wants to create an advertisement to make their product popular.

Advertising should endeavour to gain the goodwill of the public on the basis of the merits of the goods or services advertised. Direct comparison with competing goods or firms and disparaging references are in no circumstances permitted.

Methods of advertising designed to create confusion in the mind of the consumer as between goods by one maker and another maker are unfair and should not be used. Such methods may consist first the imitation of the trademark or name of the competitor or the packaging or labelling of goods; or another is the imitation of advertising devices, copy, layouts or slogans.

No advertisement are likely to bring advertising into contempt or disrepute should be permitted. Advertising should not take benefit of the superstition or ignorance of the general public.

Advertising should be truthful, avoid distorting facts and misleading the public by means of implications and omissions. For instance, it should not mislead the consumer by false statements as to:

- the services accompanying purchase, including delivery, exchange, return, repair, upkeep etc.;
- the quality of the value of competing goods or the trust worthiness of statements made by others.
- the price of the merchandise, its value, its suitability of terms of purchase;

- personal recommendations of the article of service, testimonials which are fictitious and/or fraudulent or the originals of which cannot be produced must not be used. Anyone using testimonials in advertisements is as responsible for the statements made in them as he would be if he had made them himself; and
- the character of the merchandise, i.e., its utility, materials, ingredients, origin etc.;

Advertising should be designed as to conform not only to the laws but also the moral, aesthetic and religious sentiments of the country in which it is published.

No advertisements should offer to refund money paid.

No advertisements of talismans, charms and character-reading from photographs or such other matter as will trade on the superstition of the general public shall be permitted.

Indeed, vulgar, suggestive, repulsive or offensive themes or treatment should be avoided in all advertisements. This also applies to such advertisements which in themselves are not objectionable books, photographs or other matter and thereby lead to their sale and circulation.

No advertisement should be permitted to contain any claim so exaggerated as to lead inevitably to disappointment in the mind of the public. Special care is called for in the following cases:

- Advertisements inviting the public to take part in lotteries or competitions such as are permitted by law or which hold out the prospects of gifts. Such advertisements should state clearly all the conditions for the lottery or competitions or the conditions for the distribution of the gifts.
- The publication of employment notices requiring fees for application forms, prospects, etc. and security deposits should be forbidden except when such advertisements emanate from Governmental or quasi-Governmental sources.
- Advertisements inviting the public to invest money — such advertisements should not contain statements which may mislead the public in respect of the security offered, rates of return, or terms of amortisation.
- Advertisements addressed to those suffering from illness. In this respect the Code of Standards of Advertising in relations to medicine must be adhered to.

CODE OF ETHICS

The following are the code of ethics for advertising which are issued by advertising council of India Code of Ethics for Advertising

Along with the development of a very complex distribution system, the requirements of a market economy, faced with the need for ensuring a regular flow of mass-production, have given rise to the development of new methods of sales promotion.

Of these, advertising has proved itself to be of inestimable value for producers and distributors as well as for consumers. It enables the former to maintain contact with customers who are widely scattered and frequently unknown.

The legitimate function of advertising is the advocacy of the merits of some specific products or services recognizes this code which is intended to be applied in the spirit as well as in the letter and should be taken to set out the minimum standards to be observed by the parties concerned. This Code does override all ethical standards in advertising laid down by individual organisations, but it does not supersede the stan1dards of practice laid down by individual organisations as incumbent upon their own members and applying to their own particular trade or industry.

Unacceptable Advertisements

In advertising field, because of some nature or characteristics advertisements are not accepted by Times of India group. These nature are following:-Unacceptable Advertisements

- Advertisements claiming that advertisers have spiritual powers to cure or mitigate illness by tantra, puja, talisman, rites, etc.
- Box No. advertisements which call for copies of testimonials, certificates and enclosures such as photographs, catalogues and literature. However, open address advertisements calling for these documents are acceptable.
- Advertisements offering personal services or any kind of social contacts.
- Advertisements regarding house-keepers, companions, pen friends, massage service or massage house, etc.
- Accommodation/premises advertisements emanating from an estate agent should clearly mention Agent/Estate Agent in the text of the advertisement.

- Vacancy and accommodation advertisements containing references to any sect, cast or community.
- Advertisements from matrimonial bureaus/agencies.
- Loan advertisements for extension of business are accepted but loan advertisements of a private or personal nature are not accepted.
- Advertisements regarding buying/selling of telephones.
- Advertisements regarding availability of rooms on an hourly hire basis.
- Matrimonial advertisements containing reference to dowry/ life companionship.

In other countries also individual newspapers have formulated their own code. For instance, in the USA, a newspaper The Detroit News has listed in its code some classes of advertisements as unacceptable. The following are the classes of advertising that are unacceptable. In other countries individual newspapers have evaluated their own code.

COMMITTEE REPORT IN ADVERTISING

There are some committee report in advertising which are following below:-

- Advertising should be so designed as to conform to the laws of the country and should not offend against morality, decency and religious susceptibilities of the people.
- Notwithstanding anything contained herein, this code is subject to such modification/direction as may be made/issued by the Government of India from time to time.
- Advertisers or their agencies must be developed to produce evidence to substantiate any claims or illustrations.
- No advertisement should be permitted:
  - — which derides any race, caste, color, creed, nationality except wherein such usage would be for the specific purpose of effective dramatisation, such as combating prejudice;
  - — which is against any of the objectives, principles, or provision's of the Constitution of India;
  - — which will tend to incite people to crime or to promote disorder, violence or breach of law;

— which presents criminality as desirable, or furnish details of crime or imitation thereof;

— which would adversely affect friendly relations with foreign States;

— which exploits the national emblem, or any part of the Constitution, or the person or personality or national leaders or state dignitary;

— No advertisement should contain references which are likely to lead the public to infer that the product advertised or any of its in gradients have some quality which is not capable to being developed.

— No advertisement shall be permitted the objects whereof are wholly or mainly of a religious or political nature; advertisements must not be directed towards any religious or political end or have any relation to any industrial dispute:

— Visual and verbal representation of actual and comparative prices and costs that must be accurate and should not mislead on account of distortion.

— Advertisements should not contain disparaging reference to another product or service.

Case Study

Note : knowing more about "Mediums of Advertisement" reader can study documentation process of Microsoft company by visiting their site : www.members.microsoft.com

http://www.icmrindia.org/casestudies/catalogue/Marketing/MKTG048.htm

http://www.lucidview.com/publications/Retail_Marketing_Mix_Case_Study(LucidView).pdf

http://www.thetimes100.co.uk/case-study—sponsorship-marketing-mix—41-131-1.php

http://www.bized.co.uk/compfact/times100/exams/4_203_1854_2791_7925.htm

http://www.essays.se/about/case+study+of+marketing+mix/

13

Role of Communication

This chapter includes the key concepts that are described below:-

- Introduction
- Impotance of Communication
- Aims of Communication
- Principles of Communication
- Features of Communication
- Categorization of Communication
- Communication Process
- Difficulties in Communication Process
- Role of Communication
- Current Status of Communication in India
- Essential Factors
- Discrimination The Discrimination in Advertising
- Functions of Communication
- Qualitative Aspects of Communication
- Essentials in Communication
- Reasons for the growing Importance of Communication
- Remedies in Communication
- Rule of Five
- Today's Role
- Goals and Objectives of Mass Communication

INTRODUCTION

In the present competition world, every business is working efficiently when it has good communication skills. Communication is one of the most relevant factor for any business organization. That is why, every business used to find new and interactive ways of communication. It is, therefore, the most difficult challenges-for managers to ensure effective communication among the people in the enterprise and outside. To meet this challenge, every manager spends about 80 per cent of his time in communicating.

Almost all conflicts involve communication problems, as both a cause and an effect. Misunderstandings, resulting from poor communication, can easily cause a conflict or make it worse. Further, once a conflict has started, communication problems often develop because people in conflict do not communicate with each other as frequently, as openly, and as accurately as they do when relationships are not strained. Thus communication is central to most conflict situations.

For an efficient communication, it must require two person—First person, i.e., speaker who speaks and the second person, i.e., the listener who listen to the speaker. Sometimes there are third parties: in-between people who carry messages from one person to another, or the media, for example, which has such transmission of information as its primary goal. Problems can develop at all three of these sources.

Some times it happen that when people of different cultures interact with each other then the speaker is not able to make himself clear that what he actually wants to say convey to the listener. In this situation, people can either misunderstood the speaker or take him in a wrong manner. Either way, people often get confused about other people's messages. This is especially common when people from different cultures try to communicate. Even if their languages are the same, culture acts like a lens through which we see and interpret the world. If their cultures are different, it is easy for the same statement to mean one thing to one person and something different to someone else. Thus intercultural communication is especially prone to errors.

Listeners also are sources of communication problems. People often fail to listen carefully. They may assume they know what the other person is saying or will say (because they have heard it before, or they assume that one person is "just like" another person from the same group). Also, when people are in conflict, they often concentrate more on what they are going to say in response to their opponent's statement, rather than listening to their opponents' words with full attention. The result, again, is misunderstandings, and often unnecessary escalation of a conflict.

Third parties can make communication better, or they can make it worse. Skilled third parties can help speakers clarify what they are saying, and they can help listeners hear what is really meant. They can act as go-betweens, carrying messages between people who cannot or will not meet face-to-face.

Presence of skilled and efficient third parties help the speaker and listener to understand the matter in an efficient way. But some time these third parties, i.e., media in order meet their goal make the matter worse to be understood by others.

While communication, a gap can occur due to which a communication problem may exists. It happens because the user don't make useful information available to us. Instead they tell us a life story and pass on a lot of information that won't help us solve the problem, all while leaving out the critical nuggets of data. Then the IT employee wonders why and spends significant time chasing users down and trying to gather the missing details needed to work the issue.

During a communication process several problem occurs but some times these problems are not because of lack of information but because of ambiguous and mal functions process which is not properly defined. It is suggested that, in our hypothetical conversation, that if an IT help desk employee has to regularly perform the same tasks and if the information necessary for success is challenging to gather from users, then the solution should be in doing something to ensure the proper information is collected and that the users know what's needed and expected. That's a communication process. And a well-defined communication process does a couple things: It sets clear, unambiguous expectations and provides a known mechanism to accomplish the activity it defines. It also needs to be reasonable and usable, to be fully successful. Perhaps the IT help desk would deploy a standard form, for example, which collects all of the information required to resolve a class of issue. At that point, once the user population has been made aware of the form and process, it is reasonable to expect the users to take advantage of the tools and instructions provided.

Now, if our information communication process is in place and communicated effectively and sufficiently, yet the people to whom the process applies neglect to do their part, we no longer have a communication problem.

In simpler terms, we can say that communication is process by which two people interact with each other and exchange their ideas. It help them in expressing their ideas, emotions, and feeling to others.

It may be stated that communication is the process of exchange of information, ideas, feelings and understanding among human beings. It is the process of conveying meanings. It is a systematic process of conveying, listening and understanding something between two or more persons through words, figures, symbols, pictures, body language etc.

Faulty communication process leads to several problems in any business organization. Due to this communication several goods projects can lead to failure and produce no result, which in turn effect the organization in a bad way. Communication is the exchange and flow of information and ideas from one person to another. It involves a sender transmitting an idea to a receiver. Effective communication occurs only if the receiver understands the exact information or idea that the sender intended to transmit.

Studying the communication process is important because you coach, coordinate, counsel, evaluate, and supervise through this process. It is the chain of understanding that integrates the members of an organization from top to bottom, bottom to top, and side to side.

IMPOTANCE OF COMMUNICATION

Communication is one of the basic functions of management in any organization and its importance can hardly be overemphasized. It is a process of transmitting information, ideas, thoughts, opinions and plans between various parts of an organization. The importance of communication in managing can hardly be over-emphasized. It is the life-stream or life-line of modern business management. No manager can effectively perform his functions without effective communication system. The success of all managerial functions depends on successful communication. As we studied that perfect and ideal communication is foundation of sound management including sound communication system is indispensable for small, medium, large as well as multinational organizations sound communication system is essential for every organization following points described the importance of communication:

Avoidance of Ignorance

In the communication regime, the news or information to be transmitted variated because of several causes which completely lead to misunderstanding of the information. According to W.H. Whyle, "The greatest enemy of communication is the illusion of it." Sometimes, parties receive no information or incomplete information and remain ignorant of exact information. Consequently, misunderstanding, confusion and illusion creeps up in the minds of the concerned parties. In order to remove and avoid misunderstanding, illusion or ignorance, effective communication system is a must.

Building Image or Goodwill

In a business organization, for the purpose of making their goodwill and image in the society, communication plays the most important role as it represent the image of the company to the society. For this purpose an organization appoints P.R.O. and managers. Business houses disseminate plethora of information for building their goodwill and image. Information relating to financial performance, sales and export performance, launch of new products, foreign collaboration) award won, social welfare activities etc. are usually disseminated to the shareholders, and public at large. Radio, TV, newspapers, magazines usually contain such advertisements. Press conferences are held and interviews are given by the big business leaders.

Democratic Management

In modern times, management of organizations specifically companies is done on democratic principles. Owners select or elect their representatives to manage the organisation. Employees, consumers and other stakeholders are given participation in the management of the organisation. They all share information, participate in discussion, consultation and decision-making. All this is possible only when a sound communication system is in place.

Effective Control

No manager can exercise the effective control of organisational activities without proper communication system. For controlling, manager has to take the following steps :

Step I Convey the objectives, plans, procedures, budgets or other standards for performance.

Step II Collect the information about actual performance.

Step III Compare the actual performance against the standard and find out the deviation, if any.

Step IV At final stage it is important to take corrective action to bring the performance as per the standards.

In this process, there should be exchange of information between the manager and his subordinates.

Essentials for Leading

Although communication applies to all phases of managing but it is particularly important in the function of leading. No doubt effective leadership requires an efficient system of communication in the organisation. A good leader may direct or lead his subordinates only when an efficient system of communication is present. It brings both the leader and the subordinates in close contact to each other. A leader have the ability to make their orders and directives which are more necessary with inviting opinions and suggestions which are from their subordinates which needs the effective communication.

Enhances Motivation and Morale

Effective communication system plays crucial role in enhancing the level of motivation and morale of employees. With the help of effective communication instruction, directions, orders, praise, solutions to the problems etc. can be effectively conveyed. Similarly, suggestions, opinions, ideas, problems, grievances, complaints can also be received in positive mind set by the managers. Such a condition greatly enhances level of motivation and morale of employees.

Effective Organising

Organising function cannot be performed without effective communication system. Communication is at the very heart of the process of organising. Organising involves many activities including delegation and decentralization of authority, assigning responsibility, and establishing relationships among the members of the organisation. As name suggested organizing functions are held by the organization which have no capability to performed without any communication system. For all these activities, manager needs to have communication system in place. Hence, it can safely be concluded that the success of organising function largely depends on sound communication system.

Effective Staffing

Communication is equally important in the staffing function. Recruitment, selection, induction, training, performance appraisal and so on are the main activities in staffing function. None of these activities can be effectively completed without the help of effective communication system.

Facilitates Change

In order to survive in the competitive world, an organization has to facilitated change as it has no other exception. Hence, people in organisation discuss the need and scope of change and introduce change. Managers prepare members of the organisation to accept change. This all cannot be possible without effective communication.

Facilitates Coordination

Coordination of work is impossible without communication. Coordination is the act of coordinating, making different people or things work together for a goal or effect. With the help of effective communication system, information, thoughts, opinions and ideas, etc., can be exchanged and commonly understanding can be developed. A manager needs to coordinate among all the departments and individuals in the organisation. He needs to ensure vertical, horizontal and external coordination. This all is impossible without communication system.

Facilitates Decision-making

Effective communication system is a prerequisite for making sound decisions. The quality of decisions largely depends on the quality of information. Moreover, effective communication system also helps in communicating decisions to the persons concerned.

Implementation of decisions also requires constant flow of communication between managers and subordinates.

Facilitates Planning

Effective planning occurs when everyone responsible for it has access to complete information affecting areas of planning. In fact, planning requires extensive communication among the executives and the other personnel, who translate the plans into action. Communication is necessary in executing a planned programme. Without communication, planning may miserably fail. Organisational objectives, policies, programmes, practices, procedures and strategies are conveyed to the concerned people in the organisation so that they may strictly follow them.

Good External Relations

Sound relations with the external world to the organisation is also essential in this age. Hence, every organisation needs to maintain relations with customers and their organizations, shareholders, trade unions and trade organizations, competitive organizations, government agencies etc.

Sound Human and Industrial Relations

An efficient communication process, helps in maintaining mutual corporation and understanding which leads to sound human and industrial relations. According to Robert D. Berth, "It is impossible to have human relations without communication." It is a fact that a large number of industrial disputes take place because of communication gap between the managers and subordinates. But through communication, managers can make the subordinates understand the objectives plans, policies, programmes, rules etc. Similarly, subordinates can also convey their views, opinions, suggestions, problems, complaints, grievance to managers.

AIMS OF COMMUNICATION

The fore most purpose of communication process is to influence the action of the others in respect of benefit of the organization. It enables us to understand others and to make ourselves understand. Without communication we cannot live or work together in an organised way. It is a flux that binds people together in an organisation. The basic purpose of communication is to facilitate and lubricate the organisation. It helps management in planning effectively and controlling efficiently. John G. Clover has outlined the following important purposes of communication :

- To keep employees informed.
- To provide employees with orders and instructions in connection with their duties or jobs.
- To solicit information from employees which may aid management.
- To make each employee interested in his respective job and in the work of the company as a whole.
- To express management's interest in its personnel.
- To reduce or prevent labour turnover.
- To indoctrinate employees with the will to work and with the benefits derived from their association with the company.
- To instill each employee with personal pride in being a member of the company.

Goals of Commounication in an Organization are stated below:

- to identify the importance of effective communication in several circumstances.
- to charity that it a multi-dimensional regime.
- recognize that communication involves problem solving and decision making
- recognize that speech is an important tool for thinking, learning, and communication
- always view and interpret visual information critically.
- practise the behaviours of effective speakers
- always speak clearly and confidently in a various range of situations
- clarify the listening as an active and constructive process
- practise the behaviours of effective, active listeners
- listen effectively in a variety of situations
- always identifying the writing as a constructive and meaningful process

- practise the behaviours of effective writers
- write confidently in a variety of formats
- to clarify the reading as an active, constructive process
- practise the behaviours of effective strategic readers

PRINCIPLES OF COMMUNICATION

A brief description on some of the basic principles of communication are follow below :

Principle of Adequacy : Communications should be adequate and complete, not broken or incomplete. Inadequate communication delays action. It spoils understanding as well as good relations. Efficiency of both the communication and recipient is affected.

Principle of Attention : The recipient's attention to the communicated message must be drawn to make the communication effective. The communication is always meant for action. Mere words may not help. An executive should first show the way his men surely will follow. People think according to their heart and feelings not with their mind, this theory was proposed by Dale Beach. Hence, good manner has to decide the time of communication. This decision of times requires to reduce the effect of emotions and moods of an individual.

Principle of Clarity : The communication message should be clear. It should be communicated in simple, easy and commonly understood language. It is the speaker who makes them meaningful and it is the receiver who interprets them. Therefore, whatever is conveyed should be conveyed in unambiguous clear words.

Principle of Consistency : The communications should be consistent with the plans, policies, programmes and objectives of the enterprise. Communications should be consistent among themselves. Inconsistency creates confusion. Better coordination is achieved by consistent communications.

Principle of Feedback : Communication is a two-way traffic. Messages, policies, programmes, directions, opinions etc. are communicated downward. Grievances, complaints, suggestions etc. are communicated upward. Both are necessary in an organisation. Thus communication is also termed as a two-way process. It follows the principle of 'give and take'. It is meant for being communicated. The steps which are involved in two way traffic should be calmly watched received sympathetically and incorporated wherever and whenever necessary. Oral communication is regarded better as compared to written communication since the former provides more opportunity for feeding back than the latter.

Principle of Integration : Communication is a means to attain the objectives of the enterprise. It tries to get cooperation of all to see that the work is accomplished satisfactorily. As far as possible it should be based on the policy of integration of efforts in order to avoid confusion and help in better understanding. It should help in achieving a genuine spirit of cooperation among the personnel of the organisation.

Principle of Informality : The executive should try to remain informal in his behaviour with subordinates. But in a certain situation, he may bid good bye to informality and become formal in his relations and conduct.

Principle of Time : It is very important to give the information at proper or perfect timing. Without any specific timing, there is no value of information which are provided with the help of communication. Wrong choice of time may not have the desired impact on the recipient .

FEATURES OF COMMUNICATION

Communication process comprises several features some of them are stated below:

- Communication is a process where people exchange this ideas, emotions and feeling. So it can be regarded as an interactive process .
- It is all pervasive function of management. In other words, it is performed by all the managers and employees across the organisation.
- The subject-matter of communication is some message expressed through words, data, symbols, body language, pictures, figures etc.
- It involves at least two persons, one of whom is the source or sender and another is receiver of information.
- It may be formal or informal.
- It may be oral, written or gestural.

- Communication may be intentional or unintentional.
- It is a two-way process. It essentially involves dialogue for its success.
- It is a dynamic process which is adapted in accordance with the prevailing situation.
- communication can take place, i.e., downward, upward, horizontally and diagonally too.
- It involves exchange of information, opinion, idea, meaning and understanding among human beings.
- Its main object is to elicit desired response from the receiver.
- It is a social process.

CATEGORIZATION OF COMMUNICATION

Communication may be classified on the following basis :

- On the basis of organisation structure.
- On the basis of mode of expression.
- On the basis of direction.

On the Basis of Organisation Structure : On the basis of organisation structure, communication may be of two types :

- Formal communication.
- Informal communication or 'grapevine'.

Formal Communication

When communication flows through any suitable and established medium then it is said to be a formal communication. In other words, communication which travels through the formal chain of command or lines of hierarchy of authority is called the formal communication. It establishes the single path of communication which links the various positions. Thus, it is deliberately and consciously established by the management. Members of the organisation are expected to communicate through these formal channels. It can be in several direction, i.e., upward, horizontal or downward.

Benefits—Benefits of formal communication are stated below:

- It helps in maintaining direct contact with the subordinates. Thus, facilitates control by superiors.
- It helps in maintaining the lines of authority in the organisation.
- It helps in maintaining discipline.
- It helps in the fixation of responsibility and accountability.
- facilitated a direct flow of communication.

Limitation—Formal communication face several limitations too. Some of them are stated below:

- It takes a lot of time to communicate through this process.
- It creates a bottleneck in the flow of information because almost all information is channeled through a single executive.
- It distort the free flow of information in an organization.
- It has deficiency of personal relationship between the members of the organization.
- Organizational distance is a big barrier in the free flow of communication. Hence, there is possibility of distortion of facts when the message passes through various levels.
- The distortion of facts may be possible in upward communication also, since a person working in a subordinate capacity is likely to report to his superior.

Informal Communication

When flow of communication takes place informally between the members of the organization this type of communication is said to be informal communication. It is personal communication in nature and not a positional communication. It does not flow along with the formal lines of authority or formal chain of command. It is even not regulated by the formal rules and procedures.

Informal communication channels are not established by the management. Such channels on account of natural desire of people to socialise and communicate with others. In other words, informal communication arises out of social interaction of people. Herbert Simon has rightly stated that "informal communication system is built around the social relationships of the members of the organisation."

This informal flow of communication is also known as "Grape Vine". In this type of communication the flow of information is in upward direction. It transmits information about what people are doing. It often leads to rumours in the organisation. Keith Davis has identified the following four different networks for transmitting information via the grapevine:

- Single strand- In the single strand, one person communicates with only one person.
- Gossip chain- In gossip chain, every member talks with every one else, usually about personal matter.
- Probability chain-In it communication is random.
- Cluster chain-In it messages are transmitted selectively. Grapevine generally operates like a cluster chain. Grapevine may move in the fashion of a long chain. It should be remembered here that in a cluster chain, only a few persons are active communicator and such persons are known as liaison agents.

Benefits—Informal communication has grabbed several advantages in it. Some of them are stated below:

- It is effective means of communicating organizational rules, values, morals, traditions and history.
- It fulfill the urge of the member of the organization.
- It may provide feed back to managers on their actions and decisions.
- It is dynamic and reacts quickly to the change in the circumstances.
- It bridges the gap made during formal communication.
- It works as a powerful and effective tool of communication.
- Informal communication is faster in speed than formal communication.
- It may disseminate the tentative view point of management on any important issue.
- It helps improve decision-making.
- It is more flexible.

Limitations—Limitations of informal communication are stated under:

- It leads to leakage of secret information.

- It can also misguide the member of the organization.
- It carries inaccurate, half-truth or distorted information.
- It is difficult to believe on information.
- It may cause misunderstanding.
- It is difficult to fix responsibility for the information.
- It spreads rumours and promotes gossips.

Communication on the Basis of Direction : On the basis of direction communication can be categorized into four:- :

- Downward communication,
- Upward communication,
- Horizontal communication,
- Diagonal communication.

Downward Communication

When communication flows from higher to lower hierarchical management, i.e., from top level management to lower level of management. This type of communication is called downward communication. In other words, when messages are transmitted from superiors to subordinates along with the chain of command, it is said to be downward communi-cation. Such communications may be in the form of orders, instructions, policies, programmes, directives, praise, reprimands etc. According to Katz and Kahn, the major objectives of downward communication are as follows:

- To provide information about the rationale of the job.
- To give information about organisational procedures and practices.
- To tell the subordinates about their performance.
- To provide ideological type information to facilitate indoctrination of goals.
- To avoid the employees with their particular work which are directed towards the accomplishment of the organizational goal.

Benefits—Downward communication has grabbed several advantages in it. Some of them are stated below:

- It helps an executive to use his authority effectively.

- It helps to tie the different levels of hierarchy together.
- It helps in explaining company policies, pro-grammes, rules, procedures etc. to the subordinates.
- It helps in preparing the people to introduce change.
- It increases the effectiveness of upward communi-cation through feedback.
- It removes misunderstanding and suspicion.

Limitations—Limitations of downward communi-cation are stated as under:

- It also lead to misunderstanding of the message conveyed as it flow through every level of management .
- It is a time consuming as it flows through every level of management it require a lot of time.
- It tends to be faulty and inaccurate because of the sender's carelessness, poor communication skills, decoding etc.
- It tends *to* promote one-way or authoritative communication.
- Some managers at various levels tend to filter or screen or manipulate messages for their personal ends and gains.

In order to increase effectiveness of the downward communications, following steps may be taken :

- It should be consistent with the duties, responsibilities, capacities and decision-making abilities of the receiver.
- It should be specific to time.
- It should be consistent with the organisational goals and objectives.
- It should be consistent with the organisational policies and practices.
- The information to be transmitted should be clear it should not be fake.

Upward Communication

Upward communication is that type of communication in which information or message is transmitted from lower level to management to the top level of management in the organization hierarchy. In this communication the information is transferred from blue collar workers to white collars managers. In other words, when the communication flows from subordinates to superiors along with the chain of command, it is called upward communication. Such communication may be on the form of progress report, problems, suggestions, opinions, ideas, requests, grievances, complaints, appeals, explanations etc.

Upward communication may be of two types :

- *Voluntary upward communication i.e.* voluntarily from subordinates. Such communication include opinions, ideas, suggestions, grievances, complaints, appeals.
- *Feedback upward communication i.e.* feedback or response communication from subordinates. Such communications include progress report, follow-up reports, and information reports desired by the superiors.

Benefits—Upward communication has several benefits. Some of them are stated below:

- It help in creating new and innovative ideas no.
- It enables managers to evaluate the impact of communication.
- It allows subordinates to express their problems, grievances and appeals.
- It promotes innovative ideas.
- It promotes feeling of belongingness among the subordinates.
- It increases receptiveness of information.
- It enables managers to know the progress of the work done by subordinates.

Limitations—Upward communication face a lot of difficulties. Some of it limitation are mentioned below :

- Some subordinates tend distort communication for their personal interests.
- Subordinates may not provide all the information. They may transmit the information which may please their subordinates.
- Superiors usually do not encourage the subordinates to pass on information to them.
- Superiors may react negatively on some upward communications.

- Subordinate tend to communicate upward the information which is favourable to them.

Horizontal or Lateral Communication

Horizontal communication is referred as that type of communication when it takes place within the employees of same level. The interaction is made between only on the same level of management same level of management not within all levels of management.

In other words, when communication takes place between two or more persons of the level or position of the same department or other departments of the organisation, it is known as horizontal communication. Such communication is more of an informal nature. The main object of such communication is to inter-departmental or inter-unit coordination.

Benefits—These are the advantages of horizontal communi-cation are as follows :

- It helps in resolving inter-departmental conflicts quickly.
- It facilitates inter-unit or inter-departmental coordination.
- It leads to non-repetition of the tasks..
- Horizontal communication leads to immediate transfer of information.
- It promotes joint problem solving.
- It encourages peers to share information.
- It develops informal and congenial work environment.

Limitations—Limitations of horizontal communication as stated below:

- The success of such communication depends on the willingness of people to share information.
- Difference in approach and vision of peer may cause distortion in communication.
- In this communication subordinates used to hid the information which they think is not them which in turn affect the organizational goal.

Diagonal Communication

Communication in inter-departments of the organization is

known as Diagonal communication. Such communication is in between people who are neither in the same department nor on the same level of organisational structure. It takes place when members cannot communicate effectively through other channels. For example, the cost accountant, who is interested in conducting a distribution cost analysis may ask sales representatives to report directly to him. When sales representatives send report directly to the cost accountant it is diagonal communication. They need not send report first to the marketing manager who may, in turn, send the report to the cost accountant. The flow of communication is diagonal rather than vertical. It helps to save time and to speed up action, though it violates the principle of unity of command.

On the Basis of Mode of Expression : Types of communication classified on the basis of mode of expression are stated below:

- Written communication.
- Oral or verbal communication.
- Gestural or non-verbal communication.

Written Communication

When information is expressed or forwarded on papers, i.e., in written then it is said to be written communication. It may be expressed even through groups, charts, diagrams, pictures with or without words. It is, therefore, sometimes the communication in black and white. Example of written communication are circulars, notes, memos, report, brouchers, etc.

Benefits—Benefits of written communication are stated below:

- It must not be ambiguous and fake.
- It ensures little risk of unauthorised alteration in the messages.
- It help in communicating from the companies situated at far off places.
- It ensures transmission of information *in* uniform manner, *i.e.* everyone concerned has the same information.
- It tends to reduce misunderstanding, conflicts, and disputes.
- It is an ideal way of transmitting lengthy messages.
- It provides time to think before communicating.

- It is suitable to convey message to a large number of persons at the same time.
- It provides a permanent record of communication for future reference.
- It is taken as a legal evidence by the Courts.

Limitations—Limitations of written communication are stated below:

- It is rigid and does not provide any scope for making alterations for inaccuracies that might have crept in.
- It tends to ineffective and unimpressive in case of poor drafting.
- It is time consuming.
- It distort the privacy of the subject-matter.
- Messages tend to be lengthy when expressed in writing.
- It may be interpreted in a different manner by different people.
- It is quite costlier.
- It fails to provide feedback immediately.
- It encourages red-tapism because involves many formalities.
- It is very formal and lacks personal touch.

Oral Communication

The communication that are made by verbally method, i.e., just by speaking it is said to be oral communication. This is also known as Verbal Communication. The basis of communication is the interaction between people. Verbal communication is one way for people to communicate face-to-face. Some of the key components of verbal communication are sound, words, speaking, and language.

When message is expressed through the words of mouth or spoken words, it is said to be oral communication. It may take place either through face-to-face conversation or through any electronic mode such as telephone, cellular phone, intercom etc. Oral communication may be in the form of one-to-one conversation meeting, group discussion, joint consultation, announcement, group meeting, speech, lecture, radio and TV programme.

Oral communication has been given a lot of consideration as there is not written proof of. It is because of the fact that it is regarded as a most powerful and effective mode of communication. Haimann has rightly pointed out that "the human voice can impart the message with meaning and shading which even long pages of written words simply cannot convey."

Benefits—Benefits of oral communication are stated below:

- It establishes a personal touch and leads to better understanding.
- Misunderstanding or doubts can be removed then and there.
- It is more effective than written communication.
- It is economical or less expensive as compared to written communication.
- It is flexible and the messages can be changed to suit the needs and response of the receiver.
- Immediate feed back or reaction motivation or response of the receiver can be taken.
- It is not time consuming.
- It provides opportunity of active participation *to* the listener.
- It is of very much use when any emergency occurs.

Limitations—Limitations of oral communication are stated below:

- It has the tendency of being distorted.
- It does not provide sufficient time for thinking before conveying the message.
- It does not avail any written proof regarding the subject matter.
- This communication is much influenced by the behaviors of the people.
- It has language problems. One may intend to convey something, but due to his way of speaking, it may convey something else.
- It may prove less effective amid of formal relations.
- It is not suitable for lengthy messages.
- Different perception of sender and receiver of the message may cause conflict.
- It is less reliable.

- It involves high cost in case the receiver of the message is at a distant place.

Non-verbal Communication and Gestural

The communication in which messages are transmitted from one person to another person not in written or oral but by the gestures of the body. This type of communication is called non-verbal communication. Movement of lips, wink of an eye, the ware of hands, nodding of head, facial expressions, tone of voice, frown on face or any other movement of body or body parts may be used to transmit the message. People also read body language to understand the feelings or thoughts of another person. Nonverbal communication (NVC) is usually understood as the process of communication through sending and receiving wordless messages.

NVC can be communicated through gesture and touch (Haptic communication), by body language or posture, by facial expression and eye contact. NVC can be communicated through object communication such as clothing, hairstyles or even architecture, symbols and infographics. Speech contains nonverbal elements known as paralanguage, including voice quality, emotion and speaking style, as well as prosodical features such as rhythm, intonation and stress. Dance is also regarded as a nonverbal communication. Likewise, written texts have nonverbal elements such as handwriting style, spatial arrangement of words, or the use of emotions. However, much of the study of nonverbal communication has focused on face-to-face interaction, where it can be classified into three principal areas: environmental conditions where communication takes place, the physical characteristics of the communicators, and behaviors of communicators during interaction.

Gestural mode is regarded one of the most important modes of communication. It conveys feelings, emotions, attitudes of a person. It also effectively conveys the reactions and responses of the listener of the message.

Selecting Mode of Communication : The most important part of the communication process is the selection of appropriate made of communication through which the information is transmitted. This requires a lot of coordination as one has to calculate all the merits of and demerits of every mode of communication and then he opts for the most suitable one. But, in general, verbal communication is more effective mode of conveying ideas, feelings, suggestions, information, messages, etc. However, as a matter of fact, no organisation can depend entirely upon one mode as both are complimentary to each other.

Written communication may be preferred to convey lengthy messages to a large number of persons scattered over distant places and where the information is required to be repeated for purposes of repetition and record. Oral communication may be the only available method to be used to convey emergency messages and where personal touch is required. Oral messages may be supported by gestures, demonstrations, etc. to make communication effective.

COMMUNICATION PROCESS

Communication regime can be defined as a process transmitting the message of the sender to the receiver in such a manner that the receiver never face any problem to understand the sender's message. The importance of effective communication is immeasurable in the world of business life. From a business perspective, effective communication is an absolute must, because it commonly accounts for the difference between success and failure or profit and loss. It has become clear that effective business communication is critical to the successful operation of modern enterprise. Every business person needs to understand the fundamentals of effective communication.

The most relevant and significant ingredient of TQM is effective communication process. The manner in which individuals perceive and talk to each other at work about different issues is a major determinant of the business success. It has proven been proven that poor communication reduces quality, weakens productivity, and eventually leads to anger and a lack of trust among individuals within the organization.

As we know that effective communication pave the way of better understanding so the communication process should be so efficient that it help in sharing the views of two persons. Communication help a lot to the individuals, professionals to groom themselves and make themselves quite more presentable .

The communication process is made up of four key components. Those components include encoding, medium of transmission, decoding, and feedback. There are also two other factors in the process, and those two factors are present in the form of the sender and the receiver. The communication process begins with the sender and ends with the receiver.

The sender is an individual, group, or organization who initiates the communication. This source is initially responsible for the success of the message. The sender's experiences, attitudes, knowledge, skill, perceptions, and culture influence the message.

The first foremost step a sender has to face in the communication process is the encoding process, i.e., encoding the information of sender to the receiver of information.

In order to convey meaning, the sender must begin encoding, which means translating information into a message in the form of symbols that represent ideas or concepts. This process translates the ideas or concepts into the coded message that will be communicated. The symbols can take on numerous forms such as, languages, words, or gestures. These symbols are used to encode ideas into messages that others can understand.

When encoding a message, the sender has to begin by deciding what he/she wants to transmit. This decision by the sender is based on what he/she believes about the receivers knowledge and assumptions, along with what additional information he/she wants the receiver to have. It is important for the sender to use symbols that are familiar to the intended receiver. A good way for the sender to improve encoding their message, is to mentally visualize the communication from the receiver's point of view.

While transmitting his message or information, a sender has to use some medium through which he conveys his message. These mediums are called channels. These channels or medium can be written or oral. Most channels are either oral or written, but currently visual channels are becoming more common as technology expands. Common channels include the telephone and a variety of written forms such as memos, letters, and reports. The effectiveness of the various channels fluctuates depending on the characteristics of the communication. For example, when immediate feedback is necessary, oral communication channels are more effective because any uncertainties can be cleared up on the spot. In a situation where the message must be delivered to more than a small group of people, written channels are often more effective. Although in many cases, both oral and written channels should be used because one supplements the other.

Sometime message distortion takes place and it is so because sender opted for an inappropriate channel to transmit his message it might have nit reached to the correct receiver whom the sender wants to convey. That is why senders need to keep in mind that selecting the appropriate channel will greatly assist in the effectiveness of the receiver's understanding. The sender's decision to utilize either an oral or a written channel for communicating a message is influenced by several factors. The sender should ask him or herself different questions, so that they can select the appropriate channel. Is the message urgent? Is immediate feedback needed? Is documentation or a permanent record required? Is the content complicated, controversial, or private? Is the message going to someone inside or outside the organization? What oral and written communication skills does the receiver possess? Once the sender has answered all of these questions, they will be able to choose an effective channel.

Once the suitable channel is chosen for conveying the message of the sender, next step in the communication regime is decoding which is conducted by the receiver of the message. Once the message is received and examined, the stimulus is sent to the brain for interpreting, in order to assign some type of meaning to it. It is this processing stage that constitutes decoding. The receiver begins to interpret the symbols sent by the sender, translating the message to their own set of experiences in order to make the symbols meaningful. Successful communication takes place when the receiver correctly interprets the sender's message.

The message which is transmitted by the sender is directed only to the receiver of the message. These receiver can be individual or individuals. The extent to which this person comprehends the message will depend on a number of factors, which include the following: how much the individual or individuals know about the topic, their receptivity to the message, and the relationship and trust that exists between sender and receiver. All interpretations by the receiver are influenced by their experiences, attitudes, knowledge, skills, perceptions, and culture. It is similar to the sender's relationship with encoding.

The last step in the communication process is the feedback. It is regarded as the last link in the communication chain. It helps to the sender to the sender to know that how effectively and clearly his message is conveyed or transmitted to the receiver. After receiving a message, the receiver responds in some way and signals that response to the sender. Feedback is a key component in the communication process because it allows the sender to evaluate the effectiveness of the message.

Communication process is the sequence of identifiable steps that are necessary to complete exchange of informance, ideas and understanding among the human beings. Usually the basic steps or elements involved in communication process are as follows :

Source of Communication

Source of communication includes the idea, opinion, any plan, thought and several other.

Sender or Communicator

Sender or communicator is the initiator of the process of communication. He is the person who intends to convey or transmit an information/message to some other person. Sender is usually the source of communication. He initiates the process of communication by defining the idea, coding it and selecting the media for transmission.

Communicatee or Receiver

While going through the communication process, it is noticed that the presence of a receiver is a must in the communication regime to whom the sender send his message. He is the person who is to receive, interpret, understand and respond to the message. The communicator, therefore, must properly identify and understand the communicatee in order to ensure effectiveness of the message.

Message

Message is the most important point of the communication as it is the matter for which a sender arid a receiver interred with each other. It may be some idea, information, thought or emotion. It may be expressed in written, oral or gestural form.

Encoding

Encoding means transforming or translating the message into some language or code understandable to communicatee *i.e.* receiver of the message. Once the message is prepared by the sending the encoding of the message by the sender of the information. At this step, sender transforms the message into words, data, symbols, figures, pictures, gesturals or other code or language so that the intended receiver may understand it properly.

Channel or Medium

As the step of encoding finished, the next step is to select a suitable channel or medium for transmitting the information by the sender to the receiver. The sender can choose among a number of media such as face-to-face conversation, telephone calls; letters, e-mail, fax, photographs, meetings, organisation manuals, news releases, press conferences, advertising on TV, radio and newspapers, and magazines. While selecting a medium, sender should weigh its advantages and disadvantages. A sender should always choose a medium which is free from barriers or disturbing influences so that the message can surely and safely reach to the intended receiver and catch his due attention.

Message Transmission

Once the channel of communication is chosen the next step is to convey the information to the communicate, i.e., transmission of the message. Step at which the message is put into the course of transmission from sender to the receiver. The sender should ensure complete and safe transmission of the message.

Receiving and Decoding

No message accomplishes its purpose unless it is understood by the receiver. Hence, the next step in the process relates to "understanding of the message after receiving it. Where the message has been encoded, decoding should take place. Decoding means translation or transformation of message into an understandable language. But perfect decoding is nearly impossible in our word of many languages and cultures. The chances of successful decoding are enhanced if the receiver knows the language or terminology or code used in the message. It becomes easier, if the receiver understands sender's purpose and background of the message.

Response or Action and Feed Back

As we know that without having the feedback no one can condusle. The effectiveness of the process in the same way without getting the response we can not say about the effectiveness of the communication process. The main object of communication is to elicit desired response or action from the receiver of the message. Hence, communication process remains incomplete or ineffective unless it elicits desired action or response. The receiver, therefore, should give feedback of the message. It enables the sender to know whether the message has been successfully received and has created the desired impact. As soon as the feed-back of the response is received, the process of communication is said to be completed.

The communication process is the perfect guide toward achieving effective communication. When followed properly, the process can usually assure that the sender's message will be understood by the receiver. Although the communication process seems simple, it in essence is not. Certain barriers present themselves throughout the process. Those barriers are factors that have a negative impact on the communication process. Some common barriers include the use of an inappropriate medium (channel), incorrect grammar, inflammatory words, words that conflict with body language, and technical jargon. Noise is also another common barrier. Noise can occur during any stage of the process. Noise essentially is anything that distorts a message by interfering with the communication process. Noise can take many forms, including a radio playing in the background, another person trying to enter your conversation, and any other distractions that prevent the receiver from paying attention.

If communication process is implemented effectively in an organization then it will result to sound and healthy communication within all the members of the organization. It has been proven that individuals that understand the communication process will blossom into more effective communicators, and effective communicators have a greater opportunity for becoming a success.

DIFFICULTIES IN COMMUNICATION PROCESS

In a communication process, every managers tries his best to make his communication process effective, but still several difficulties occurs in a communication process. Hence, communication fails to elicit desired effect or response. There are several barriers to communication. A few among them are as follows:

Language Barrier : Language is also the major cause of communication distortion. For instance, one knows English but the other does not know. Both cannot communicate themselves with each other effectively. In addition, there are large numbers of specialised fields such as systems analysis, computers, operations research, etc., in which technical jargon or vocabulary is used to communicate messages. This factor also contributes to poor communication.

Filtering Information : Sometimes, communicator filters or screens information. He tends to convey only that part of information which the receiver would appreciate. For instance, a subordinate tends to pass on information which his superior would appreciate. This practice tends to distort communication.

Undisclosed Assumptions : Due to the hidden suppositions, the receiver of the message may have some assumptions (regarding the message) which are different from the assumptions of the communicator. This may lead to incorrect action or lack of action on the part of the receiver of the message.

Complex Organisation Structure : One of the important aspect of problem in the communication process is the complex nature of an organization. Long chain of command, large span of control, several layers of management, confusing relations between line and staff officers etc. create distance between the sender and receiver of the message. Consequently, message tends to be distorted or diluted and ultimately becomes less effective.

Poorly Expressed Message : Some times the messages conveyed are poorly or badly transmitted which may lead to problem in the communication process. Wrong choice of words and phrases, faulty construction of sentence, ambiguous language, lack of coherence etc. are the main causes of poor expression of message. Sometimes, communicator speaks very fast and in haste. Sometimes, he omits certain essential facts. All these create a big barrier to communication.

Inadequate Attention or Half Listening : Some time the problem that occur in the communication process is due to the half-listening nature of the people. They don't listen to the interaction properly and then misunderstood the massager information. Inattention may arise because of over business of the communicate or because of the message being contrary to his expectations and beliefs. The simple failure to read notices, minutes and reports is also a common feature. Whatever be the reason, communication remains only a one-way process and there is no understanding of the message, if the receiver pays little attention to the message. In the words of Joseph Dooher, "Listening is the most neglected skills of communication . . . half listening is like racing your engine with gears in neutral. You use gasoline but you get nowhere."

Different Backgrounds : Different individuals often interpret the same communication differently because of their different backgrounds. Thus, when people with different knowledge and experience try to communicate, they often have trouble in getting their meaning across.

Resistance to Change : It is a general tendency of human beings to stick to old and customary patterns of life. They may resist change to maintain *status quo*. Thus, when new ideas are being communicated to introduce a change, it is likely to be overlooked or even opposed. This resistance to change creates an important obstacle to effective communication.

Barriers due to Lack of Mutual Trust : Communication means sharing of ideas in common. "When we communicate, we are trying to establish a commonness." Thus, one will freely transfer information and understanding with another only when there is mutual trust between the two. When there is a lack of mutual trust between the communicator and the communicate, the message is not followed. Credibility gaps, *i.e.* inconsistency in saying and doing also cause lack of trust which works as a barrier to effective communication.

Status Barriers : Sometimes the designation or position of the members in an organization may also lead to difficulties in the communication process. In addition, many superiors do not like to listen patiently to their subordinates. Similarly, a subordinate usually hesitates to seek classifications and express his views and suggestions. In such situations, effective communication becomes a distant dream.

Emotional Attitude : Emotional behavior of the people is also major factor of barrier in the communication process.

Semantic Barriers : Semantic barriers means the barrier caused by the meanings of the words or symbols. Different people may derive different meaning from the same words or symbols. Difficulties in communication arise when the sender and receiver of the message use the same words or symbols in different senses.

ROLE OF COMMUNICATION

Communication with the people is necessary in any society and in any form of government. It is much more so in a democracy where the government depends on popular backing. People must be told about the government plans, programmes, policies, activities, successes, achievements, etc., so as to involve them and to get their willing participation. Also, communication from the people-reaction of the people to the policies and programmes-must reach the policy--makers and administrators to enable them to modify or change the programmes accordingly.

In the ever growing economy of India, it need a lot of consideration towards the mass communication. Mass communication media in India have made significant strides during the 43 years since Independence. They have played an significantly role in disseminating information and ideas, and in providing instruction and entertainment to our people in a purposeful and effective manner.

CURRENT STATUS OF COMMUNICATION IN INDIA

Todays mass communication can be classified into two categories, i.e., traditional techniques and modern techniques:

- Traditional media-pup-petry, folk dance, folklore, community singing, rural theatre, etc.;
- Print-printed word, pictures, etc., which appeal to the sense of sight (newspapers, periodicals, publications, advertisement, etc.);
- Audio-Visual-appeal to both visual and auditory sense (television, films);
- Outdoor media-printed word and visual (posters, cinema slides, hoardings, neon signs, etc.);
- Radio-sense of sound;
- Oral communication-public meetings, group discussions, individual contacts, etc.

ESSENTIAL FACTORS

Communication is a tool for management. Communication as transfer of message service to management through its various functions, has to employ a number of tools and techniques like other disciplines. As such, there is no point of surprise that for solving many communication problems, alternative media for transmission of messages are available. These modern mechanical devices both in verbal and written communication are meant to remove the drawbacks of traditional media by evolving new tools of superior quality and more scientific in nature and use. It is to remember that several previous tools or mediums of communication though in significant use, a numerous latest tools and techniques have been developed by replacing those old and previous tools which brought—many communication technologies.

DISCRIMINATION THE DISCRIMINATION IN ADVERTISING

Despite these advances, the country is still behind the norms laid down by UNESCO for adequate information services for the developing countries. Take radio, which reaches the largest number of people in India. The number of radio sets is far below the minimum laid down by UNESCO, i.e., one set for five persons. In this respect, we are also far behind even some Asian countries such as Japan, Kuwait, Jordan and Iran.

The cost of a radio receiving set is a major constraint for the poorer section of our people living in rural areas and city slums. The solution, therefore, lies either in providing subsidized receiving sets to this vulnerable section of the society, or to expand community listening facilities with adequate arrangements for the maintenance of community sets. The people who live below the poverty line, and who need information more than any other section of society, should be reached by this powerful medium.

Television is still a largely urban and semiurban-oriented medium in the country. A TV set is beyond the reach of an average middle class family. The need, therefore, is to bring down the cost substantially. Even with the reduction of price, TV sets still would be beyond the reach of the poorer sections of the country. The supply of subsidized sets to groups of people, or installation of community TV sets with proper maintenance facilities is a possible way out. These facilities can be provided in the areas which are already covered by TV network at present, and which are likely to be covered in the near future.

Today, the circulation of 1800 daily newspapers in India is about two crore. Compared to the UNESCO norm of ten daily newspapers for 100 persons the number in India is too low. Also the daily circulation of newspapers is largely urban-oriented. Fifty per cent of the total circulation of daily newspapers is centered in four metropolitan cities of Delhi, Calcutta, Bombay and Madras. The daily newspapers, therefore, do not reach the bulk of our rural population.

As the literacy rate has increased a lot in our country so the newspaper can also provide information to the people. Facilities to start such newspapers, therefore, need to be provided if the newspaper medium is to reach people living in semi-urban and rural areas.

For expansion of such newspapers in the country, there is need for substantial increase in indigenous production of newsprint. Limited annual availability of such newsprint is a serious bottleneck to the growth of newspapers. Simultaneously, these newspapers should be provided with facilities such as supply of subsidized news, publicity material, printing machinery, etc.

At present, India is leading in the newsprint because of the material deficit. It was only after independence that the National Newsprint and Paper Mills Ltd., Nepa Nagar, Madhya Pradesh, emerged as a newsprint producer. By 1982, two other newsprint mills had come into operation. These were the Mysore Paper Mills in Karnataka (a State Government Undertaking) with a capacity of 75,000 tones of newsprint, and the Kerala Newsprint Project (now Hindustan Newsprint Ltd.) of the central public sector undertaking, Hindustan Paper Corporation, with a capacity of 80,000 tones per annum. Consequently, the domestic production of newsprint increased from 1.02 lakh metric tones in 1981-82 to 2.72 lakh metric tones during 1989. The remaining requirement of the country was met by imports, which increased from 2.01 lakh metric tones in 1982-83 to 2.68 lakh metric tones in 1988-89. The total newsprint requirement for 1988-89 was of the order of 5.40 lakh metric tones. Of this 2.72 lakhs, was met through indigenous production.

Newsprint is allocated to newspapers and periodicals in India in terms of the Newsprint Allocation Policy, which is announced by the Ministry of Information and Broadcasting for each licensing year. The basic entitlement of newsprint for a newspaper is largely determined on the basis of actual consumption of newsprint, or white printing paper, or both during the previous year, its average circulation, average number of pages, average page area, and the number of publishing days.

Several professional and social norms have to be traced while the allocation of newsprint. For instance, a newspaper is declared eligible only if it has shown a regularity of 90 per cent in case of a daily newspaper, and of 66-2/3 per cent in case of any other periodicity. Newsprint is also allocated to:

- printing of low-priced books for promotion of education, and
- Advertising agencies,
- newspapers for their trail printing,
- printing of college and school magazines.

The allotment of newsprint from different sources is made in the light of such factors as quantity of newsprint likely to be available, and the need to maintain adequate buffer stocks. Accordingly, a newspaper, with an entitlement of less than specified tones, has the option to obtain indigenous or imported newsprint either in part or in full. In the case of newspapers, whose entitlement is above that limit, the allocation is made on a package basis, comprising indigenous and imported newsprint. Periodicals, which are regular in publication, are allowed to exercise their choice from the glazed newsprint subject to its availability. Their requests are, however, considered on merit having regard to the paper's circulation, targeted readership and other relevant factors. In the case of a newly-started newspaper or periodical, only indigenously-produced newsprint is allocated. Further entitlement is released only after necessary proof is furnished, as to how the initial quota of indigenous newsprint has actually been utilised by the newspaper concerned.

Imported and indigenous newsprint is sold at different prices. To fix the prices for imported newsprint, the Union Ministry of Information and Broadcasting had set up a Price Fixation Committee. As regards the indigenous newsprint, the prices are fixed from time to time by the mills concerned in consultation with the Ministry of Industry.

Several documentary films and advertisement have been made in our country in our country but could not approach a large number of people. It is because of deficit of proper exhibition amenities in out country. In cinema halls, we have 0.8 seats for 100 persons as compared to the UNESCO yardstick of two seats for 100 persons.

The Film Enquiry Committee recommended that the country should have at least one cinema house for 20,000 people. The present number is far less than this norm. The existing cinema houses are also unevenly distributed, with the result that more than 55% of our rural population has to travel 15 km to find a cinema house. There is, therefore, an urgent need for building more cinema houses with even distribution, and touring and open air theatres within the country. The diversion of a part of the entertainment tax, allocation of sites at concessional rates, and other forms of encouragement would help in building more cinema houses in the country. However the need of more cinema houses will have to be reviewed in the context of emergence of Video age.

At present India's book production has increased a lot and also improved quality wise. This has resulted in higher cost of book-production and also considerable wastage of effort on the part of the author, the publisher and the printer. The smaller towns and villages, at present, remain outside the reach of the book-world. It is, therefore, necessary to produce better and more books, and also in large numbers. This will bring down the cost of book-production, and enable a larger number of people in the country to buy books.

FUNCTIONS OF COMMUNICATION

The purpose or function of communication in an organisation is to provide the information to the individual or group about the subject. Function of communication varies according to different levels of management. Top management informs policies to the lower level through middle level. In turn lower level informs top level the reaction through middle level. Information exchanges flow vertically, horizontally and diagonally across the organisation. Becoming informed or informing others is the main purpose of communication.

Examination of activities to form an idea or judgement of the worth of task is achieved through communication. Communication is a tool to appraise the individual his contribution to the organisation. Evaluating one's own inputs or another's outputs or some ideological scheme demands an adequate and effective communication process.

Communication is essential to provide directions by the top management or managers to lower level. Directing others or being directed or instructed cannot take place without complete communication process. The managerial function of directing includes giving orders to employees immediately subordinate to do a task, stop it or modify it. Directing others may be communicated either orally or in writing. An order may be command order, request order or implied order. Communication includes indirectly to the organizational objectives. It includes directly to the satisfaction of an individual requirements which are compatible with organizational goals and objectives.

A complete communication process is necessary in influencing others or being influenced. It implies the provision of feedback which tells the effect of communication. Motivational forces in an individual are to be provided and then stimulated through communication. Motivation is a behavioural concept through which one may try to understand why people behave as they do. Motivation is the result of interaction among three groups of factors such as

- influences working within the individual,
- influences working within the organisation,
- influences working in the external environment.

Communication discharges several incidental and neutral functions. Many pieces of communication are not directly connected with the accomplishment of the objectives of an organisation.

The importance of personal safety on the job has been greatly recognised. A complete communication process is needed to teach and educate the workers about personal safety on the job. This communication helps the workers to avert accidents, risks etc. and avoid cost, procedures etc.

A business enterprise cannot survive by remaining aloof from the rest of society. There is interrelationship and interdependence between society and an enterprise operating in society. Public goodwill and confidence are essentially created among the public. It is the communication with its multi-media approach has to project the image of the firm in society. Through an effective external communication system an enterprise has to inform society about its goals, activities, progress, social responsibilities, etc..

The employees of the organisation are to be oriented with the organisation structure. Communication helps to make people acquainted with the co-employees, superiors and with the policies, objectives, rules and regulations of the organisation.

Recruitment process implies face-to-face or oral communication. Effective decision-making is possible when required and adequate information is supplied to the decision-maker. Communication, either verbal or written, helps the process of decision-making. In general everyone in the organisation is to be provided with necessary information so as to enable him to discharge his own tasks effectively and efficiently.

QUALITATIVE ASPECTS OF COMMUNICATION

The initial purpose of communication is to keep people informed. Communication is a reciprocal alternative two-way and a continuous social process. It should serve the organisational objects. To accomplish this, the management adopts an effective media and network of communication. To make it effective, the communicator must possess certain qualities, understand the receiver, convey the message and get to act on it. Practical experience in the field makes both the sender and receiver to reach perfection. Communication translates organisational information into the language commonly understood in the organisation. Lack of feedback, interaction and effective decoding of signs or words into receiver's capability are the important problems in communication. But they do not alter the basic essentials for successful communication. Wilbur Schramm was proposed for any communication to be transmitted effectively from source to receiver, whether the source is personal or, non-personal, the message must meet the following three requirements which are follows as:

- It must be so designed and delivered as to gain the attention of the receiver.
- It must use signals that are understood in the same way by both source and receiver.
- It must arouse needs in the receiver and suggest some way of satisfying these needs that is appropriate to the receiver's group situation when moved to make the desired response.

Knowing the audience or receiver in the case of written communication is important. However, the important principles of communication are discussed under the following paragraphs. These are essentials or factors which are to be considered while initiating communication to achieve the objective of communication.

In the communication process, message is the very subject matter of communication. Clarity of ideas, facts, opinions in the mind of communicator should be clear before communicating. It is a thinking process to conceive the subject. The message is always subject to the test of principle of clarity. It is to be encoded in common, in the direct and simple and easily understandable language. So that the receiver is able to understand it without doubt and difficulty.

Information is different from communication. All communi-cations contain information while all information cannot communicate a message. The word information is comprehensive in which communication is a special kind of transmitting message in symbolic form. The sender first collects and keeps before him the relevant information concerning a particular or group or people. Principle of effective communication is to have information and communicate in symbolic form.

Communication processes the clarity when it is expressed in language and transmitted in a manner that can be comprehended by the receiver. This theory was proposed by Koontz and Donnell.

The subject matter to be communicated must be adequate and full which enables the receiver to understand the central theme or idea of the message. Incompleteness of message may conclude in misunderstanding the subject by the receiver. The decision-making process would be delayed and actions may be delayed when the message is incomplete.

The objective of communication is to draw the attention of the receiver. An effective communication changes the behaviour of the receiver. The process is not complete just by transmitting ideas, facts or opinions. Effective communication calls that it must create interest and pay proper attention to the message and to act accordingly. Action speaks louder than words. The changes which are made in effective communication always effect the receiver. This is the underlying principle of attention.

The message transmitted should not be contradictory. The subject matter of communication is said to be consistent when it is in agreement with the objectives and policies of the organisation. The thinking, action or happenings should be according to the same organisational rules and principles. Communication is said to be effective when it is consistent than when it is varied or contradicted. Consistency can be achieved if the communicator keeps in his mind the broad objectives, policies and programmes of the enterprise. There should be some linkage and compromise between communications. One communication should not conflict with the previous communication. Conflict and inconsistency create confusion, chaos ultimately resulting in delay in decision-making and action.

Achieving common goals of the enterprise is the objective of group activities. Communication as a tool of management should strengthen the enterprise. Communication is only a means rather than end. The transmitter and receiver have to use the communication tool as a means to an end not an end itself so it promotes integrated efforts of the organisation. On the basic of the principle of integrity Koontz and Donnell observe : "The purpose of managerial communication is to support understanding by individuals as they achieve and maintain the cooperation needed to meet enterprise goals. All communications should be framed and transmitted in such a way as to support the integrity of the formal organisation."

"The most effective communication concludes when managers utilize the informal organization to supplement the communication channels of the formal organization". This concept was proposed by Koontz and Donnell.

Informal communication is called grapevine. It is a kind of communication. It occurs on account of informal relationship between the persons. This relationship grows up spontaneously from personal interest, group interest, social and other non-formal relations. Informal channel is the most effective one and transmits information with surprising speed. Informal organisation should be utilised properly to communicate a message. It supplements formal communication channel.

An effective communication demands two-way communi-cation, i.e., vertical — upward and downward. It should not always be downward movement from the superior to the subordinates. In such a case communication cannot produce its desired goals. The reaction and responses of the receiver are equally needed to achieve the purpose of communication. A manager should thus not only speak, inform, instruct and order, but should also be prepared to listen, understand, answer, amend and interpret. Thus it involves two-way traffic or process and the process is complete.

After transmission of the message in the communication process, the receiver is the kingpin who has to act on the message. The receiver must understand the subject. This is the main purpose of communication. The sender must use such language which may easily be understood by the receiver. The message should be simple, clear and short lines. Killian suggested "communicate with an awareness of the total and physical and human setting in which the information will be received. Ask what, when and in what manner you would like to be communicated with if you were in a similar environment and position."

The major objective of communication is to make the message reach at an appropriate time. It is not just the transmission of ideas, opinions etc., by the superior to the subordinate for the sake of communication. They should be conveyed at right and proper time. Sending before time or after would not serve the purpose of communication. A delayed message is stale or historical and has no importance. Simplicity is the best and easiest way of understanding and response in communication. With the help of simplicity, the communicator must try to achieve the principle of effectiveness. In simplicity, it refers to the language used should be simple and only common words be used which doesn't mean using colloquial English.

Simplicity is the feature which meets to all situations. Yet another principle of effective communication is communication network. It is the channel or path by which exchange of transmission of ideas, facts etc. flow to and from the officially designated positions in the organisational structure. Formal communication has a set network which determines fixed route for information movement. The network covers downward, upward, horizontal line of communication. In a downward line the message moves from top to bottom and *vice versa* in the case of upward line. Horizontal line is for personnel in one department and personnel of equal, lower or superior position in another department. Both vertical and horizontal lines should be used for effective communication, but distance should be less as possible.

There are two media for transmitting a message. They are oral and written media. Both have their own merits and demerits. *Oral communication* is more effective for some messages and similarly written communication in other circumstances. The principle of strategic use of media is to be adopted. The need, objective and the receiver are the factors should be kept in mind in selecting a medium.

Though the last but the most important key or principle to effective communication is to obtain feedback from the receiver. Knowing acceptance or rejection as to the message transmitted is probably the most important method of improving communication. The principle of feedback promotes two-way communication. Feedback is a process to ascertain whether or not the receiver properly understood the message. It helps to know the reaction of the receiver of the message. In which superior has to listen, answer, interpret and amend the message. Interface and interaction are possible in feedback. It avoids errors in transmission of message and invoking effective participation of the subordinates. Thus feedback enables the communicator to take initiative in order to know reactions regarding the effectiveness of communication.

ESSENTIALS IN COMMUNICATION

The essential of effective communication are more useful in personnel management. Most communications are designed to meet the demands of current situation.

The message must have meaning for the receiver, and it must be compatible with his value system. It must have relevance for him. In general, people select those items of information which promise them the greatest regards. The content determines the audience.

The message must be put in simple terms. Words must mean the same thing to the receiver as they do the sender. Complex issues must be compressed into themes, slogans or stereotype that have simplicity and clarity.

Communication is an unending process. It requires repetition to achieve penetration. Repetition with variation contributes to both factual and attitude learning. The story must be consistent.

Established channels of communication should be used those channels that the receiver uses and respects. Creating new ones is difficult. Different channels have different effects and serve effectively in different stages of the diffusion process.

Communication must take into account the capability of the audience. Communications are most effective when they require the least effort on the part of the recipient. This includes all the factors of availability, habit, reading ability and receiver's knowledge.

Job of communication is to help and promote human relations, making use among other things of medium or media. There can be no mutual understanding without communication and mutual understanding in human relations is possible through communication.

- Empathy is feeling with the other person expressed by speech. Sympathy is feeling sorry for him expressed by words.
- Dialogue is a process of conversation or speech with purpose. It involves exchange of ideas. It is for influencing behaviour. Conciliation and compromise are generally involved. Dialogue is a democratic, civilized and constructive weapon. It takes the form of discussion, criticism and deliberation. Others' viewpoints should be considered and there is no place for monopoly of the conversation in dialogue.
- Persuasion is a process of convincing and motivating to get the things done. Speech is one of the methods to persuade a person. A sense of human interest on the person who is being persuaded will understand and appreciate the cause and effect of his action.

There are three process which are used in communication process.

The new information order of the world information transmission is the process of getting things done. In complex business organizations, effective decisions depend upon collection, storage and supply of information. Information giving and information taking is a continuous process in organizations.

The object of transmitting information is to change the behaviour of the recipient. Communication is aimed to influence, to persuade, to motivate or activate towards desired goals.

The main reason for conflict in interpersonal situation is lack of mutual understanding. The problems of communication are really the problems of understanding people. Possibly the most important managerial function to bridge the gap is communication, without it mutual understanding cannot be achieved.

Use of Querries : "Does the communicator recognise that technologists and scientists must come to grips with certain concrete problems the solutions for which would permit the lean "third world countries' people look near fat cats in rich countries?"

- Can the "New Information Order" check more effectively the sources (of information) which feed the Third World Countries so that they can get only such information as will help the growth in the long run?"
- What can be done against the bottleneck that is developing between the unlimited information capacity of modern

communication systems and the limited reception and assimilation rate of individuals ?

- Can communicators help in encountering the danger of over-population ?
- Can communicators arrest the dangerous tendency towards overurbanization ?
- What can be done to educate children, adolescents and adults to be fit citizens in a materially stationary civilization on a high culture?
- Can communicators create awareness among the people of 'developing countries' ?

What can be done about 'Information pollution? Some of the elements which contribute to Information Pollution are : political lies, political scandal, character assassination, rigging the elections, interference in judicial administration, pornography, violence and sex via audio-visual media, and many similar or other pollutions."

REASONS FOR THE GROWING IMPORTANCE OF COMMUNICATION

The reasons for the growing importance of communication can be judged from the following points:

Facts, figures, of past and present are to be provided for quick and effective decision-making. The primary basis is communication through which an effective network supplies information, helps in arriving at quick decisions. Problem defining, alternative courses of action, selecting best course of action are all possible only with necessary information supplied to the decision-maker. In its absence it may not be possible even for the top management to formulate broad policies and objectives. The middle level management supplies which helps top management to take meaningful decisions. On the other hand, objectives and goals cannot be achieved unless the top management can effectively communicate to lower levels.

Communication promotes management process. Communication also promotes managerial efficiency. This efficiency lies in the manner in which an individual or group is informed towards general objects. These managerial function like planning, coordination, control and motivation, etc., cannot be discharged without communication.

The modern complex organizations are large in size having a large number of people working in the organisation to achieve common goals. The organisational structure shows many levels of organisational hierarchy both tall network, flat network. This always leads to a problem of coordination. An effective system of communication promotes to better coordination. It helps a lot in coordination. Coordination is essential between groups, channels which is necessary for the efficient functioning of the entire organisation. It is the communication which promotes to better coordination.

Smooth and uninterrupted working of an enterprise is to a great extent dependent on a good communication network. Communication assumes a greater role in this direction. Communication is the basic to existence of an organization from birth of organization on through its life. This theory was proposed by Herbert G. Hicks. Corrective decision-making and efficiency of the organisation is based on information supply. If the messages are not flowing freely across the organisation, smooth functioning and unrestricted working of the organisation are not possible.

Communication is necessary for achieving job satisfaction. Management conveys messages which promote mutual understanding. Reception and recognition provide job satisfaction to employees. Two-way communication creates confidence which leads to job satisfaction. Efficient managers with good communication skills promote job satisfaction to employees. Openness, frank expression of opinions are necessary in this direction.

Morale and good human relations in the organisation are essential to achieve goals of the organisation and to promote its goodwill in the public. An effective system of communication builds good morale and improves human relations. Participatory communication is the best technique of morale building and motivation. Proper communications between the interested parties reduce the points of friction and minimize those that inevitably arise. Management at every work level is primarily charged with the responsibility of seeing that proper procedures are established for sympathetic interchange of information between all parties concerned."

Communication plays an important role in these three types of roles. In case of inter-personal role a manager has to interact always with subordinates. In information role a manager has to collect information from various people and supply necessary information to others both inside and outside the organisation. A manager in decisional role has to communicate decisions to others. Thus it is through oral or written media of communication the managers discharge their interpersonal, informational and decisional roles.

REMEDIES IN COMMUNICATION

Following are the remedies that can be taken to present the distortion of communication:

Clarity and Completeness : In order to communicate effectively, it is very essential to know the 'audience' for whom the message is meant. The message to be conveyed must be absolutely clear in the mind of the communicator because if you do not understand an idea, you can never express to someone. The message should be adequate and appropriate to the purpose of communication. The purpose of communication, itself, should be clearly defined.

(a) Training of Employees : The employees should be trained to understand the objectives, rules, policies, authority relationships and operations of the enterprise. It will help to understand each other, minimise conflicts and distortion of messages.

(b) Suitable Channel or Medium : In order to have effective and sound communication the most important selection of suitable or appropriate mode of communication. A judicious combination of written, oral and gestural modes as well as formal and informal channels should be used for maximum effectiveness.

(c) Motivation, Mutual Trust and Confidence : The communication should be made in such away it encourage communicate towards its tasks which in turn leads to the accomplishment of organizational goal. A sense of mutual trust and confidence must the generated to promote free flow of information.

(d) Sound Organisational Structure : To make communication effective, the organisational structure must be sound and appropriate to the needs of the organisation. Attempt must be made to shorten the distances to be travelled through for conveying information.

(e) Consistent Behaviour : To avoid credibility management must ensure that their actions and deeds are in accordance with their communication.

(f) Gestures and Tone : The way you say something is also very important along with the message for gestures such as a twinkle of an eye, a smile or a handshake, etc. convey sometimes more meaning than even words spoken on written. Thus, one should have appropriate facial expression, tone, gestures and mood, etc. to make communication effective.

(g) Use of Informal Communication : As informal communication, sometimes is of great use at various leads of management so it should also be implemented in relation to the formal communication in the organization.

(h) Empathic Listening : In order to have effective communication one should be good listener as it enhances the interaction between sender and receiver of the information. Superiors should develop the habit of patient listening and avoid premature evaluation of communication from their subordinates. This will encourage free flow of upward communication.

(i)Participation : The management should promote the participation in communication. Subordinates should be invited to participate in the decision-making process so that cooperation nay increase and communication barriers are removed.

(j) Feedback : Communication is not complete unless the response or reaction of the receiver of the message is obtained by the communicator. The effectiveness of communication can be judged from the feedback. Therefore, must be encouraged and analysed.

(k) Proper Language : To avoid semantic barriers, the message should be expressed in simple, brief and clear language. The words or symbols selected for conveying the message must be appropriate to the reference and understanding of the receiver.

RULE OF FIVE

Rule of five includes all these expectations of receiver which have to be considered during the communication process. Theses includes: (i) receiving, (ii) understanding, (iii) acceptance, (iv) action, and (v) feedback. The communication is regarded effective and successful if these five steps are completed efficiently.

Communication Network

Communication network refers to the pattern of interconnecting lines of communication that exists in an organisation. Communication network are based on two things, i.e., needs of the organization and also on the attitudes of the senior-subordinate relationship.

Types of Communication Network—Communication networks can be categorized into four sects. They are as follows :

- Wheel network,
- Chain network,
- Free-flow or decentralised network,
- Circular network.

Wheel or Star Network : When there is no direct communication between the members in the organizationthis type of network is called wheel network. It is also known as star network. They communicate with other members through one superior or manager *i.e.* hub of the wheel. The manager acts as the central point like the hub of a wheel. All the members of the organisation exchange information, and throught though the hub of the wheel *i.e.* manager. Such a network is also known as 'autocratic network'.

Chain Network : When communication flows in the hierarchy of management, i.e., along the chain of command then it is said to have chain network of communication. In other words, where communication flows in direct vertical line of hierarchy of management it is said to be chain network communication. It is usually two-way communication from top to bottom and bottom to top of the hierarchy of management. But there is no scope of horizontal communication in this network.

Free-flow or Decentralised or all Channel Network : Free-flow network is one in which lines of communication are not structured. Every member of the group can communicate freely, and frankly with all other members of the group. Thus, there is no restriction on the flow of communication and hence it is a more of a nature of informal network.

Circular Network : Circular network of communication is one in which communication moves in circular way. In this network, each individual can communicate with the person on his immediate right or left but not with any other person in the organisation or group.

TODAY'S ROLE

In modern days the emphasis is on recognition of dignity of labour and authority. Workers are not to be treated as a commodity. They are part and parcel of the organisation having partnership relationship. The concept of master-servant relationship has lost its significance. They are copartners of the enterprise. A successful management is one which must understand the needs, attitudes and feelings of the worker. As such the emphasis is on human relations, which implies better understanding of workers. This emphasises at the same time the significance of two-way traffic in communication. Therefore, the growing recognition of human relations and to maintain good human relations with workers and a host of other factors have necessitated an effective communication.

Social responsibility of management cannot be ignored. The responsibilities imply the obligations which a business house owes to society. There are four important groups such as owners of the business, i.e., the shareholders, customers, employees and the society at large. These people must be kept informed always about the steps taken in the discharge of its social responsibilities. Public relations emphasise a proper understanding of the nature of the public and the social environment in which an industry is operating and the changes that are constantly taking place. The word public refers to any group of people who share a common interest. Employees are public called as internal public. Relation is the outcome of mutual understanding derived from the process of sharing of the common interest. The integration of these two elements gives us public relations which is today a specialised management function.

GOALS AND OBJECTIVES OF MASS COMMUNICATION

The basic function of mass communication media is to provide information, education or instruction and entertainment to the people. The media also motivate people directly or indirectly. To discharge these functions in a meaningful and purposeful manner in any country or in any community, the mass media agencies should be clear about the broad communication objectives, which may guide their operations in their day-today work.

The national objectives should be non-political, non-controversial, and on which there is general national consensus. The objective should be to further the interests and well-being of the people as a whole, and to promote the many-sided development of the country. The objective should be a long-term one and need not necessarily change with political changes.

In a developing country like India where a lot of diversification can be seen then it's a greater problem to made a national communication policy as people of different religion, caste and language live together. Nevertheless, such a policy is essential so as to give some direction to mass media efforts. The country should also have the necessary infrastructure to implement the basic policy in the shortest possible time.

To discharge his functions in an efficient and purposeful manner, the mass communicator in India should have a clear conception of the basic ideals or values which he has to promote. He should also know something about the availability of mass media infrastructure, the gaps that exist at present in communication facilities as compared to international standards, and the effort that is required to bridge or minimize this gap.

The major goal of the India's mass communication is to inculcate the faith and strength among the people of our country towards two democratic institutions. Such as free and fair elections, rule of law, independence of the judiciary, freedom of the press, secular character of the state, etc.

The communication media should also promote under-standing and involvement of people in the socio-economic changes and developmental activities taking place in the country. The media thus can quicken the process of development. The point which the media need to emphasize is that development is perfectly possible within the democratic framework.

The mass communication agencies should also propagate nationally--needed and nationally-accepted themes which are basic to our society. A few of these are:

- it also contributed towards agricultural development,
- eradication of social evils such as drinking of liquor, dowry, etc.,
- promotion of savings, and
- it emphasize on strategic development through scientific techniques and new technologies,
- family welfare and population control, and stabilization of the population at a level consistent with requirements of national economy by reducing the present birth rate,
- any other subject mentioned in the Directive Principles of our Constitution.
- citizens need--oriented programmes-dissemination of useful information to different sections of people such as farmers, workers, artisans, students and youth; information on housing, medical care and medical facilities, travel, prices of essential commodities, self-employment and employment opportunities, educational facilities and industrial relations,

- national integrity and national unity, national cohesion and common cultural heritage despite diversity of language,: region caste and religion,
- it focused an increase of literacy rate through television and FM radio.

Our mass communication society should also contribute towards the development of rural and vulnerable section of our society. This section of the people and the areas should be identified and disparity in communication facilities should be minimized, if not eradicated. These sections and areas need information most and communication media should satisfy this requirement.

In the context of the task outlined above, the question arises whether we have an adequate network of mass communication facilities. India has made significant progress in the, field of mass communication since Independence. In radio networks also we have made devastating changes. Now use have 98 radio stations all over the country as which was only 6 in 1947.

Television, which was non-existent in 1947, is now a major communication medium with over 400 transmitters covering 67.2% of the area and 88% of the population of the country.

The Indian film industry with about 600 feature films a year is at the top of producers of films in the world. It makes one and a half times more films now as compared to 1947.

At present nearly 22000, newspaper published in our country which quite double from 1947. Books publishing has also since then.

The advertising business increased manifold since Independence. Commercial broadcasting and telecasting have made a significant difference in the field of advertising.

Case Study

Note : knowing more about "Role of Communication" reader can study documentation process of Microsoft company by visiting their site : www.members.microsoft.com

http://www.citehr.com/44751-communication-skills-handbook-case-studies.html

http://www.communicaid.com/case-studies.php

http://www.english.heacademy.ac.uk/explore/publications/casestudies/oralskills/index.php

14

Non-Commercial Advertising

This chapter includes the key concepts that are described below:-

- Introduction

INTRODUCTION

Non-Commercial Advertising is sponsored by or for a charitable institution or civic group or religious or political organization. To raise the fund, many non-commercial advertisement seek money and placed. Others hope to change consumer behavior. Therefore, the main objectives of non-commercial advertising are:

- Change activity habits
- Decrease waste of resources
- Stimulate inquires for information
- Improve public attitude
- Remind people to give again.
- Popularize social cause
- Communicate political viewpoint

So called word-of-mouth advertising is a person to person communication that is perceived as being noncommercial, concerning goods or services: it is face-to-face product related communications between and among the friends, relatives and others. Because it is noncommercial, it is commonly seen as being an unbiased source of information.

Use of Communication Process

Communication Process is undertaken as a part of

communication management and helps to ensure that stakeholders are kept regularly informed. Communication is the phenomenon of sharing ideas, thoughts, and feelings with other people and having those ideas, thoughts, and feelings understood by the people we are talking with. When we communicate we speak, listen, and observe. The manner we communicate is a learned style. As children we learn from watching our parents and other adults communicate. As an adult we can learn to improve the way we communicate by observing others who communicate effectively, learning new skills, and practicing those skills. Due to the many forms and uses of advertising, it is typical to make all-embracing generalizations about its distinctive qualities as a component of the promotional mix.

Communication is one of the most important areas of human activity. Advertising endeavors to make skillful use of the communication approach by focusing it for achievement of specified objectives. Most advertising is used in business and marketing strategies and has commercial orientation. It should be instrumental in contributing to the profit position of the company and thus justifying the investment made in it. However, the basic approach of advertising is equally relevant to the achievement of non-business and non-profit, i.e., all non-commercial and non-commercial advertising lies in advertiser's expectations from expenditure incurred on advertising and other forms of promotion.

Amplified Expressiveness : Advertising provides opportunities for dramatizing the company and its products through the artful use of print, sound and color. Sometimes, however, the tool's very success at expressiveness may dilute or distract from the message.

Impersonality : Advertising cannot be as compelling as a company sales representative. The audience does not feel obligated to pay attention or respond. Advertising is able to carry on only a monologue, not a dialogue, with the audience.

Public Presentation: Advertising is a highly public mode of communication. Its public nature confers a kind of legitimacy on the product and also suggests a standardized offering. Because many persons receive the same message, buyers know that their motives for purchasing the product will be publicly understood.

Pervasiveness: Advertising is a pervasive medium that permits the seller to repeat a message many times. It also allows the buyer to receive and compare the messages of various competitors. Large-scale advertising by a seller says something positive about the seller's size, popularity and success.

Advertising is an efficient manner to reach numerous geographically dispersed buyers at a low cost Per exposure. Certain forms of advertising, such as TV advertising, can be done on a small budget, while other forms, such as newspaper advertising, can be done on a small budget. Advertising may have an effect on sales simply through its presence. Consumers may believe a heavily advertised brand is one that offers "good value", "otherwise, why would advertisers spend so much money backing a poor product?

Effective communication is a major part in achieving your educational goals. Effectively communication is essential when it comes to about learning. Many times your instructor is the sender. Job of instructor is to send you messages that include information about the skill you need to learn. Your instructor's messages might include lectures or handouts for you.

Advertising as Communication Tool

In the present day marketing, advertising has become a communication tool for all type of business enterprises including large and small. Even non-business enterprises have recognized the importance of advertising. Advertising is a non-personal tool of stimulating the goals and services. It has acquired the distinction of being the most pervasive channels of marketing communications.

In our daily life, we perceive, listen and experience numerous products at home, in a shop, while traveling in the bus or train etc., and many talk about their individuality. Therefore, it is anything which turns person's attention towards it is termed as 'advertising' and the way through which the advertiser makes people aware, is communication. In this way advertising and communication are related to each other.

The first requirement is that the advertisement captures the attention of its audience after communicating the message to them. In other words, the advertisement has to go through the attention filter of the target audience. Advertising communication gives new information, or it may attempt to alter existing views or beliefs of the entire audiences. It is vital that the advertisement communication should appeal to them and influence their attitude, thought process and purchase behavior in favor of the advertised brand. The major objective of advertising communication is to boost up sale figures as to maximize the profits. It is one of the most important tools of modern marketing.

The elemental determination of advertising is to assist sale probability of a product or a service. Advertising as a promotional technique augments tendency to purchase, moving the prospect gradually towards the product to make a purchase decision. Of course, advertising is only one of several communication forces. It actuates the buyer through consecutive stages such as awareness, comprehension or recognition, conviction and action.

Stages of Commercial Communication

Advertising objectives may be divided into four stages of commercial communication which are explained below: -

Cognizance: The prospect must be informed about the subsistence of the brand or company in the market. Awareness is the bare minimum goal of advertising. The buying process starts after informing the consumer about the product or service.

Conception: The prospect must understand what the product is and what it will do for him. The apprehension level indicates that people are not only aware of the brand or company but they also know the brand name and can be familiar with the package or trademark. But they are not yet influenced that they want to buy.

Conviction: The prospect must be mentally convinced to buy the brand or the product. The convinced level shows brand preference and intention to buy the product in the near future.

Advertising for Social Causes

Another expression commonly used in this context is public service advertising. Such advertising may be undertaken by public bodies such as municipal corporations. It may also be undertaken by business concerns in the public interest. As the name of the company will normally appear in the advertisement, some payoff from such advertising to the company's goodwill, may be there. However, when the primary purpose of such advertising is to promote a social cause, it may be considered non-commercial. While there can be no categorical classification, it is the basic motive which matters.

Need for Public Service Advertising

A public service advertisement (PSA) or community service advertisement (CSA) is a non-commercial advertisement broadcast on radio or television, for the public interest. PSAs are intended to modify public attitudes by raising awareness about specific issues. The most common topics of PSAs are health and safety. A typical PSA is part of a public awareness campaign to inform or educate the public about an issue such as smoking or compulsive gambling.

Public service advertising campaigns are widespread around the world. Such advertising is generally produced and distributed on a cooperative basis by governmental agencies or nonprofit organizations acting in concert with private advertising and mass media companies. In most cases, the nonprofit provides the programming that is to be advertised, while the participating advertising agency and media companies provide creative services, media planning, and dissemination services on a *pro bono* basis. The military produces PSAs to recruit enlistees, in addition to paid advertising and sponsorship efforts.

Advertising has to be responsive to the social context in which it operates. It is not merely an array of techniques. Both as an area of knowledge and as a profession, advertising has scope for application beyond commercial activity. It is in this spirit that the professional advertising associations and other related forums make special efforts to identify topics and problem areas needing public attention. They also organize preparation and release of advertising campaign. Advertising agencies invariably extend the fullest cooperation in such endeavors, as a part of their professional and social responsibility.

Advertising with a central focus on the public welfare. Public-service advertising is generally sponsored by a nonprofit institution, civic group, religious organization, trade association, or political group. Typically, it is directed at some humanitarian cause, philosophical ideal, political concept, or religious viewpoint. Most public-service advertising involves the donation of time or space on part of the medium in which it is featured, although free time or space is not a prerequisite for this type of advertising. Groups such as the Red Cross, United Way, and International Ladies Garment Workers Union have sponsored a great deal of public-service advertising.

Concept of Professionalization

The phenomenon of professionalization tends to establish the group norms of conduct and qualification of members of a profession and tends also to insist that members of the profession achieve "conformity to the norm." and abide more or less strictly with the established procedures and any agreed code of conduct, which is policed by professional bodies, for "accreditation assures conformity to general expectations of the profession."

Professionalization is the social process by which any trade or occupation transforms itself into a true "profession of the highest integrity and competence." This process tends to involve establishing acceptable qualifications, a professional body or association to oversee the conduct of members of the profession and some degree of demarcation of the qualified from unqualified amateurs. This creates "a hierarchical division between the knowledge-authorities in the professions and a deferential citizenry." This demarcation is often termed "occupational closure", as it means that the profession then becomes closed to entry from outsiders, amateurs and the unqualified: a stratified occupation "defined by professional demarcation and grade."

Professions also possess power, prestige, high income, high status and privileges; their members soon come to comprise an elite class of people, cut off to some extent from the common people, and occupying an elevated station in society: "a narrow elite a hierarchical social system: a system of ranked orders and classes."

It would be most inappropriate to give a second place to non-commercial advertising. It is common practice, especially amongst government departments and some public-sector organizations, to use the expression 'publicity'. This generally has the effect of downgrading the standard of professionalism in such organizations. In most situations, the challenge of creating effective communication is possibly much greater than that in the conventional commercial context.

Case Study

Note : knowing more about "Non-Commercial Advertising" reader can study documentation process of Microsoft company by visiting their site : www.members.microsoft.com

http://www.acma.gov.au/WEB/STANDARD/pc=PC_310315

http://code.google.com/apis/adsense/docs/casestudies/hubpages.html

Bibliography

ADAC. An Assessment of On-Campus Advertising: Quantitative Research. Edmonton: Alberta Alcohol and Drug Abuse Commission, 1994. HV 5135 A86 1994

Adlaf, Edward M. and Paul M. Kohn. Alcohol, advertising, consumption and abuse: A covariance - structural modelling look at Strickland's data. British Journal of Addiction 84, no. 7: 749-757 (1989).

Ads recruit young drinkers. The Journal 23(4):9, July/August 1994.

Aharon, Sara. Alcohol Advertising on Television: An Exploration of Educational Dimensions and Curriculum Strategies. Toronto, ON: University of Toronto. on order (cdbf)

Aitken, P.P. Alcohol advertising in developing countries. British Journal of Addiction 84(12): 1443-1445 (1989).

ARF. The Path of Least Resistance: The Trend to Normalize Alcohol. Best Advice Series. Toronto: Addiction Research Foundation, 1993.

Book, Albert C. and Norman D. Cary and Stanley I.Tannenbaum. Radio & Television Commercial . 2nd edition. Lincolnwood, Ill.: NTC Business Books, 1984. BCAST HF 6146.B74B6.

Brand, Leslie, L. editor. 1988 Radio Copy Book: Ideas and Inspiration for Radio Copywriters. New York: Radio Advertising Bureau, 1986. BCAST HF6146.R3R3.

Brown, Les. Television: The Business Behind the Box. New York, Harcourt Brace Jovanovich 1971. BCAST HE8700.8.B75.

Campbell, Richard. Media and Culture: An Introduction to Mass Communication. New York : St. Martin's Press, 1998. BCAST P 92.U5C26 1998.

Casswell, Sally. Alcohol Advertising Expenditure and Exposure. Auckland, New Zealand: Alcohol and Public Health Research Unit, 1994.

David, Miles. Making money with co-op: the complete radio co-op course. New York: Radio Advertising Bureau, 1986. BCAST

HF6146.R3D38.

Evans, Jacob A. Selling and Promoting Radio and Television. New York: Printers' Ink Pub. Co. 1954. BCAST HF5439.A33E8.

Felix, Edgar Herbert. Using Radio in Sales Promotion; A Book for Advertisers, Station Managers and Broadcasting Artists. 1st ed. New York: McGraw-Hill, 1927. BCAST TK6570.B7F4.

Firestone, O. J. Broadcast Advertising in Canada; Past and Future Growth. Ottawa, University of Ottawa Press, 1966. BCASTHF6146.R3F5.

Fisher, Joseph C. Advertising, Alcohol Consumption, and Abuse: A Worldwide Survey. Westport, CN: Greenwood Press, 1993. HF 5809 .A4 F47 1993

Foreman, Robert L. An Ad Man Ad-libs On TV. Illustrated by Alphonse Normandia. New York: Hastings House 1957. BCAST HF6146.T42F6.

Goode, Kenneth Mackarness. What About Radio?. New York, London: Harper & Brothers, 1937. BCAST TK6570.B7G64.

Gorman, DM. Alcohol misuse and the predisposing environment. British Medical Bulletin 50(1):36-49, 1994.

Harrison, Larry. Alcohol advertising. In Preventing Alcohol and Tobacco Problems : Manipulating consumption, information, law and voluntary controls Vol. 2. eds. Christine Godfrey and David Robinson, 44-74. Aldershot, England : Avebury, 1990. HV 5840 .G7 M36 1990

Heighton, Elizabeth J. Advertising in the Broadcast and Cable Media. 2nd ed. Belmont, Calif.: Wadsworth Pub. Co., 1984. BCAST HF6146.B74H44.

Hettinger, Herman S. A Decade of Radio Advertising. Chicago: The University of Chicago Press, 1933. BCAST HF 6146.R3H4 1933a.

Horgan, Mavis M. The Relationship of Alcoholic Beverage Advertising and Drinking Behaviour: A Digest of the Literature. Ottawa: The Author, 1986. HF 5809 .A4 H67 1986.

Howard, Herbert H. and Michael S. Kievman, with the assistance of Darrel Holt, Kent Sidel, Mark Banks. Radio and TV Programming. Columbus, Ohio: Grid Pub., 1983. BCAST PN1991.55.H68.

Kohn, P. M. and Smart, R. G. Wine, women, suspiciousness and advertising. Journal of Studies on Alcohol 48(2):161-166 (1987).

Kohn, Paul M. and Reginald G. Smart. The impact of television advertising on alcohol consumption: An experiment. Journal of Studies on Alcohol 45(4):295-301 (1984b).

Kohn, Paul M., Reginald G. Smart and Alan C. Ogborne. Effects of two kinds of alcohol advertising on subsequent consumption. Journal of Advertising 13(1):34-40,48(1984). HF 5809 .A4 K6 1984

Kusserow, Richard P. Youth and Alcohol: Controlling Alcohol Advertising That Appeals to Youth. Rockville, MD: DHHS, Office of Inspector General, 1991. HF 5809 .A4 Y687

Lewis, Agnes L. From Crystal Sets to tTelevision. Written for General Mills, Inc. BCAST HE8696.L3.

Lockhart, Ron and Dick Weissman. Audio in Advertising: A Practical Guide to Producing and Recording Music, Voiceovers, and Sound Effects. New York : F. Unger Pub. Co., 1982. BCAST ML3790.L6.

Mad at the Ads!: A Citizen's Guide to Challenging Alcohol Advertising Practices. Washington, D.C.: Center for Science in the Public Interest, 1992. HF 5809 .A4 M33 1992

Meringoff, Laurene. Children and Advertising: An Annotated Bibliography. 1980 ed. New York, NY.: Children's Advertising Review Unit, National Advertising Division, Council of Better Business Bureaus, 1980. BCAST HF6146.T42M47.

Murphy, Jonne. Handbook of Radio Advertising Radnor, Pa.: Chilton Book Co., 1980. BCAST HF6146.R3M87.

National Association of Broadcasters. Dept. of Research. Radio Market Data Handbook; comp. by Department of Research under the direction of Research Committee. Washington: National Association of Broadcasters, Inc., 1943. BCAST HF6146.R3N28.

Neuendorf, Kimberly. Alcohol advertising : Regulations can help. In Controversies in the Addiction's Field : Volume One. ed. Ruth C. Engs, p. 119-129. Dubuque, Iowa: Kendall/Hunt, 1990. HV 5801 .C587 1990

Ogborne, Alan C. and Reginald G. Smart. Will restrictions on alcohol advertising reduce alcohol consumption? British Journal of Addiction 75(3):293-296 (1980).

Ontario Prevention Clearinghouse. Alcohol Moderation Resource Package. Toronto: The Clearinghouse, 1993. HV 5276 A369 1993.

Orlandi, M. A., Lieberman, L. R. and Schinke, S. P. Effects of alcohol and tobacco advertising on adolescents. In: B. Segal (Ed.). Perspectives on Adolescent Drug Abuse. New York, NY: Haworth Press, Inc., 1989. HV 5824 .Y68 P468 1989

Orowitz, E. M. What is Wrong With Commercial Broadcasting? New York: The EMO Co., 1932. BCAST HF6146.R3O76.

Peck, William A. Anatomy of Local Radio-TV Copy. New 4th ed. Blue Ridge Summit, Pa.: G/L Tab Books, 1976. BCASTHF6146.R3P4.

Ringold, Debra Jones. Social criticisms of target marketing: Process of product? American Behavioral Scientist 38(4):578-592, 1995.

Ruthrauff & Ryan, Inc. Human! Handle With Care. New Chicago, 1939. HF6146.R3R88.

Shoup, Hal. Alcohol advertising : Restrictions without due cause. In Controversies in the Addiction's Field : Volume One. ed. Ruth C. Engs, p. 130-135. Dubuque, Iowa : Kendall/Hunt, 1990. HV 5801 .C587 1990

Simpson, H.M., D.J. Beirness, D.R. Mayhew, and A.C. Donelson. Advertising and the alcohol-crash problem. Chap. 5 in Alcohol-Specific Controls: Implications for Road Safety. Ottawa: Traffic Injury Research Foundation of Canada, 1985. HE 5620 .D7 A456 1985

Swann, D. R. Free-alcohol policy on airlines. Canadian Medical Association Journal 139(11):1051 (1988).

The impact of product usage warnings in alcoholic beverage advertising. Journal of Public Policy and Marketing 9:16-29 (1990). HF 5809 A4 S629 1990

Wallack, Lawrence M. Media Advocacy and Public Health: Power for Prevention. Newbury Park, Ca: Sage Publications, 1993. RA 440.5 M425 1993

Whitehead, Paul C. Is advertising effective? Implications for public health policy. In Evaluation Research in the Canadian Addictions Field: Proceedings of the 2nd Annual Meeting of the Special Interest Group on Program Evaluation of the Canadian Addictions Foundation, eds. Brian Rush and Alan Ogborne, p. 131- 147. Canada: Health and Welfare Canada, 1982. HV 5809 .M4 1982

Wilford, Bonnie Baird and Jacqueline Morgan. Alcohol Advertising and Marketing: Consumer and Government Involvement. Washington, DC: The George Washington University, 1992. HF 5809 .A4 A426 1992

Index